A Nation
for
Our Children

A NATION FOR OUR CHILDREN

Human Rights, Nationalism, Sovereignty
Selected Writings of Jose W. Diokno

THE JOSE W. DIOKNO
FOUNDATION, INC.

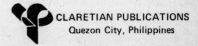

CLARETIAN PUBLICATIONS
Quezon City, Philippines

Manuscript Editor Priscila S. Manalang
Cover Design and Illustration Gilbert Torres

FOREWORD

This collection of essays and speeches of the late Senator Jose W. Diokno (Ka Pepe to so many of his friends and admirers) gives the reader an inkling into the workings of a great mind. Through them, like golden threads, run the basic beliefs and ideals that guided his life: freedom for the individual , sovereignty for the people, use of both freedom and sovereignty to establish a just society.

Behind every speech lie unseen the infinite capacity to take pains, the labor that knows neither night nor holidays, the meticulous collating and marshalling of data that swept the listeners to the conviction that there is no substitute for freedom, sovereignty, truth and justice if the Philippines is to survive.

The style is characteristic of the man: plain, logical, trenchant and convincing. It calls to mind the advice that an old practitioner once gave to a young lawyer about to argue his first case: "Speak clearly and plainly so you can be understood by the Court bailiffs; for if they understand you, at least some of the Justices will be sure to do likewise." With Ka Pepe there are no ambiguities; no one is left in doubt as to where he stood.

It is a measure of his soul's greatness that after being unjustly imprisoned for two years and released without any charges being preferred against him, Ka Pepe wasted no time in protests or recriminations but immediately proceeded to organize and guide the Free Legal Assistance Group (FLAG) dedicated to the gratuitous defense and vindication of others who, like him, should be persecuted, oppressed and denied justice. To this task he dedicated the rest of his life, even when nailed to the bed of suffering that brought him to an early grave.

JOSE B. L. REYES

September 7, 1987

PREFACE

When Jose W. Diokno died in February 1987, grief struck at many hearts. Many people feared that the heroic work he had done for the country would not be completed and still many others regretted that the service he had rendered to his people would cease abruptly.

Pepe Diokno was the quintessential nationalist; his whole life was informed by a passionate commitment to people and country. Whether it was human rights, nationalism or the U.S. military bases, he was in the forefront, fighting for the Filipino.

His labors, thoughts, ideas and actions were imbued by a deep sense of being Filipino – it was his special talent that he should inspire in his associates, acquaintances, and followers who were legion, this same feeling of deep commitment to Philippine society. As Pepe himself claimed, courage is contagious. In the final analysis it is this shared passion that will ultimately lead to a united populace, a truly popular democracy, and authentic sovereignty.

Perhaps nothing expresses better the nationalism that he espoused and willy-nilly transmitted to others than an unfinished essay, **This Land is Ours.** Written in 1978, it was never completed because too many important causes demanded his attention and efforts in the painful struggle to regain our freedom from the dictatorship. He wrote:

"This land is ours. Yet for some four hundred years, we stood helplessly by as men of other races and other creeds enjoyed our harvests, mined our riches, ran our trade. They lusted after our wealth – they got a large part of it.

Worse, they lusted after our souls – and they got part of that too. And after they had turned us into somewhat jaded images of themselves, they denied us the simple dignity of human equality. Even as our young men fought and bled and died by their side in Bataan, Filipino soldiers were given poorer food and paid less than their American counterparts.

But we learned. We pulled strings. And finally, we got our independence. It was not complete – it is still not complete – but at least we got more space to move and manueuver in. And even as we stood their scorn, and smiled, we vowed that we would never let this ignominy happen again. We are keeping that vow.

It is to remind our leaders of that vow, in these days that we face the crucial tasks of rewriting our constitution and reshaping our economic relations with the United States, that I have written this.

This land is ours. We must keep it ours. For it is not ours to give away, or lose but to enrich and ennoble and pass on to our children, for them to enrich and ennoble and pass on to theirs.

How we must and how we can enrich and ennoble the land, I hope to show in the papers that follow.

But if I do nothing else, I will be amply repaid if you will remember: This land is ours. Let it never again be taken by others. Let us make it truly ours – yours and mine and the thirty-seven million living Filipinos and the several million that will come from our loins."

Acknowledgments

The Jose W. Diokno Foundation Inc. acknowledges the invaluable assistance of:

1. Aurora De Dios / Conspectus for the photograph on the cover;
2. Sr. Eileen Laird, Maryknoll Sisters and Ed Gerlock for proofreading;
3. Claretian Fathers and Claretian Publications.

TABLE OF CONTENTS

III. PHILIPPINE SOVEREIGNTY

HUMAN RIGHTS

I. HUMAN RIGHTS

Jose W. Diokno was a man of many causes. Among his ruling passions were human rights which he defended at great risk, at a time when championing them was considered subversive by a militarized state. Thus Diokno engaged in this struggle on many fronts: in the defense of political prisoners, in the investigation and analysis of violations which took him all over the country and overseas, in his speeches, in deliberations and meetings of cause-oriented groups, and in his mission of educating our people.

His decision to organize the Free Legal Assistance Group (FLAG) resulted directly from his incarceration when Martial Law was declared. He was a senator; yet he was imprisoned without charges for almost two years. If a senator of the land could be stripped of his rights so summarily, then ordinary political prisoners would be more helpless and powerless to obtain justice. He founded FLAG to defend and protect the oppressed, the weak, the poor, the deprived.

And he never stopped. To the very end Pepe never gave up. His courage inspired other lawyers and professionals to join him. He had launched a movement which gave hope to the desperate and informed his countrymen and the world that there was a promise of freedom and justice, however difficult and painful the struggle. FLAG would henceforth symbolize the quiet heroism of its founder and members.

HUMAN RIGHTS MAKE MAN HUMAN

In concise, lucid language Diokno explains the meaning of human rights of man and of a people. He clarifies the most basic principles from which all human rights derive.

Then he describes in concrete, existential terms the increasing violations of human rights in the Philippines, blaming them largely on an excessively materialistic socio-economic system and on the anti-communist hysteria resulting from cold war propaganda.

Finally he invites the people to join the fight for their human rights against a cruel and oppressive government. He admits that what he is asking is dangerous, but:

"If we do not struggle with all that we have and do all that we can to vindicate our rights, we not only condemn our rights to death; we also condemn our hopes and our dreams, our present, and our children's future".

No cause is more worthy than the cause of human rights. Human rights are more than legal concepts: they are the essence of man. They are what make man human. That is why they are called human rights: deny them and you deny man's humanity.

Almost everywhere human rights are extolled. Yet almost everywhere they are violated, and nowhere with less shame than in our country. Here men in government, aided or abetted by foreign governments, international institutions and transnational corporations, debase the cause of human rights as they devalue our currency for ignoble purposes and with pernicious results. At times, they brazenly deny that anyone's rights have been or are being violated. When their denials begin to sound hollow even to themselves, they admit with feigned sorrow that some violations have taken place, yet quickly add that the violations do not reflect policy, but are "aberrations" caused by overzealousness in protecting national security or promoting economic development – as if Filipinos exist for the economy and the state, and not the reverse. Or they dismiss the cause of human rights with impatience, if not contempt, as an imposition of western culture alien to the Filipino soul – as if Filipinos were less human than the men and women of the West. Most often, they raise their right

---

(Lecture delivered at a Convocation on Human Rights at Siliman University on its 80th Founder's Day, August 31, 1981)

hand in solemn pledge to uphold human rights, but with their left hand create situations and bless policies and practices that trample upon these rights.

In truth, the distinguishing mark of government these days is not so much corruption or incompetence as a grim determination to displace the straightforward with the devious, and to smother thought with slogans. That government succeeds partially is due not only to its power over mass media but also to our ignorance: too many of us are not aware of our rights or of the ways we can enforce them. So it is especially urgent that we restore the cause of human rights to its pristine purity and respond to the call which the United Nations has made upon "every individual and every organ of society .... [to] ... strive by teaching and education to promote respect for these rights and freedoms ... and to secure their universal and effective recognition and observance."[1]

Human rights are enumerated in five great international documents and two great national documents.

The international documents are the Universal Declaration of Human Rights, which the United Nations adopted on December 10, 1948; its two implementing covenants: the International Covenant on Economic, Social and Cultural Rights, and the International Covenant on Civil and Political Rights, both of which took effect in 1976; the Declaration and Action Programme on the Establishment of a New International Economic Order, and Economic Rights and Duties of States, both of which the United Nations adopted in 1974.

The two national documents are our Malolos Constitution of 1898 and the Philippine Constitution of 1935. The 1973 Constitution has no place on the list, not only because it is of doubtful parentage but also because it contains provisions on executive immunity [Art. VII, Sec. 15]; on the President's right to enter into treaties or agreements disregarding the constitutional requirement that natural resources be controlled by the Filipino people [Art. XIV, Sec. 16]; the provision validating martial law acts [Art. XVII, Sec. 3(2)]; and the provision granting the President power to legislate [1976 Amendment 6].

Each of the seven great documents on human rights enumerates more than twenty human rights. Because so many are listed, many of us find it hard to grasp their scope. So let us start with the basics.

---

[1]Universal Declaration of Human Rights, enacting clause.

First. None of us asked to be born. And regardless of who our parents are and what they own, all of us are born equally naked and helpless, yet each with his own mind, his own will and his own talents. Because of these facts, all of us have an equal right to life, and share the same inherent human dignity. The right to life is more than the right to live: it is the right to live in a manner that befits our common human dignity and enables us to bring our particular talents to full flower. So each of us individually has three basic rights: the right to life, the right to dignity, and the right to develop ourselves. These are traditionally known as the rights of man.

Second. Even if we may not know who our parents are, we are never born without parents, and never live outside society, a society with its own peculiar culture, history and resources. So besides our rights as persons, we have rights as society, rights which belong to each of us individually but which we can exercise only collectively as a people. These rights are known as the rights of the people. They are analogous to the rights of man, and like the latter, comprise three basic rights: to survive, to self-determination, and to develop as a people.

Third. Once a society reaches a certain degree of complexity, as almost all societies have, society can act only through government. But government always remains only an agent of society; it never becomes society itself; it never becomes the people themselves. It is always and only an instrument of the people. Moreover, since government is composed of men, each with his own interests and his own frailties, it usually happens — in fact, it happens all too often — that government doesn't seek the people's welfare: on the contrary, it oppresses the people. These facts lead to two conclusions. One is that when we speak of national security, what we refer or should refer to is the security of the people, not of the governors; and when we speak of economic development, what we are talking about or should be talking about is the improvement of the standard of living of all the people, not the enrichment of the governors. The other conclusion is that, since government is merely an agent of the people, people have the right to change both the men who run the government and the structure and system of government itself; and when the people cannot do so peacefully, they have the right, in the language of the preamble to the Universal Declaration of Human Rights, "to have recourse, as a last resort, to rebellion against tyranny and oppression."[2]

---

[2]Paragraph three.

All the rights of man and all the rights of the people stem from those three basic principles.

From man's first basic right – his right to life – spring our rights to health, to own property, to work, to form trade unions and to strike, to social security, to rest and leisure, to move about freely within our country and freely to leave and return to it, to marry, to establish a family and to exercise the rights of parents.[3]

Analogously, the right of the people as a people to survive is the source of our people's rights to peace, to non-aggression, and to share in international trade, receiving a just price for our products and paying no more than is fair for the products of other countries.[4]

Man's second basic right – his right to human dignity – is the source of our rights to recognition everywhere as a person, to honor and reputation, to freedom of thought, of conscience, of religion, of opinion and expression, and to seek, receive, and impart information, to peaceful assembly with our fellows, to equal treatment before the law, to privacy in our family, our home, and our correspondence, to freedom from slavery, torture, and cruel, inhuman or degrading punishment, as well as from arbitrary arrest, detention or exile, to be presumed innocent of crime or wrong, to fair trial, and so forth.[5]

The analogous right of the people to self-determination is the root of our people's rights to sovereign equality in international affairs and international organizations, to freedom from all forms of racial discrimination, to political independence and freedom from colonialism, neo-colonialism, alien domination and intervention in our national affairs, to sovereignty over our natural resources and over all economic activities, to control the activities of foreign investors and transnational corporations, and to nationalize and expropriate their assets, and freely to choose and change our political, social, cultural and economic systems.[6]

Man's third basic right – his right to develop – is the source of our rights to an education, to share in the cultural life of our community, to form associations with our fellows, and to live in a

---

[3]Universal Declaration of Human Rights, articles 13, 16, 17, 22, 23, 24, 25.

[4]Charter of Economic Rights and Duties of States, Chapter 1; Declaration of Action Programme, par. 4(j).

[5]Universal Declaration of Human Rights, Art. 1, 2, 3, 4, 5, 6, 7, 8, 9, 10, 11, 18, 19.

[6]Charter of Economic Rights and Duties of States, Chapter II, Art. 1, 2, 16.

national and international order that allows all of our rights to flower and be respected.[7]

Similarly, the people's right to develop as a people implies the rights freely to choose the goals and means of development, to industrialize the economy, to implement social and economic reforms that ensure the participation of all the people in the process and benefits of development, to share in scientific and technological advances of the world, and as a former colony, to reparation and retribution for the exploitation to which we have been subjected.[8]

No one has ever doubted that the rights of the people are all of a piece. Equally so are the rights of man. But for convenience, the rights of man have been divided into two broad kinds: economic, social and cultural rights on the one hand, and civil and political rights on the other. This distinction has led to much argument about which kind should be given priority and whether one kind can be sacrificed for the other. My experience has convinced me that these arguments are silly. As lawyer for small farmers, fishermen, workers, students and urban poor, many of whom have been detained, most of whom have been threatened with detention, a few of whom have been shot and wounded when they were peacefully exercising their rights of assembly, I have learned the painful lesson that we cannot enjoy civil and political rights unless we enjoy economic, cultural and social rights, anymore than we can insure our economic, social and cultural rights, unless we can exercise our civil and political rights. True, a hungry man does not have much freedom of choice. But equally true, when a well-fed man does not have freedom of choice, he cannot protect himself against going hungry.

A more useful distinction than between economic and political rights is this: that some of man's individual rights are absolute, others are not. Rights which are absolute cannot be limited in any way under any circumstances, not even under the gravest of emergencies. Such are, for example, the rights to freedom of thought, of conscience, of religion, to be everywhere recognized as a person, to be free from torture and from cruel, degrading and inhuman treatment, and of course, the right not to be deprived of life arbitrarily. Not only may these rights never be denied, but nothing justifies imposing any limitation on them.[9]

---

[7]Universal Declaration of Human Rights, Arts. 20, 26, 27 and 28.

[8]Charter of Economic Rights and Duties of States, Chapter II, Arts. 1, 7; Declaration and Action Programme, par 4(d), (f), (p).

[9]International Covenant on Civil and Political Rights, Art. 4, par. 2.

On the other hand, other rights may be and in fact must be limited to preserve social life. Such are, for example, the right to freedom of expression, freedom of assembly, and freedom of association. To be valid, however, limitations placed on these rights must meet three conditions: first, they must be provided by law, not by executive whim; second, they must be necessary to preserve society, or protect public health, public morals, or similar rights of others; and third, they must not exceed what is strictly necessary to achieve their purpose.[10]

These rights and some others – such as for instance, the right to be free from arbitrary detention and arrest and the right to a remedy for every violation of fundamental rights – may even be denied in times of grave emergency. But to justify such a denial, the emergency must be so grave that it truly threatens the life of the nation: the existence of the emergency must be publicly proclaimed; and the denial may go no further than is strictly required by the exigencies of the situation.[11]

In the light of these principles, how well do human rights fare in our country? Let us examine first the rights of man, then the rights of the people.

Salvaging

Of the rights of man, the most basic is the right to life. Since martial law was imposed on our country, that right has been violated more and more frequently – and increasingly so after martial law was supposedly lifted. From 1975 to 1979, Task Force Detainees of the Philippines (TFDP), the church-related organization which looks after the material and spiritual needs of political prisoners, documented 341 cases of "salvaging," the extrajudicial execution of suspects by military, police and paramilitary personnel, and 176 cases of involuntary disappearances of persons arrested and not heard from again, for a total of 507 cases, an average of about 100 cases a year. In 1980, however, TFDP documented 149 cases of salvaging and 53 cases of involuntary disappearances for a total of 202 cases, twice the first five-year average. And in the first six months of this year, 1981, TFDP has documented 161 cases of salvaging and 12 cases of involuntary disappearances for a total of 173 cases, an increase of 150 over last year.

---

[10]Ibid, Art. 10, par. 3; Art. 20, 22, par. 2; Universal Declaration of Human Rights, Art. 29, par. 2.

[11]Ibid, Art. 4, par. 1.

Poor Health

Violations of other rights may not be as drastic, but they are just as deadly. Consider the right to health. Only 39 per cent of our people have access to safe drinking water. Of the ten leading causes of death, seven – pneumonia, tuberculosis, gastro-enteritis and colitis, avitaminosis and other nutritional deficiencies, malignant neoplasma, bronchitis, emphysema and asthma, and tetanus – could be prevented, or at least greatly minimized, by providing adequate public health services. Yet every year these seven claim at least 120,000 lives. Almost 80 per cent of our children of pre-school age suffer from malnutrition, in some cases so severe that by the end of 1979 it had led to mental retardation for some 1,500,000 of our children – and there is no cure for mental retardation. Yet government annually has spent the equivalent of only U.S. $3.00 per Filipino for health, while spending U.S. $15.00 per Filipino for the military. For this government, the militarization of our society has a higher priority than the health of our people and the normal development of our children.

Unemployment

This twisted sense of priorities also reveals itself in government's policies on the right to work. Despite grandiose development plans and glittering projects government has, in fact, done little to reduce unemployment, yet much to exploit our workers for the benefit of a select few in our country and their foreign partners.

Reasonably accurate data on unemployment and underemployment are hard to come by. The International Labour Office (ILO) discovered this when, with the blessing of this government, they made a study of our economy in 1974. The government supplied them with statistics which showed that 11 percent of our workforce was then unemployed. But when ILO checked that figure against other data, it was forced to conclude that the correct figure for unemployment and underemployment was between 25 per cent to 33 per cent of our work force.

Today, the government no longer publishes data on underemployment, only on those "totally unemployed." Its latest data claim that, in 1978, only 4 per cent of our work force, some 694,000 workers, were unemployed. But the same data also show that, of those employed, some 3,500,000, 10 per cent of the work force, were "unpaid family workers." Even by government statistics, then, at least 23 per cent of our workers are not gainfully employed.

Those statistics, however, understate the real situation. IBON, a non-government economic research group, reported that, in 1976, actual unemployment amounted to 44 per cent of our work force. Since then, with the oil crisis and worldwide recession, the situation has certainly not improved.

Low Wages

Whether unemployment stands at 23 per cent or 44 percent there is no doubt that it is unreasonably high. This has made it easier to exploit labor in two major ways: keeping wages low and allowing conditions of work bordering on slavery.

From the 1975 survey made by the accounting firm of Sycip, Gorres and Velayo & Co. to the 1980 survey made by Business International, every survey of wages has reported that wages in our country are the lowest in Asia, lower than in Indonesia and Thailand, although the latter's GNP per capita is lower than ours. This is the result, not of accident, but of policy. On January 4, 1974, at the Central Bank's silver anniversary celebration, Mr. Marcos promised, with great pride and determination, that:

> "Our country now has one of the lowest average wage levels ... We intend to see to it that our export program is not placed in jeopardy at an early stage by a rapid rise in the general wage level .... we shall preserve the relative position of our wage structure vis-a-vis those of competing countries."

Unfortunately this is one promise that Mr. Marcos has kept. Philippine wages were low and remain low.

Of course, low wages are not bad in themselves – as long as prices remain low. But that has not happened here. Prices have skyrocketed; and while wages have increased in money terms, increases have always come after price hikes. The result has been that real wages, the quantity of goods that wages can buy, dropped 36.3 per cent for skilled workers and 47.5 per cent for unskilled workers from 1972 to 1980. So severe has the drop been that, in 1980, the Union Bank of Switzerland reported that, to buy one month's needs, Manila laborers must work 548 hours, that is, a worker must work two months and eighteen days to feed his family for one month.

Although the policy of low wages is officially limited to industrial workers, it has adversely affected the income of farmers as well. Industrial workers must eat if for nothing else than to keep on working productively. Once industrial wages are depressed, farm product prices must also be depressed, and cannot be allowed to rise faster than industrial prices. As a result, according to government, the real income of farmers dropped 53.4 per cent from 1976 to 1979.

Exploitation

Not only are wages low, but working conditions are inhuman. Government knows this, yet allows it to continue, most often by inaction, in some cases by cooperation. Let me give you an example of the latter that was brought to my attention recently.

On May 18, 1981, 25 Filipino seamen serving on the crew of the vessel MS Saudi Independence, of Saudi Arabian registry, went on strike with the help of the International Transport Federation, an international seamen's union. Like all Filipino contract workers abroad, by government decree they received only 30 per cent of their wages, 70 per cent being remitted by their employer to their families in order to augment government's foreign exchange receipts. Because the seamen had been travelling in colder climates than they were used to, much of this 30 per cent went to buy clothing. To compound their difficulties, food aboard ship was grossly inadequate. For ten months our seamen had complained. Two captains of the vessel, one a German, the other a Filipino, a Filipino first mate and a Filipino radio operator all lost their jobs because they supported the seamen's complaints. On the last 25 days of the last voyage before they went on strike, the seamen's food ration was reduced to one dried fish and some rice daily for each crew member.

The seamen's right to refuse to work under such conditions seemed undeniable. In fact, a Dutch Court ruled, on the day after the strike began, that the ship owner should provide food for the striking seamen, and a week later it ruled that the owner could not remove the seamen forcibly from the ship.

Then the Marcos government stepped in. On May 30, Philippine Coast Guard Commander Commodore Brilliante C. Ochoco suspended the seamen and confiscated their licenses. On May 31, Atty. Oscar Torres of the National Seamen's Board went to Holland to convince the seamen to give up their strike. He failed. On June 1, Philippine Labor Attache Manuel Cruz warned the crew that the strike and the intervention of the International Transport Federation were illegal. Eleven days later, on the strength of an affidavit of the same Atty. Oscar Torres of the National Seamen's Board, that the

strike was illegal and contrary to Philippine National policy, the
Dutch Court reversed its earlier decision, and ordered the seamen to
end their strike. Ironically, this decision was handed down on June
12, Philippine Independence Day. Today the seamen have no jobs
and face administrative charges before the Coast Guard to boot.
This is how the Marcos government protects Filipino workers
against exploitation.

Suppressing Dissent

The list of human rights violations is interminable. So let me
wind up with one more right: the right of peaceful assembly.

On February 1, 1981, some 3,000 peasants from barrios of
Guinayangan, Quezon, marched towards town to hold a public
meeting to protest the low prices of coconut products, the high
prices of prime commodities, and the abuses of the military. They
had a permit to hold the meeting. As they approached the town, a
platoon of the 232nd PC Company, led by Sgt. Carlos Zamora,
blocked their path and ordered them to disperse. The people refused
to do so, showing their permit. Then some soldiers fired into the
crowd. Two died and 16 were wounded.

This was not an isolated incident. On June 14, a group of some
2,000 unarmed farmers from the town of Bassud, Camarines Norte,
peacefully marched towards Daet, the capital of their province, to
attend a rally to protest the June 16 "elections." Just outside the
town, a platoon of the 242nd PC Company commanded by Capt.
Joseph Malilay and some soldiers fired at the ground in front of the
marchers, mindless of the injuries that ricocheting shots could
cause; and other soldiers fired directly into the crowd. Four were
killed and twenty-one wounded. The organizers of the rally
protested to Mr. Marcos, and demanded an impartial investigation
of the crime. To insure the integrity of the investigation, they
demanded that Capt. Malilay and the Provincial Commander, Lt.
Col. Nicasio Ma. Custodio, who had issued a distorted report of the
incident, be relieved temporarily from their command. Their
protests were never answered. Instead, on June 26, 1981, Mr.
Marcos ordered their arrest, and they were arrested on July 31, 1981
by the very PC officers whose temporary relief they had sought.

Why are the rights of man so blatantly violated? Surely not all
the men who commit these crimes – and heinous crimes they are –
are evil. Why do they behave so?

Of the many possible reasons, I believe two are decisive.

The first explains why otherwise decent, churchgoing men depress wages and exploit workers: they do so simply because that is what the economic system we live in demands. Excessively materialistic, the system stresses efficiency, profits and competition, ignores whatever cannot be expressed in pesos and centavos, and honors a man more for what he has than for what he is. And since our economy is underdeveloped, these pernicious aspects are intensified: the struggle for a livelihood is harder in an underdeveloped economy, and the temptation to disregard the welfare of others and think only of oneself and one's family is stronger. Time and again churches have spoken out against the evils of the system, but the evils continue because the system and our underdevelopment encourage them. So we must seek ways to modify, if not change, the system.

The second reason explains why otherwise good men salvage and torture and shoot into unarmed crowds of peaceful marchers: they do so simply because, influenced by U.S. mentors and cold war propaganda, the military mind believes that communists are enemies, who will use every means, legal or illegal, to overthrow the government: and from the premises, which are not wholly unreasonable, the military mind jumps to two wrong conclusions: first, that communists should not be allowed to exercise legal rights; and second, that anyone who opposes or criticizes government is a communist sympathizer, and so were not reluctant to break up the march, even though it meant shooting into unarmed crowds.

Two other examples of this mentality are Mr. Enrile's branding a pictorial protest against military brutality that was shown in a catholic school as communist propaganda, though the photographs were factual, and Mr. Marcos' issuing Presidential Decree 1804, denying permits for public meetings to persons who are facing charges for rebellion, sedition or subversion, though they have not been convicted.

The military mind probably does not realize it, but its mentality is the very same mentality it attributes to the communists whom it would exorcise and the very opposite of the democratic mentality it would uphold. For the essence of the democratic mind is that it respects the freedom of all – communist, fascist or "apathist" – to exercise their human rights that all may hear "the thought we hate."

Unfortunately, the totalitarian mentality is not limited to the regime. The temptation to silence voices that disagree with us afflicts us all. We must constantly guard against it, lest we too succumb to it.

Let us turn now to the rights of the people. How well do they fare?

Our Survival Not in Our Hands

The people's most basic right, the right to survive as a people, is no longer in our hands. In 1979, Mr. Marcos put our survival into the hands of the U.S. military. That year, Mr. Marcos gave the United States "unhampered control over military operations involving U.S. forces" in the Philippines and the authority to take part in "security activities" outside the bases. By so doing, Mr. Marcos allowed nuclear weapons to be brought in, assembled and stored in our country, and thus made us a prime target for nuclear attack in case of war between the U.S. and the Soviet Union, a war which events seems to bring perilously close. He also allowed the U.S. government to intervene in our internal affairs, for to participate in "security activities" outside the bases amounts to nothing less than that.

Economic Policy Decided by Aliens

Equally important, Mr. Marcos has abdicated the power to lay down national economic policy to the World Bank, the IMF and the Asian Development Bank. It is these institutions, rather than Mr. Marcos or his technocrats, who are shaping our economy – and doing so to meet the demands of international trade, not our people's needs. That is understandable: international trade is their primary concern, not our economic development. What is not understandable is that any government calling itself Filipino should ever permit such a situation to develop. Because of this abdication, for example, the Central Bank allows the importation of luxuries and other non-essential commodities, though we are so short of foreign exchange that our external debt jumped from U.S.$2 billion in 1972 to over U.S. $14 billion today. Because of this also, although the Central Bank is aware that foreign investors borrow the equivalent of U.S. $8.33 for every U.S. $1.00 that they bring into the country – so that we are in fact financing foreign investments, instead of their financing themselves – and it did adopt regulations to limit these borrowings, the Central Bank nevertheless exempted such giants as General Motors, Ford Philippines Mfg. Co., and others from these regulations.

There are other examples – but these are more than enough to prove the point. U.S. government control of our survival and world Bank-IMF control of our economic policy are the main reasons why the Filipino people have lost their freedom and become impoverished. Of course the immediate visible cause is the martial rule, but martial rule itself is merely the means for foreign control to institutionalize itself. Not Mr. Marcos alone is to blame for martial rule though he alone declared it: for he could not have effectively imposed it all these years without U.S. military and economic aid. And not Mr. Marcos alone has benefited from martial law, although it has indeed kept him in power long beyond his term of office: for it has also quashed the resurgent nationalist aspirations of our people and allowed the U.S. government and transnational corporations not only to continue to exploit our land, but to intensify their exploitation. Without martial law, the institutions of freedom – free press, free elections, free assembly, and independent courts – could not have been dismantled. And without that dismantling, it would not have been possible either for the U.S. government to obtain and maintain total control over our survival nor for the World Bank, IMF, and transnational corporations to dictate economic policy and exploit our economy and our people.

But if Mr. Marcos and foreign interests bear the bulk of the blame, we are also to blame. For too long, too many of us have limited ourselves to privately criticizing the situation or going along with it, as Rizal said, "begging with our eyes for a share of the booty," or raising our hands in hapless surrender. Before it is too late, we must change the situation.

How can we do so?

There are two strategies we could follow: either convince the government to change policies or change the government. However, as long as elections remain as farcical as they have become under martial law, it is unrealistic to expect to change the government through elections, and to change it through violence could be justified only as a last resort, after all peaceful efforts to convince government to change policies have failed. So the question is, how can we convince government to change policies?

In two ways: one as individuals, the other as a group.

As individuals, we can refuse to accept meekly the violations of our rights and those of others. We can go to law against those who trample on our rights and stand witness when the rights of others are trampled upon. We can initiate or join protests, petitions and public demonstrations against abuses. At the very least, we can publicly show our sympathy for the victims of abuse and our condemnation of the abuses. If we have a way with words, we can write about what is happening; if we have a talent for music, we can compose and sing songs of freedom; and we can always speak the truth. Never mind if our words and our songs are not heeded. They will linger in the air, and one day they will be heard.

Such activities do no violence to the moral rule that it is better to suffer than to do injustice. That rule correctly commands us to do no injustice; it does not advise us to suffer all injustices – at least not when, by so doing, we make it easier for similar injustices to be inflicted on others. One reason why the PC dared to fire at unarmed marchers in Daet on June 14 is that they had done so in Guinayangan on February 1, and done so with impunity. For the same reason, without passing judgment on Salvador Reyes, the Radio Veritas correspondent who withdrew his charges against Mayor Caruncho and some policemen of Pasig, I am apprehensive that this withdrawal may lead to similar abuses against others.[12]

So we can act effectively as individuals. But we can act even more effectively as a group. Ninety years ago Rizal reminded us that "ang isang tingting ay madaling baliin, nguni't mahirap ang isang bigkis na walis." (A single stick is easy to break, but not a whole broom.) The time is now for us to heed this advice, to go beyond the confines of our family and close friends and open ourselves to people: people from all walks of life, of all religions and all ideologies. We must learn to work with them to redeem our rights both as individuals and as a people. For these purposes, we must help others see reality and organize themselves. We must work as organizations, and with other organizations here and abroad devoted to the same noble cause of human rights. We must create new ways of voicing the aspirations of our people and of making those aspirations heard.

I know that what I am asking you to do is hard and dangerous. There are many who have been imprisoned and not a few who have been tortured or killed for defending their rights and those of our people. I am myself afraid, so I know most of us are also afraid for ourselves and for our families. But some years ago, I read one of T.A. Collins' poems, and his lines have served me well:

While fear remains my Hope can yet abide.

x x x

But should Fear pass on some wild panic night,

---

[12]Salvador Reyes was mauled by the policemen of Pasig Mayor Caruncho. The incident was shown on TV.

What if I saw in the calm, certain dawn
My Hope had fled the light?

Let us then welcome, not shun fear.

Of course there is no guarantee that we will succeed. No one can give us a guarantee except God – and we have no right to demand guarantees from Him. All we can do is fight the good fight and leave the outcome in His hands, confident that we have done the best we could and that He in turn will do what is best for us.

If these words discourage you, so be it. They are not meant to do so, only to warn you of the dangers that lurk ahead. It is extremely dangerous to defend our rights. But it would be infinitely worse not to do so. If we do not struggle with all that we have and do all that we can to vindicate our rights, we not only condemn our rights to death; we also condemn our hopes and our dreams, our present, and our children's future.

Which course shall we choose?
Only you can answer.

A FILIPINO CONCEPT OF JUSTICE

". . . our language establishes that there is a Filipino concept of justice . . . broader than western concepts of justice, for it embraces the concept of equity . . ."

What is justice?

Through the ages, great minds have tried to answer the question – with conflicting results. Some have argued that justice is what the strong impose and the weak accept; others, that on the contrary, justice is what puts limits on what the strong can impose; still others see no conflict between these two views, for the first describes the real, and the second the ideal in whose image the collective conscience of mankind gradually transforms the real. The debate goes on.[1] John Rawls, for example writes:

> Justice is the first virtue of social institutions, as truth is of systems of thought. A theory, however elegant and economical, must be rejected or revised if it is untrue; likewise laws and institutions no matter how efficient and well-arranged must be reformed or abolished if they are unjust.[2]

In reply, Edgar Z. Friedenberg cites the lawyers' phrase "justice under law," and, after noting that the phrase suggests an "unpleasant sexual" imagery, adds:

> It is not customary for Law to yield to Justice; if Law is to perform its social function, Justice must yield to Law ......

(Paper Presented to the Seminar on the Administration of Justice in the Philippines: Focus on the Poor, Sponsored by the Management Education Council, the College of Law, and the Law Center of the University of the Philippines, August 7-8, 1981)

[1] Eugene Kamenka and Alice Erh-Soon Tay, eds., *Justice,* London: Edward Arnold (Publishers) Ltd., 1979.

[2] John Rawls, *A Theory of Justice,* Cambridge, Mass.: Harvard University Press, 1973, p. 3.

The relationship of law to justice is not even ambiguous; it is essentially negative.[3]

There is no unanimity either on how to distribute the burdens and benefits of social life, that aspect of justice which today is usually called social justice. In days of old, social costs and benefits were distributed mostly according to rank. Today no one seriously advocates that method of distribution, but it is still followed in many countries ruled by dictators and in other countries; its vestiges remain, for example, in the deference paid to rank and in the perquisites of office (a larger room, a carpeted floor, a better car, and so on). And some do still urge distribution according to "merit," which in many cases is a thinly disguised form of distribution by rank. The focus of the debate today, however, is on whether distribution is to be according to deeds or to needs. Since Marx, the formula "from each according to his abilities, to each according to his needs" has been so often urged that it has become almost banal. Yet who is to determine what are abilities, what are needs, and what deeds are worth? Doctors cure us when we feel sick. Are they entitled to more than farmers who provide the food we must eat to stay healthy? We lawyers spend more years in study than do garbage collectors. Does society need our services more than theirs? We could argue these questions till doomsday and fail to reach agreement.

Yet justice must somehow be done or attempted to be done if society is to hold together. The alternative would be anarchy or dictatorship; and having experienced both, we Filipinos want neither. The question of what justice is is more than theoretical, it is eminently practical – and urgent. Somehow we must seek to answer it, however short of perfection our answer may be.

Fortunately, your invitation has considerably lightened our task. You invited me to "discuss a model or paradigm of justice upon which we can evaluate existing laws, policies and institutions that seek to attain social justice in the Philippines."[4] In so wording your invitation, you make it clear that you hold justice to be at least one measure of law; that your concern is not with justice in general, but with social justice; that you expect, not a detailed

---

[3]Edgar Z. Freidenberg, "The Side Effects of the Legal Process," in *The Rule of Law,* Robert Paul Wolff, ed., New York: Simon and Schuster, 1971, p. 37.

[4]Letter, dated March 12, 1981, of Dean Froilan M. Bacungan of the U.P. College of Law and Chairman Raul P. de Guzman of the U.P. Management Education Council.

program of action, but a set of standards or principles on which to base evaluations; and since it is "existing laws, policies and institutions ... in the Philippines" that you wish to evaluate, that you expect those standards or principles to be relevant to the now and here, and to reflect, or at least not to violate, the common aspirations of our people.

In short, our task is to explicate a Filipino concept of social justice for today and, one hopes, for tomorrow.

But first we must quiet a niggling doubt. We have been dominated by the West for so long; our political institutions, our laws, our educational system, all are copies of Western patterns; and advertising, television programs, books, magazines and newspapers emanating from the West have deeply affected our values. In these circumstances, can we hope to find a concept of justice native to us Filipinos?

I suggest that we can, if we look to our language and to our history.

Tagalogs, Ilongos, Cebuanos and Pampangos use a common word for justice, *katarungan,* derived from the Visayan root *tarong,* which means straight, upright, appropriate, correct.[5] For us, therefore, justice is rectitude, the morally right act; and because it also connotes what is appropriate, it embraces the concept of equity, for which we have no native word, and for which on the rare occasions that we use the concept, we employ the Spanish derivative *ekidad.*

For "right," we use *karapatan,* whose root is *dapat,* signifying fitting, appropriate, correct. The similarity in meaning of the roots of our words for "right" and "justice" indicates that, for us, justice and right are intimately related.

On the other hand, for "law" we use *batas,* a root word denoting command, order, decree, with a meaning disparate from that of the roots of our words for "justice" and "right." Our language, then, distinguishes clearly between law and justice; it recognizes that law is not always just.

In this our language resembles English. English also links the words "justice" and "right," since it derives "justice" from the Latin *"ius"* which means right; and separates "justice" from "law" since it

---

[5]The succeeding data on language are based on Jose Villa Panganiban, *English-Pilipino Dictionary,* 1938-1966, Mimeoscript by Limbagang Pilipino; and *Random House Dictionary of English Language,* Unabridged Edition, Jess Stein and Laurence Urdang, Random House, New York.

derives law from the old Norse word *"log,"* which means something laid down or settled. But English does differ from our language in two respects: our term for justice, *katarungan,* is native to us, the English term is imported; our word for justice includes the concept of equity, the English word does not.

Our language differs from Spanish and other continental languages in another respect. In the latter, the word "right" – the Spanish *derecho,* the Italian *diritto,* the French *droit* and the German *recht* – means both right as well as law in general; and this could connote three things: that law must respect right, or that what is law is right, or that law and right ought to be inseparable. This ambiguity is absent from our language.

On the other hand, we use the word *kapangyarihan* both for "power" and for "authority;" and this creates a similar ambiguity, for it could mean that power confers authority, or that authority confers power, or that power ought not to be divorced from authority. This ambiguity is absent from English, Spanish and other continental languages. Lately, however, we have tended more and more to distinguish between naked power and authority, using the Spanish *poder* or the Tagalog *lakas* (which means strength, intensity) to signify naked power, and *kapangyarihan* to signify authority.

Two more points need to be made. One is that our language employs the same word, *katarungan,* for both justice and fairness, as it does for both justice and equity. And although we use a native word, *karapatan,* for right, we use a Spanish derivative, *pribilehiyo,* for privilege. So it seems logical to conclude that the fundamental element in the Filipino concept of justice is fairness; and that privilege and naked power – two of the worst enemies of fairness – are alien to the Filipino mind.

The last point is that Tagalogs have a root word *tuwid* that is an almost exact equivalent of the Visayan root *tarong.* Yet Tagalogs chose *tarong* as the root of our word for "justice," *katarungan;* and use *tuwid* to form *katuwiran,* meaning straightness (not rectitude), and *katuwiran* or *katwiran,* meaning reason, argument, with overtones of self-justification or excuse as in *mangatwiran, magmatuwid,* and cognate words. So we Filipinos know that not every justification is just.

In summary, our language establishes that there is a Filipino concept of justice; that it is a highly moral concept, intimately related to the concept of right; that it is similar to, but broader than, western concepts of justice, for it embraces the concept of equity; that it is a discriminating concept, distinguishing between justice and right, on the one hand, and law and argument, on the other; that its fundamental element is fairness; and that it eschews privilege and naked power.

These ideas, you may complain, are too general to be of much use. And you would be right.

As Chaim Perelman points out, concepts of justice differ, but underlying them all is justice as "a principle of action in accordance with which beings of one and the same essential category must be treated in the same way."[6] Perelman's principle of justice is similar to Aristotle's principle of "treating equals equally and unequals unequally but in proportion to their relevant differences."[7]

Both accord with the Filipino concept of justice as fairness. But, as Perelman also points out, both are formulas of formal, not concrete justice, because neither tells us what constitutes essential or relevant equality in a category, nor how to form categories, nor in what way to treat each category. In fact it would seem that these are principles of reason, derived from the principle of identity, rather than principles of justice. That is why, in Perelman's words, "every system of justice will finally depend on values other than the value of justice;" and "law will be judged by means, not of formal justice, but of concrete justice, that is, of a particular conception of justice which assumes a settled scale of values. In effect, we shall not condemn or reform in the name of justice, but in the name of a vision of the universe."[8]

To discern the Filipino vision of the universe that puts flesh on the bones of the concept of justice our language expresses, we need to turn to the history of our people. That history may be described as a continuous and continuing struggle to create a just society:

<< A society, first, which is not only independent but in which the people are sovereign:

Procure the independence of your fatherland ... because its independence constitutes your very freedom, its advancement your perfection, its greatness your own glory and immortality.

---

[6]Chaim Perelman, "Concerning Justice," in *The Idea of Justice and The Problem of Argument,* John Petrie, trans., London: Routledge & Kegan Paul, 1963, p. 16.

[7]W.D. Ross, trans., *Nicomachean Ethics,* V, 1129-1138 in *The Basic Works of Aristotle,* ed. by Richard McKeon, New York: Random House, 1941, pp. 1002-1022.

[8]Perelman, op. cit., p. 26.

Do not recognize the authority in your fatherland of any person who has not been elected by you and your fellow citizens because all authority emanates from God, and as God speaks through the conscience of each individual, only the person whom the consciences of the people as a whole designate and proclaim can wield true authority.

Procure for your country a republic, never a monarchy: the latter exalts one or several families and founds a dynasty; the former creates a people noble and dignified through reason, great through freedom, and prosperous and glowing through labor.[9]

>> A society, second, which respects the freedom and the equal dignity of all:

Maitim man at maputi ang balat, lahat ng tao'y magkakapantay, mangyayaring ang isa'y higtan sa dunong, sa yaman, sa ganda ... nguni't di mahihigtan sa pagka-tao.

x x x

Ang kamahalan ng tao'y wala sa pagkahari, wala sa tangos ng ilong, at puti ng mukha, wala sa pagka-paring kahalili ng Diyos, wala sa mataas na kalagayan sa balat ng lupa; wagas at tunay na mahal ang tao, kahit laking-gubat at walang nababatid kundi ang sariling wika, yaong may magandang asal, may isang pangungusap, may dangal at puri; yaong di napaaapi't di nakikiapi; yaong marunong magdamdam at marunong lumingap sa bayang tinubuan.

Paglaganap ng mga aral na ito at maningning na sumikat ang araw ng mahal na Kalayaan dito sa kaaba-abang Sangkapuluan at sabugan ng matamis niyang liwanag ang nangagkaisang magkakalahi't magkakapatid ng ligayang walang katapusan, ang mga ginugol na buhay, pagod, at mga tiniis na kahirapa'y labis nang natumbasan.[10]

---

[9] Apolinario Mabini, "El Verdadero Decalogo," in *La Revolucion Filipina,* Teodoro M. Kalaw, ed., Manila, Bureau of Printing, 1931, Vol. I, pp. 106-107.

[10] Emilio Jacinto, "Ang Mga Aral ng Katipunan," in Jose P. Santos, *Buhay at mga Sinulat ni Emilio Jacinto,* n.p.: 1935, pp. 61-63. Following is a rough translation:

4. The color of a man's skin, be it black or white, is of no importance, for all men are created equal; a man may best his

>> A society, third, which protects workers and tenants, opposes oppression, exploitation and abuse, and seeks to eliminate poverty:

> Ipagtanggol mo ang inapi at kabakahin ang umaapi.[11]
> Bahaginan mo ng iyong makakayanan ang sino mang mahirap at kapuspalad.[12]

When did you begin to consider the government as unjust to the people? – 1930.

Why? – Because of the abuses against the people. The needs of the laborers were ignored. The leaders paid no attention to the people.

x   x   x

Then the basic problem was one of poverty or having enough to live? – Having enough, but without abuses.

x   x   x

It was poverty, then, and abuses which caused your discontent? – No, it was more. There was a root cause behind everything. Nothing could solve our problem except independence ... Freedom was the solution .... There was no other answer to the abuses and the poverty. With independence the leaders would cease to be powerful. Instead, it would be the

---

neighbor in intellect, wealth or looks .... but they are one in their humanity.

13.   A man's dignity lies not in his power of dominion over others, his aquiline nose or Caucasian face, his priestly closeness to God, or his high social position in this earthly life; a man who is pure and true, though unlettered and uncivilized, with nothing more than his word of honor, goodness of heart, honesty and integrity, who will never countenance oppression against himself or others, who is sensitive and has an abiding love of country, is the truly worthy man.

When these ideas firmly take root and the golden rays of Freedom shine forth on the subjugated Isles, and spread their glorious light among all our countrymen in unending happiness, then each life sacrificed and all manner of hardship and suffering shall have been more than worth it.

[11]Emilio Jacinto, ibid. Following is a rough translation:

8.   Defend the oppressed and fight the oppressor.

[12]Andres Bonifacio, "Katungkulang Gagawin ng mga Z. Ll.B" [Duties of the S(ons) of the P(people), in *Dekalogo ng Katipunan,* p. 1. A rough translation follows:

8.   Share all that you have with the poor.

people who were powerful. The people would have their freedom. We would have our own lands; they would no longer be the monopoly of the proprietarios and of the government officials. As it was, we had nothing.

The problem, in short, was poverty and power? – You might say that; that was our belief. Under independence, no one would be powerful, because the people would exercise power.[13]

>> A society, fourth, which is united in brotherhood and self-reliant:

> Ang tunay na kabanalan ay ang pagkakawanggawa, ang pag-ibig sa kapwa, at ang isukat ang bawa't kilos, gawa't pangungusap sa talagang katwiran.[14]

Ano ang nararapat nating gawin? Ang araw ng katuiran na sumisikat sa Silanganan, ay malinaw na itinuturo sa ating mga matang malaong nabulagan ang landas na dapat nating tunguhin .. Ytinuro ng katuiran, na huag nating sayangin ang panahon sa pagasa sa ipangakong kaguinhawahan na hindi darating at hindi mangyayari. Ytinuro ng katuiran ang tayo'y umasa sa ating sarili at huag antain sa iba ang ating kabuhayan. Itinuro ng katuiran ang tayo'y magkaisang loob, magkaisang isip at akala, at ng tayo'y magkalakas na maihanap ang naghaharing kasamaan sa ating bayan.[15]

---

[13]"An Interview with Salud Algabre," in David R. Sturtevant, *Popular Uprisings in the Philippines, 1840-1940,* Ithaca: Cornell University Press, 1976, pp. 290-291.

[14]Emilio Jacinto, op. cit. A rough translation follows:
3. True holiness lies in charity, love of one's fellowmen, and in seeing to it that every act, move or word is done in accord with what is right.

[15]Andres Bonifacio, "Ang Dapat Mabatid Ng Mga Tagalog," in *The Writings and Trial of Andres Bonifacio* by Teodoro A. Agoncillo, 1963, p. 69. A rough translation follows:
What, then, must we do? The day of reason/righteousness slowly rising in the East clearly shows our long-blinded eyes what path we must take. Reason/righteousness teaches us not to waste time relying on promises of prosperity which will never be fulfilled and will never happen. Reason/righteousness tells us to depend on ourselves, not to wait for others to give us our livelihood. Reason/righteousness teaches us to unite in feeling,

>> In short, a moral society:

To erect the true edifice of our social regeneration we must radically change not only our institutions but also our ways of being and thinking. We need an external and internal revolution at the same time; we must establish our moral education on more solid bases and abjure the vices that for the most part we have inherited from the Spaniards.[16]

Independence alone is not enough; we must also have a moral government, a very moral government, one that governs with truth and without deceptions, sincerely obeying the laws and fulfilling its promises to the people; a government opportunely progressive, one neither too backwards nor too advanced, but adjusted to the degree of culture and the growing needs of the people, because extremes are vicious; in short a very patriotic government, one that seeks the common good and not the good of an individual or a privileged class.[17]

What set of principles or standards can translate this Filipino concept of a just society into a Filipino model of social justice? Let us approach this question indirectly by asking: How is social injustice committed?

I suggest that social injustice is committed in three ways: first, by not having a system of law at all, written or unwritten, or one so flawed that people do not know what their legal rights and duties are; second, by not enforcing law fairly; and third, by enacting law that does not pursue the social values that constitute the Filipino vision of a just society, or that adopts means which subvert those values.

The first two deal with matters of form or procedure; the last, with matters of content or substance. But all are of equal importance: for, as Lord Lawton said, "Doing what is right may still result in unfairness if it is done in the wrong way"[18] or as our

---

thought, dreams and aspirations so that we may have strength to face the evil that reigns in our Motherland.

[16]Apolinario Mabini, "A Mis Compatriotas," op. cit., Vol. I, p. 105.

[17]Apolinario Mabini, "Cual Es La Verdadera Mision de la Revolucion Filipina?," op. cit., Vol. II, p. 57.

[18]Maxwell v. Department of Trade, I.Q.B. 523, 440 (1974).

own Emilio Jacinto said, "Ang gawaing magaling na nagbuhat sa pagpipita sa sarili at hindi sa talagang nasang gumawa ng kagalingan ay di kabaitan.[19] This is, incidentally, what due process means: doing the right things in the right way.

Let us, then, examine each of these ways of committing injustice to formulate standards on which to evaluate laws, policies and institutions.

A total absence or breakdown of a system of law is extremely rare. I cannot, in truth, point to any society, not even a society of thieves, which does not have some system of rules, written or unwritten, that governs relationships among its members and provides a mechanism by which equilibrium is restored when those relationships are willfully breached.

But having a system is not enough; the system must work. To do so, it must meet the following minimum requirements:

(1) The authority of the law-maker must be recognized by the majority of the people as legitimate, and the laws enacted must not exceed the limits on the authority imposed by the prevailing consensus;

(2) Laws must be published or made known to the persons who are to be affected by them; one of the prime causes of the people's anger at the Emperor Caligula, we are told, is that he had "the laws inscribed upon a pillar so high that the people could not read them."[20]

(3) Laws must not be changed so often or so quickly that people cannot reasonably base plans on them;

(4) Laws must be understandable and not contradictory, and must not prescribe acts beyond the capacity of the people or against their conscience.

This is the set of standards that constitutes the first part of a Filipino concept of social justice.

What happens when these standards are persistently breached so that, although there is not total breakdown, there is a general deterioration of the system of law? Lon Fuller describes the results in these words:

. . . A situation begins to develop, for example, in which though some laws are published, others, including the most

---

[19]Emilio Jacinto, op. cit. A rough translation follows:
   A good deed born of self-denial, rather than a genuine desire to do good, is not real goodness.
[20]William Seagle, *Men of the Law — From Hammurabi to Holmes*, New York: The MacMillan Co., 1947, p. 14.

important, are not. Though most laws are prospective in effect, so free a use is made of retrospective legislation that no law is immune to change ex post facto if it suits the convenience of those in power. For the trial of criminal cases concerned with loyalty to the regime, special military tribunals are established and these tribunals disregard, whenever it suits their convenience, the rules that are supposed to control their decisions. Increasingly the principal object of government seems to be, not that of giving the citizen rules by which to shape his conduct, but to frighten him into impotence. As such a situation develops, the problem faced by the citizen is not so simple as that of a voter who knows with certainty that his ballot will not be counted. It is more like that of the voter who knows that the odds are against his ballot being counted at all, and that if it is counted, there is a good chance that it will be counted for the side against which he actually voted.[21]

Lon Fuller wrote those lines seventeen years ago; he based his description on events that had taken place in Nazi Germany; yet his description fits our present situation almost perfectly. Under the circumstances he describes, the voter has to make a choice: either, as Fuller says, "to stay with the system and cast his ballot as a kind of symbolic act expressing the hope of a better day," or to boycott the polls, as millions of Filipinos did in April and June of this year, despite threats of prosecution and acts of harassment. In either case, the social injustice perpetrated is undeniable.

I should skip the second part of our model – the set of standards that would foster fairness or at least prevent unfairness in the enforcement of law – since that topic has been assigned to other speakers.

I cannot resist the temptation, however, paraphrasing Judge Joseph Hutcheson,[22] to point out that, in my years at the bar, I have learned to classify court decisions into six types: the analytic, product of the study and analysis of the law, its policy, and the facts of the case; the intuitive, product of a hunch, the feeling of what is right for this case, which is thereafter reasoned out; the aleatory, like those of Rabelais' Judge Bridlegoose, product of the toss of a coin or the throw of dice, resorted to out of the indolent

---

[21]Lon Fuller, *The Morality of Law,* New Haven: Yale University Press, 1969, pp. 40-41.

[22]Joseph C. Hutcheson, Jr., "The Judgment Intuitive," in *Law and Philosophy,* Edward Allen Kent, ed., New York: Appleton Century Crafts, 1970, pp. 408-409.

desire to avoid the hard work of thinking the issues of the case through; the pusillanimous, product of fear or apprehension of displeasing authority that could block or retard promotion; the venal, product of bribes sometimes offered, but of late often demanded; and the asinine, product of an ass.

The second part of a Filipino concept of justice should, I propose, incorporate standards to eliminate or, given the frailty of men, to drastically reduce the last four kinds of judgments. It should also include standards to infuse courage, competence and integrity into lawyers, and competence, industry and respect for the rights of suspects into policemen.

We come now to the last part of a Filipino model of social justice. By what standards should we judge the content of "laws, policies and institutions that seek justice in the Philippines?"

The first standard is that every law, policy and institution must respect, if it cannot promote, both the individual rights of man and the collective rights of the people.

The rights of man are set out clearly and comprehensively in our constitution, in the Universal Declaration of Human Rights and its two implementing covenants, and in sundry declarations of the United Nations on torture, on slavery and forced labour, on refugees, on territorial asylum, on the rights of the child, on the rights of mentally retarded persons and the like. Respect for these rights is essential if we are to approach the Filipino aspiration for freedom.

The rights of the people have only recently achieved legal recognition. People as national communities have three basic rights: the right to survive; the right to external and internal sovereignty; and the right to development. From these three basic rights flow such rights as freedom from aggression and from intervention in internal affairs; the rights to territorial integrity, political independence, sovereign equality and international social justice; the right freely to choose their economic, as well as their political, social and cultural systems, and the means and goals of development, without outside interference in any form whatsoever; full permanent sovereignty over all national wealth, natural resources and economic activities, which includes the right to regulate and supervise foreign investment and the activities of transnational corporations, and to nationalize, expropriate or transfer ownership of foreign property; and finally, the right – and the duty – to end colonialism, neo-colonialism and all forms of foreign occupation and domination, and the economic and social consequences thereof, as a prerequisite for development.[23]

Every law, policy and institution, must be scrutinized to determine if it impairs or violates any of the rights of the people. To reject this standard is to reject Filipino aspirations to sovereignty, independence and self-reliance.

Yet, given the present condition of Philippine society, these standards are not enough.

In addition to the denial of human rights and of the people's rights, our society today is characterized by a third malady: poverty and inequality. What the degrees of poverty and of inequality are, and whether they are abating or increasing may be disputed – but not even the most obsequious follower of what used to be called a new society and is now called a new republic (as if the word "new" were a perfume that overcomes the stench of the old), no one – I repeat – could honestly deny that there is too much poverty and inequality in our land.

This poverty and inequality cannot be blamed on the vast majority of those of our people who are afflicted by them. In a mixed but capitalist-biased economy such as we have, a person's income is the result of four factors: the amount of income-producing property he owns, his skills, his productivity, and the market value of his skills. Most economists would add a fifth factor for this "new" Republic: closeness to the executive power. There isn't much anyone can do about market value.

What skills a person has, moreover, and their quality and productivity are products of his education, his genes, and his health; and his education is, for the most part, the result of what nutrition his parents could afford to give him during the formative years of childhood. A person's skills and productivity, therefore, depend on the wealth and income of his parents.

So, too, is the income-producing property he acquires: for he can acquire property by inheritance as well as by purchase, or, dishonestly, by extortion, bribery, political influence, fraud or theft. But inheritance depends on the wealth of parents and, as we

---

[23]Charter of Economic Rights and Duties of States, Chapters I and II, Art. 1, 2, 7 and 16; see also, *inter alia,* the United Nations Declaration on the Granting of Independence to Colonial Countries and People; the Conventions on the Prevention and Punishment of the Crime of Genocide and on the Non-Applicability of Statutory Limitations to War Crimes and Crimes Against Humanity; and the Declarations of the Elimination of All Forms of Racial Discrimination and on Social Progress and Development.

have shown, so does, in large measure, the capacity to earn income with which to buy property.

As a rule, the poor are poor and unequal because they are born poor and unequal. And this poverty and inequality spawn oppression, exploitation and abuse. Plutarch pointed this out more than two thousand years ago:

> A mere law to give all men equal rights is but useless, if the poor must sacrifice those rights to their debts, and, in the very seats and sanctuaries of equality, the courts of justice, the offices of state, and the public discussion, be more than anywhere at the beck and bidding of the rich.[24]

To attain the Filipino concept of social justice, then, laws, policies and institutions must, besides promoting respect for individual and collective human rights, also consciously strive, by effective means:

One, to eradicate poverty, at first in its most degrading forms and effects and afterwards in all its forms;

Two, to select a means of developing and using our natural resources, our industries and our commerce to achieve a self-directed, self-generated, and self-sufficient economy, in order to produce enough to meet, at first, the basic material needs of all and, afterwards, to provide an increasingly higher standard of living for all, but particularly for those with lower incomes, and to provide them with enough leisure to participate creatively in the development and enjoyment of our national culture; and

Three, to change those relations and structures of relations between man and man, between groups, and between communities that cause or perpetuate inequality, unless that inequality is necessary to improve the lot of the least favored among our people and its burden is borne by those who heretofore have been most favored.

These three standards complete the third part of a Filipino model of social justice.

These standards embody two different principles: the first, a principle of reparation that looks back to repair the injustice inflicted by society on the poor and the oppressed; and the second and the third, a principle of change that looks forward to effect the internal and external revolutions of which Mabini wrote, in order to

---

[24]Plutarch, "Poplicola and Solon Compared," in *Great Treasury of Western Thought,* Mortimer J. Adler and Charles Van Doren, eds., New York: R.R. Bowker Company, 1977, p. 869.

attain the aspiration that Jacinto articulated: that a Filipino's worth, who he is, should not depend on what he was.

Neither principle advocates nor intends to abolish all inequality nor to achieve mathematical identity in sharing social costs and benefits. I do not think it realistic to pursue such objectives. Nature, chance and accident do cause differences; these differences do produce inequalities, and though we are achieving more and more control over nature, we cannot change nature, nor eliminate chance or accident. But we can change human relations and actions; and therefore, we can see to it that whatever inequalities remain in our society are not caused by our relations with each other or our actions toward each other.

There is, moreover, so strong a streak of individuality in the Filipino psyche that I believe we would rebel at any attempt to impose uniformity upon us. Most of us would not, for example, accept wearing one unchanging style of clothing as the Chinese people accepted the drab uniformity of Mao jackets. Of course, if nothing else were available, we would have no choice; but our goal is not, and never should be, to narrow the people's choices, but to expand them, to increase man's needs, not merely to satisfy them.

Finally, neither principle seeks to do away with government or law. On the contrary, it is through honest government enforcing just laws that the principles would be translated into actual justice. I do not know of any other way.

Because the principles are distinct, though complementary, conflicts may arise from time to time in applying them. That would not diminish their value. It would simply call for the exercise of wisdom and statesmanship.

Let us now formulate a Filipino concept of social justice, valid for today and hopefully for tomorrow.

Social justice, for us Filipinos, means a coherent, intelligible system of law, made known to us, enacted by a legitimate government freely chosen by us, and enforced fairly and equitably by a courageous, honest, impartial, and competent police force, legal profession and judiciary, that first, respects our rights and our freedoms both as individuals and as a people; second, seeks to repair the injustices that society has inflicted on the poor by eliminating or at least reducing poverty as rapidly as our resources and our ingenuity make possible: third, develops a self-directed and self-sustaining economy that distributes its benefits to meet, at first, the basic material needs of all, then to provide an improving standard of living for all, but particularly for the lower income groups, with time enough and space to allow them to help create and to enjoy our culture; fourth, changes our institutions and structures, our ways of doing things and relating to each other, so that whatever inequalities remain are not caused by those institutions or structures, unless inequality is needed temporarily to favor the least favored among us and its cost is borne by the most favored; and fifth, adopts means and processes that are capable of attaining these objectives.

Are these standards impossible to meet? If you mean meet completely and immediately, they are. But only yesterday in world time, it was thought impossible to land on the moon. And not too long ago, Aristotle one of the wisest of men, justified slavery as natural and listed torture as a source of evidence. So standards thought too high today may well turn out to be too low tomorrow. But whether they do so or not is not really important. What Nikos Kazantzakis said of freedom can be said of justice: the superior virtue is not to receive justice, it is to fight relentlessly for it – to struggle for justice in time, yet under the aspect of eternity.

MARTIAL LAW IN THE PHILIPPINES

What has martial law done to the Filipinos? How have national and local organizations responded to the cruelties or harshness of martial law? The work of Task Force Detainees of the Philippines (TFDP) on behalf of political prisoners and their families, is described. TFDP was organized by the Association of Major Religious Superiors in the Philippines.

Thank you for inviting me to address you tonight. It is an honor wholly undeserved; and it comes on a date specially significant to me: for six years ago tonight, martial rule was imposed upon my country, the Philippines. Night fell on our land, and we have yet to glimpse the dawn. But now and then, a spark lights up in the darkness: the lamp of freedom flickers still, despite every effort to quench it. You of Amnesty International have helped us keep it alive. For that, we Filipinos owe you a debt we can never repay. But we can, and we do, say "Thank you."

Martial rule came to the Philippines, as it had come to other developing countries, with solemn assurances to a stunned people that, though drastic, it was temporary; that it was needed to preserve our democracy from communist subversion; and that from its crucible would emerge a new society.

As the shock wore off, we Filipinos learned to our sorrow, as other people had learned to theirs, that martial rule is self-perpetuating; that it is needed only to install dictatorship; and that it serves only to fortify the very structures of external dependence and internal colonialism, of privilege and exploitation, that had made ours a society of the greedy and the needy.

Since tonight is the sixth anniversary of martial rule, it is appropriate to tell you something of what it has done to our people, and how we are striving to free ourselves from its yoke. Perhaps our experience may be useful to others.

There is much to tell, and little time to tell it. So I shall limit myself to one area of our experience: the field of political prisoners. I do so not just because this is the area of your special

---

(Lecture delivered at the Amnesty International's International Council Meeting 1978, Cambridge, England, on September 21, 1978)

concern, but because, more clearly than any other area, it reveals the ugliness of martial rule.

The problem of political prisoners is not new to us Filipinos. But martial rule gave it new dimensions.

First, the number of political prisoners was unprecedented. In the first few weeks of martial rule, not less than 30,000 were thrown into military stockades. A year and three months later, 10,000 still languished behind barbed wires, without charges or trial.

Second, it was obvious that many, if not most, of these political prisoners were not subversives in the sense of having taken up arms against government or being members or supporters of the Communist Party. Most, in fact, eschewed violence; their crime consisted mainly of having criticized the corruption and inefficiency of the government before martial law, and in advocating reforms or changes in our social structures. Since most citizens agreed with those criticisms and reforms, most citizens were poignantly aware that they too were vulnerable to arrest.

Third, the conditions of detention were wretched. Detention centers were overcrowded; sanitary facilities, poor; medical attention, inadequate; food, meager and unpalatable.

Fourth, many political prisoners had been tortured -- particularly the poor, the young, the illiterate, the obscure. Several were kept for long periods in solitary confinement. Others died under brutal questioning. Torture had three objectives: to extract information, to extort confession and to instill terror. It achieved all three.

Fifth, most political prisoners were married. When the husband was detained, his wife was reduced to living on charity, and his children forced to drop out of school. When the wife was detained -- and in some cases, both husband and wife were -- the children were left motherless.

The regime tried to deny or disguise the facts. "No one, but no one," it insisted, "has been tortured." And no one was arrested without "sufficient evidence of guilt." Detention was not imprisonment, it said: it was rehabilitation. However, the fact that political prisoners were so numerous made it impossible to hide the truth for long.

Once known, the facts clamored for remedies. Efforts by individuals on behalf of individual prisoners would not be enough. Such efforts inevitably neglected those without money, influence, connections or friends, yet they were the ones who most needed attention. To be effective, efforts had to be planned, persistent, coordinated and concerted -- in a word, organized -- to seek justice for all political prisoners and not only for one or for some.

Yet any attempt to organize such efforts appeared doomed to failure.

Martial rule seemed all powerful; its definition of subversion, all-embracing; and this combination instilled such fear of arrest -- not only because of the consequences to oneself, but more so because of the consequences to one's family -- that erstwhile friends of political prisoners turned their backs on them; some relatives went so far as to deny their kinship; and families of political prisoners hesitated to work together: they were not sure they could trust each other, and were apprehensive that the military might taint them with guilt by association, and prevent or delay the release of their loved ones. In this climate, who would dare join an organization for political prisoners? Who would support it with funds?

Besides, what could such an organization do? It could not appeal to the press, for all mass media were controlled; it could not demonstrate, because peaceful assembly was forbidden; it could not petition Congress, because Congress had been shut down; and it could not go to law, because the courts had been emasculated. What power, then, could the organization hope to have? How could it exert pressure on the regime?

To make matters worse, martial rule was supported by the government of the United States, which doubled both military and economic aid, trained many of the officers who interrogated and tortured prisoners, and supplied sophisticated weapons of surveillance and repression. How could any organization hope to prevail against so formidable an alliance?

One institution could: the Catholic Church. However, the Catholic hierarchy made no move to organize efforts on behalf of political prisoners. Apart from warning against the use of torture, the Bishops' Conference did not touch the problem. It adopted a policy of "critical collaboration" with the regime which in practice turned out to be, for most bishops, very active collaboration and very little criticism.

Fortunately, another group within the Church -- the Association of Major Religious Superiors in the Philippines -- not so powerful as the Bishops' Conference, but still a significant part of the Church, saw the gravity and urgency of the need. The Association created Task Force Detainees of the Philippines, and called for volunteers from religious orders. Response was immediate. One year and three months after martial law was imposed, the problem of political prisoners would, at last, receive organized attention.

That it took so long is an index of how much martial law had stunned our people. That the Church, as an institution, failed to act, indicates the depths to which institutions can become compromised by the establishment. But that a group of valiant priests and nuns did act, gives hope that, in areas where ordinary citizens may fear to tread, men and women of religion will dare.

How did Task Force Detainees of the Philippines surmount the obstacles I have mentioned: the fear of arrest, the absence of means to exert effective pressure on the regime, the alliance between the regime and the government of the United States?

The answer is that it didn't. It just went ahead in spite of the obstacles. And in doing so, it found that the obstacles somehow no longer looked so formidable. For the sources of strength of martial rule are also sources of weakness.

Take fear, for example. When a regime relies exclusively or mainly on fear to maintain itself in power, it becomes weakest when it looks strongest. For, in time, people learn that, even if they are afraid, they can nevertheless do what they should, and when they do, fear's power over them is lost.

That is what happened to Task Force Detainees of the Philippines. Fear of arrest still assails members of the task force. Everyone who works for Task Force Detainees of the Philippines knows that he may, for that reason alone, be arrested. No one wants to be arrested -- particularly those who have been arrested before. But they have all learned to live with their fear, and not to let it stop them from doing their job -- a job they believe is worth doing and has to be done. That there are lawyers who are ready to defend them, and that their families will be helped if they are detained, relieves them of some anxiety. But they draw strength, most of all, from each other's determination.

Inspired by their example, families of political prisoners flocked to the task force; information poured in; political prisoners, upon release, volunteered their services; donations trickled in; other groups offered help. Fear is contagious, but courage is not less so.

In a similar fashion, Task Force Detainees of the Philippines learned that, although martial law gave the regime total control over the instruments of power, there was one source of power martial law could not provide: truth. Truth is the power of the powerless; and it becomes increasingly powerful as the regime, grown arrogant, begins to underestimate the intelligence of the people, to continue to deny or distort reality, to exaggerate accomplishments -- in short, to lose all credibility.

How Task Force Detainees of the Philippines exposed and spread the truth on behalf of political prisoners I shall discuss in a moment. But first let me take up the last of the obstacles: the alliance between martial rule and the government of the United States.

That alliance continues, despite the Carter policy on human rights which, in my country, is subordinated to the economic and security interests of the United States. Economic and military aid still flow from the United States to the dictatorial regime; and if symbolic cuts have been made in the amount of military aid, these have been more than made up for by increased assistance loans granted by international agencies over which the United States exercises decisive influence.

But continued support of the regime by the United States has also meant greater dependence by the regime on the United States; and dependence impairs freedom of action. It is this dependence that gave Task Force Detainees of the Philippines an unexpected weapon.

By exposing the wretched conditions of detention, the widespread, systematic use of torture on political prisoners, and the rampant violation of their basic rights, Task Force Detainees of the Philippines helped awaken public opinion in the United States to the iniquity and injustice, the hardship and degradation, that support by their government helps the martial law regime perpetrate on the Filipino people. American public opinion has exerted pressure on the United States government; and has caused the latter, in turn, to exert pressure on the martial law regime to curb its excesses. What had seemed to be a bar to one path, turned out to be a gate to another.

In dealing with the problems of political prisoners, Task Force Detainees of the Philippines viewed its role as being not so much to solve problems as to arouse and heighten consciousness; the consciousness of political prisoners and their families; the consciousness of the military; and the consciousness of the people.

This view of its role implied certain norms of conduct that limited the scope of its work but which also increased its effectiveness.

The objective of arousing the consciousness of political prisoners and their families required Task Force Detainees of the Philippines, first, not to make decisions for them, but to support the decisions they themselves made, to the extent compatible with its capabilities and the scope of its ministry; and second, to perform only such functions as they could not do themselves, and to turn over such functions to them as soon as they were ready to perform them.

Consequently, Task Force Detainees of the Philippines set the priorities according to what political prisoners and their families considered their most pressing needs. This led to a more effective use of its limited resources, and created stronger bonds of trust between it and those it sought to help. More important, the knowledge this gave political prisoners that they could make decisions and that their decisions would be respected; that the task force viewed them as human beings and not as mere objects of charity, enhanced their dignity, and reduced one of the worst effects of prolonged detention -- the feeling of impotence, of being a non-person -- that assails every political prisoner.

In time, political prisoners adopted their own rules of conduct within prison; organized and assigned common chores among themselves; devised means of letting the outside world know if anything untoward was happening within the prison, even when visits were curtailed; produced their own handicrafts; and secured better prison conditions by concerted action ranging from making demands on prison officials to hunger strikes.

In these matters, Task Force Detainees of the Philippines played a purely supportive role: to make the public aware of prison conditions, the prisoners' demands for improvement, and the sacrifices and hardships they were undergoing in pursuit of the demands.

As I mentioned earlier, families of political prisoners were hesitant about working together and apprehensive about meeting with military authorities. So at the start, it was the task force that notified relatives of arrests reported to it; inquired about the whereabouts of political prisoners not taken to detention centers; verified from the military what were the charges against them; and followed up petitions and papers for their release. The task force also initiated conversations among families, and they came to know each other better, to trust each other, and eventually to work closely together. Lately, families of political prisoners formed an association called KAPATID (Brother); and the association has not only taken over the functions I have just mentioned, but it is, at the same time, waging a campaign for a general and unconditional amnesty for all political prisoners.

The objectives of arousing the consciousness of the public and of the military itself required Task Force Detainees of the Philippines, first, to document, with care and thoroughness, the injustices and abuses done to political prisoners, and to disseminate the facts as widely as possible; and, second, to make sure that all actions on behalf of political detainees were non-violent and clearly moral, regardless of whether the regime considers them unlawful or not.

Following these norms, Task Force Detainees of the Philippines developed sources of information; encouraged the making of reports to it of all violations of rights of detainees; made sure they were accurate; and, if the victims agreed, made the information public. Normally, this was done by filing complaints or reports with the officers concerned and their superiors; furnishing copies to the ministry of defense and to the local and international press; reproducing the complaints and documentation in church publications; discussing them in seminars held in schools and colleges, in reflection meetings in religious houses, and in every other available forum.

In 1976, Task Force Detainees of the Philippines printed a volume describing the situation of political detainees in the Philippines. The second volume appeared in 1977; the third is in preparation. Since 1977, the task force has also published biweekly up-dates and quarterly reports on the situation.

These publications are not flattering to the regime and, of course, are not authorized by it. But so far it has not taken punitive action against Task Force Detainees of the Philippines. I suppose it has weighed the adverse reactions that arrests based on the publications would cause locally and internationally, together with the limited circulation of the publications, and has decided, so far, to leave Task Force Detainees of the Philippines alone.

In addition to publications, Task Force Detainees of the Philippines has tried to keep public attention focused on political prisoners by organizing mass public prayers for them, and by seeing to it that mass actions organized by other victims of martial rule learn of the plight of political prisoners and the connection between that plight and other injustices under martial rule.

The regime, of course, considers these demonstrations unlawful, even if they are peaceful. To organize them, to address the crowd, or just to be in the crowd, invites arrest or even bodily injury, for on occasion the regime has used water cannons, clubs and electrically charged cattle prods to disperse demonstrators. But this is a risk that has to be taken -- and it is being taken.

How successful has Task Force Detainees of the Philippines been? An honest answer is: not half as successful as it would like to be.

The tasks of supplying political prisoners with the food, medicines, clothes, blankets, pillows, and other things they need that prison authorities do not supply; of helping families of needy political prisoners set up small businesses to provide for themselves; and of seeing their children through school, have not proved too difficult. They are mainly matters of organization and funds, with funds the critical element.

Task Force Detainees of the Philippines obtained seed funds from
the Association of Major Religious Superiors in the Philippines.
However, its attempts to raise additional funds from lay sources in
the Philippines have not been quite successful. Perhaps this is
because the wealthy, who have the money, are afraid of reprisals
from the regime; perhaps there are other demands upon them they
cannot ignore; perhaps they are reluctant to help persons who have
been branded as subversives; or perhaps they are simply selfish:
after all, it is hardly possible to claim deductions from income
taxes for contributions for political detainees.

Whatever the reasons may be, the result has been that Task Force
Detainees of the Philippines has had to cut its administrative
expenses to the bone, and to appeal to the generosity of foreign
non-governmental groups and of men and women of good will
abroad to finance particular programs. I am told that less than ten
per cent of Task Force Detainees' funds have come from Filipino
sources. The picture is not flattering to us, but it would be a
disservice to you and to the Filipino people to gloss over or distort
this fact.

As you of Amnesty International know, the problem of funds
plagues all who seek justice for political prisoners. But it is a
problem that we must never stop trying to solve.

In the task of providing legal services to political prisoners, Task
Force Detainees of the Philippines was helped by a group of
lawyers, members of a union for civil liberties, who learned of its
existence and offered their services without compensation.

In the beginning, the legal aid group had only five members
clustered around the nation's capital. Today it counts some fifty
members, with at least one in every region of the country. The
group defends, not only political detainees, but also slum dwellers,
laborers, farmers, tribal people and students -- anyone who has been
victimized by martial law and can find no one to defend him. Task
Force Detainees of the Philippines assisted the growth of the legal
aid group by co-sponsoring seminars to hone their skills, financing
travelling expenses, assuming the cost of equipment for
reproducing legal materials, and the like.

Recently, the legal aid group published a pamphlet explaining
the legal rights of political prisoners under martial rule, and
excerpting relevant Philippine laws and international accords. Task
Force Detainees of the Philippines helped find funds for printing
the pamphlet and has distributed copies to lawyers, judges, political
prisoners, persons whose work with the disadvantaged makes them
peculiarly liable to arrest, and to the military themselves,

particularly those in charge of detention centers and military prisons.

Other needs of political prisoners have not been as simple to meet.

In detention centers away from the nation's capital, conditions remain wretched. In some areas, Task Force Detainees of the Philippines has discovered that military authorities use political prisoners as household servants without pay. Conditions under detention in these areas are so bad, that detainees found even this type of bonded servitude preferable.

Torture continues. The regime has been forced to admit that acts of torture have been committed, to issue statements condemning and disavowing torture; and to go through the motions of prosecuting some soldiers whom prisoners have pointed to as having tortured them. Since these prosecutions take place in military courts, most cases are ultimately dismissed or result in acquittals. Where penalties have been imposed, they have been light: little more than slaps on the wrist. Nevertheless, the incidence of torture has declined.

But as torture declined, a more terrible tactic emerged; unofficial executions. Suspected dissidents are arrested and vanish. Sometimes, the military claim they were killed in armed encounters, but in these cases, when relatives claim their bodies, they bear marks of torture. In other cases, the military simply deny having arrested them, and maintain they "went underground" to evade arrest.

Task Force Detainees of the Philippines has yet to find a way to prevent or minimize unofficial executions. Where witnesses have seen the arrest, they are too frightened to testify; where bodies are recovered with telltale signs of torture, it is often impossible to identify the torturers. And in some cases where responsibility might have been fixed, families have refused to prosecute. Task Force Detainees of the Philippines still has much to do to arouse public consciousness.

Yet a glimmer of hope came last April. Task Force Detainees of the Philippines received a report that a political prisoner had been taken to a military hospital where he had died shortly after admission, apparently from severe maltreatment under questioning. Though the caller did not give his name, he identified himself as a military man, and his knowledge of the facts, including his description of the injuries, left no doubt that he was telling the truth. So perhaps the efforts of Task Force Detainees to arouse public consciousness, including that of the military, have not been totally unsuccessful.

It is time to summarize the lessons experience with political prisoners under martial rule has taught us Filipinos that may be useful to others.

The most encouraging lesson is that dictatorship can be fought without resort to arms. Whether it can be defeated is, unfortunately, another matter. But some of its excess can be curbed, some of its rigors mitigated, through organized, determined and intelligent efforts of those who are not dismayed by the apparent hopelessness of the task, who are willing to run risks, to extend the limits of what freedom the regime allows, who force the regime to face the immorality of its conduct, who draw strength, not from the power of violence, but from the power of truth.

Another lesson we have learned is that the fear martial rule instills would not be half as effective -- indeed martial rule itself might not have been successfully imposed -- had the people not harbored an earlier fear that martial rule fed on.

In my country, this was the fear of communism. It distracted us from noticing and aborting the militarization of our society that started in the 1950's. It was exploited to discredit nationalist demands for reform in the 1960's, and to justify the imposition of martial law in 1972. Today, it hampers efforts to help political prisoners and to act in unity against the oppression that is martial rule.

Fear need not be of communists: it may be of terrorists, or of a militant minority seeking secession or independence, or of gangsters or mere non-conformists. Whatever its cause, fear -- carefully nurtured by the establishment -- hardens into the belief that communists, terrorists, secessionists, gangsters, dissenters, anarchists -- call them what you will -- have forfeited their humanity, and so have forfeited their rights. Seen as posing extraordinary dangers, they justify extraordinary remedies: national defense becomes national security; military values infiltrate civil society; the inevitable result is military rule or some other variant of dictatorship; and in the process, human rights blur and evanesce.

Please do not misunderstand me. The point I wish to make is not that the danger feared is imaginary -- it may well be very real. The point is that there are dangers we do better to live with than to try to eliminate. Fear is a powerful motive, but an unreliable guide. It can create evils more monstrous than those it seeks to avoid. It can kill freedom while trying to preserve it.

Two justifications for authoritarianism in Asian developing countries are currently fashionable.

One is that Asian societies are authoritarian and paternalistic and so need governments that are also authoritarian and paternalistic; that Asia's hungry masses are too concerned with providing their families with food, clothing, and shelter, to concern themselves with civil liberties and political freedoms; that the Asian conception of freedom differs from that of the West; that, in short, Asians are not fit for democracy.

Another is that developing countries must sacrifice freedom temporarily to achieve the rapid economic development that their exploding populations and rising expectations demand; that, in short, government must be authoritarian to promote development.

The first justification is racist nonsense. The second is a lie: authoritarianism is not needed for developing; it is needed to perpetuate the status quo.

Development is not just providing people with adequate food, clothing, and shelter; many prisons do as much. Development is also people deciding what food, clothing and shelter are adequate, and how they are to be provided. Authoritarianism does not let people decide: its basic premise is that people do not know how to decide. So it promotes repression, not development, repression that prevents meaningful change, and preserves the structure of power and privilege.

The Philippine experience under martial rule is a case in point.

Before martial rule, despite formal independence, the Philippines was essentially a colonial society. It still is.

The hub of economic, political and social activity was Manila. It still is.

Wealth and power were concentrated in a few hands. They still are.

The distribution of income was extremely uneven, it has become worse. Thirty-nine per cent of our families then lived -- if one could call it living -- below the poverty threshold. Today, 48 per cent do -- more than 20 million Filipinos.

Before martial rule, there had been some industrialization based on the import substitution model, but the economy was still basically an export economy. Martial rule intensified the export orientation of the economy. It based its entire development program on export promotion. So our land, labor, raw materials and capital are increasingly devoted to meeting the requirements of foreign markets instead of domestic needs; we export food though our children are underfed.

Under martial rule, our foreign debt swelled from U.S. $2 billion in 1972 to U.S. $7 billion in 1978. The major cause of the increase is the infrastructure program of the regime, a program designed to enable the military to deploy its forces quickly and to provide exporters and foreign investors with public facilities that reduce their costs, but which the people pay for in increased taxes and higher commodity prices. And, naturally, increased foreign debt means increased foreign influence over national policy.

Before martial rule, foreign capital dominated strategic sectors of our economy, and the national policy was to eliminate or at least reduce that domination. Martial rule reversed the policy. It opened the economy to foreign investment; and, as consequence and inducement, decreed that labor become competent while remaining docile and cheap. The economy, it is true, has expanded, but wages have contracted; real per capita GNP has grown 14 per cent since 1972, but in the same period, real wages declined 29 per cent. Today, 90 per cent of all workers in all sectors of our economy are paid wages that the regime itself describes as "below the minimum subsistence level."

Under martial rule, the rich have become even richer, and the poor hungrier.

Martial rule, then, has maintained the status quo with a vengeance. To do so, it has used its power of arrest and detention, not only on those suspected of subversion, but on little people of our society seeking a better life: laborers struggling for just wages; farmers striving for land; slum dwellers hungering for a home; students pursuing academic freedom; tribal peoples protecting ancestral lands, traditions and culture; and, recently, urban voters marching peacefully to protest the insolent frauds that had made a mockery of what the regime had promised would be a free election.

Little people -- not suspected communists -- have made up the bulk of political prisoners in the Philippines. They are living proof that you cannot enforce economic and social rights unless you have civil and political rights.

The experience of the Philippines has also been the experience of other developing nations in Asia. A recent book on Southeast Asia reports that:

> In each state the governing elite has established a more or less authoritarian political structure making it impossible for opposition groups to capture power by constitutional means. Opposition leaders are arrested or absorbed; newspapers are controlled; and potentially independent mass organizations undermined and supervised, when not banned. Elections, when they are held, always take place in circumstances ensuring victory for the government ... In the absence of effective

constitutional opposition, the most serious resistance comes from insurgents ...[1]

And it also reports that:

In spite of the growth in aggregate output and the rise in average per capita incomes in real terms, mass poverty and unemployment remain acute problems.[2]

Regardless of what dictators and social scientists may say, Asians know that loss of freedom does not lead to a better life. On the contrary, Asians know that life cannot become better -- it cannot even be good -- unless people are free.

Asians harbor no illusions that freedom will lead automatically to a good life. We Filipinos, for example, had freedom before martial law; yet, as I have indicated, life for the masses of our people was far from good, though it was better than it is today.

For our people to have a good life, the structure of our economy must change: our resources must be used and developed to meet first the needs of the majority, before supplying the demands of foreign countries for our products, and of the well-off at home for luxuries. Such a change will hurt vested interests, Filipino and foreign alike. Naturally, they will try to prevent it. That is why martial rule was imposed in the first place.

To make the change, then, the people must wrest power, but unless the people are free, there may be only one way to do so: the way of violence and bloodshed.

Even after the people have gained power, the change will be possible only if the government that the people install is not destabilized by foreign capital or foreign governments which may find their interests threatened by the change.

Is it realistic to hope for such forbearance? At one time, I confess, I was certain it was not. Today, I am not so sure.

For I have seen you of Amnesty International and other people throughout the world unselfishly help us vindicate human rights despite martial rule: some with funds, some with moral support,

---

[1]Harold Crouch, "Southeast Asia in 1977 -- A Political Overview," in *Southeast Asian Affairs 1978,* Institute of Southeast Asian Studies, ed. by Kernial S. Sandhu and others, Singapore: Heineman Educational Books (Asia) Ltd., 1978, pp. 10-11.

[2]Chia Siou Yue, "Economic Development," in ibid, p. 18.

others with manifestations of solidarity, and still others risking their safety to learn and report the truth about my country.

I have witnessed the international press accurately report events that the martial law regime had tried to conceal or distort.

These things have made me realize how much people need each other and how willingly people respond to people across the boundaries of nations and states.

And they have given me hope that, just as people around the world helped us struggle against the oppression perpetrated by our government against us, they will also help us fight the oppression perpetrated by other governments against us, even, perhaps, when the government is their own; that the concern people have shown for Filipino political prisoners will encompass Filipino aspirations for national and social liberation.

I should close, but there is a memory locked in my heart that begs to be shared. It is the memory of a young couple -- not yet in their thirties -- whom I saw some months ago in a large hall that had been converted into a military courtroom, waiting for the case to be called in which they stood accused with some ninety other young people.

I had met the young man before martial law. He was a university student, a leader: brilliant, articulate, involved. That day in the courtroom he sat in a rattan chair, almost motionless, staring blankly ahead, his mouth half open, totally oblivious to the people and the chatter around him; for he had been detained under martial law; punished so repeatedly and so brutally, and subjected to so large a dose of what the military call the truth serum, that his mind had cracked. He is confined, to this day, in the mental ward of a military hospital.

Behind him stood his wife, straight and proud, one hand lightly resting on the crown of his head, the other touching his shoulder tenderly yet defiantly, ready to spring on anyone who might still wish to hurt her husband.

As I looked at the couple, I saw in them the face of every Filipino; and I knew then that martial law could crush our bodies; it could break our minds; but it could not conquer our spirit. It may silence our voice and seel our eyes; but it cannot kill our hope nor obliterate our vision. We will struggle on, no matter how long it takes or what it costs, until we establish a just community of free men and women in our land, deciding together, working and striving together, but also singing and dancing, laughing and loving together.

That is the ultimate lesson.

OUR CULTURAL MINORITIES AND DEVELOPMENT PROJECTS

This speech shows that human rights are universal; that they apply not only to the majority, but also to the cultural minorities whose very survival is endangered by "development" projects, such as dams to be built on their ancestral lands. It was delivered at a time when fear of the three-year-old martial law regime was still very strong.

I want to thank you for the great honor and the privilege that you have given me in inviting me this afternoon. You see, this is the first time that a civic group in Manila has had the balls to invite me to speak before them. I have spoken before one other civic club but it was the Cavite Rotary Club and you all know that the Caviteños really have them well-placed.

Frankly, I am sorry to say that in the Greater Manila Area, I have not found very many people who can stand up – especially the men – who can stand up and say that they are truly men. I find that our women are more men than our men.

Seriously speaking, my friends, I really want to thank you for inviting someone who has been imprisoned by the martial law regime, because it is not often that someone who has been behind barbed wires for two years is given a chance to speak to an audience that is willing to listen to him even only for a few minutes.

When I received your invitation, I was faced by an embarrassment of riches. I didn't know what to talk about. There are so many things in our society today that demand that they be spoken about. For example, there is the hunger strike of my former companion inside who is still inside, Senator Aquino.[1] Why is he on a hunger strike? How long will it last? What is he fighting for? Should we or should we not help him? Now, this is a challenging question.

Then again, there is the very, very important problem that is happening today, right this minute, in Zamboanga where you have the Muslim leaders meeting with the government leaders. What is the fight in Zamboanga and in Mindanao all about? What do our

---

(Speech before the Thursday Club of Quezon City, April 17, 1975)
[1]The late Senator Aquino went on a hunger strike to protest his trial by a military tribunal and the death sentence passed on him.

Muslim brothers want? Is there anything that we can do to stop the bloodshed in that area? That is another subject that demands attention.

And then, there is Mr. Marcos' announcement last night that he is changing or at least restudying our foreign policy vis-a-vis the American government. To what extent should we change? When should we stop, steer away from the United States? Go closer to Japan? Go closer to Russia? Go closer to China? What should be our foreign policy? These are vital questions.

Maybe one of the questions that we should also discuss is: Should we listen to the foreign policy of our distinguished Secretary of Foreign Affairs, Mr. Romulo, whose latest problem is a dance marathon with an eighty-year-old Australian about the *tinikling*[2]? This is the way our foreign policy is being conducted. Now, these are vital problems.

There is also something closer to home, because many of you are businessmen, managers and entrepreneurs. The new Labor Code poses many problems. Is that Labor Code really a Labor Code or an anti-Labor Code? Do we really respect the rights of labor or are we trampling on those rights?

This afternoon, I would like to discuss one of these problems.

I have chosen this problem for several reasons: first, because I think it is not well known and it deserves to be known by our people; second, it is still at a stage where something can be done, but if nothing is done, we may have another Mindanao in Luzon. I am referring to the problem of the Chico River Basin Development Project in Kalinga-Apayao and Bontoc provinces.

Many years ago, the government made a study and decided that four dams should be built in the Chico River and Pasiw River in Kalinga and in Bontoc province. There is one dam that is to be built at Bontoc, Bontoc, and they call it Chico I, another dam at Sadanga, Bontoc, Chico II; another dam at Basao, Kalinga, that is Chico III; and the biggest at Lubuangan, Kalinga, Chico IV. These dams are supposed to develop 70,000 kilowatts of electric power. They are also supposed to irrigate the entire Cagayan Valley area. And so from the purely economic point of view, these projects sound as if they were economic development. That is one side of the matter.

But now, let us look at the other side. To go through with these four dams will mean that you will take out 5,000 Bontoc and Kalinga families from their homes; you will take them out from

---

[2]A native dance.

where they have lived from time immemorial and put them in the lowlands where they will die a slow death. It means that we will destroy 1,500 of our rice terraces.

But more important than the destruction of homes, more important than the displacement of people, is the fact that we are being forced to change the way of life of people who are genuinely Filipinos. We Christians of the lowlands proudly call ourselves Filipino. But the truth of the matter is: The true Filipinos are our brothers in Kalinga and Bontoc. They have maintained their culture, their way of life, their beliefs, their religion, for more than one thousand years. They were already here long before the Spaniards arrived. And now because of progress, they are to be uprooted and brought to the lowlands. One of the most important scenic wonders of the world – our rice terraces – are going to be in part destroyed. But more valuable than these are the religious beliefs of the people of Bontoc and Kalinga.

For them the big trees and forests in their environment are their churches. They pray there, beseeching help from their God. The spirits of their ancestors are alive, buried in their ancestral grounds. The entire history of their race is written in their rice terraces. And so these people are prepared to fight to the death rather than give up their land.

I bring up this problem because there are so many lawyers here. We can say that a good case can be made for the Kalingas and the Bontocs. For instance, as early as 1901, the U.S. Supreme Court through Justice Holmes in the case of Carino vs. Insular Government decided: "A native title to land in the Province of Benguet in the Philippine Islands which for more than 50 years prior to the treaty of peace with Spain on April 11, 1899, a native Igorot and his ancestors had held in accordance with Igorot custom as private property should be recognized by the Insular government although no document of title has issued from the Spanish Crown."[3] And this was not all. What he said was: " ... every presumption is and ought to be against the government in a case like the present."[4] Now, this was decided by the United States Supreme Court in 1909.

For our part, we lowlanders enacted legislation about the year 1965 in which we declared it to be the policy of the state to foster, accelerate and accomplish by all adequate means and in a systematic, rapid and complete manner the moral, material,

---

[3]Mateo Carino vs. Insular Government of the Philippine Islands, *Philippine Reports,* Vol. 41, pp. 935-936.
[4]Ibid., p. 941.

economic, social and political development of the non-christian Filipinos and to render real, complete and permanent the integration of all of said national cultural minorities into the body politic. We ruled that it was the Commission on National Integration that should promote community life, that should aid the national cultural minorities and, in general, further their agricultural, industrial and social development. And in that 1972 document that the Supreme Court and Mr. Marcos say is our new Constitution, in that very document, it is stated "the state shall consider the customs, traditions, beliefs and interests of national cultural communities in the formulation and implementation of state policies."[5]

Now, I ask: Are we considering the customs, traditions, beliefs and interests of the Kalingas and the Bontocs when we force them to get out of where they have lived from time immemorial and to live a life which for them is not living? Are we advancing their moral, social, economic and material well-being by uprooting them from their way of life and their culture? Is it not that we Christians are looking at them as if they were ignorant and lower than we are? And yet, who are the real Filipinos – they or we? Is our culture genuinely ours? Our culture is a mix of Chinese, Spanish, American, Japanese elements. Whereas our Kalinga and Bontoc brothers have their own unique civilization.

We talk about community, but is there any community in the lowlands that is as well organized as a Bontoc or Kalinga community?

We talk about passive resistance and knowing our rights. I will give you an example of what the Bontoc women did to the surveyors of the National Power Corporation when the surveyors went to Sadanga to survey the land. Let me read to you an account of what happened: "The women drove out the National Power Corporation team who came to survey and drill."[6] How did they do this? Did they use arms? Did they use guns? This is what they used. I will read to you: "The women removed their *tapis* (a kind of skirt) knowing that the lowland men would not touch them in public nor even look at them if they were naked. It is a cultural taboo. They advanced on the engineers nude, armed only with their garden tools; the engineers fled in sheer embarrassment. A helicopter had to be flown to pick up their abandoned equipment."[7]

---

[5]1973 Philippine Constitution, Art. XV, Sec. 11.
[6]The Signs of the Times. Association of Major Religious Superiors of Men and Women, June 1974.
[7]Ibid.

Now, let us ask ourselves: Can we in the lowlands do what the Bontoc women did? Do we have the courage to stick up for our rights as these Bontoc people and Kalinga people whom we, in our arrogance, consider as less civilized than we are? And yet, let us remember one thing: how much can they do alone? Sure, their men and women are very brave Kalinga and Bontoc. Yet, can their weapons prevail against the modern weapons of the Armed Forces of the Phlippines? If the government decides to push through these projects and get them out and these people resist, is there a chance for them or will there be another Mindanao in Luzon?

But more important than that – and the reason why I wanted to bring this problem to you is because in my mind, this problem points to one of the most important questions that each of us has to ask himself and answer for himself – what do we mean by development and growth? Do we mean only that we will become richer? Do we mean only that we will have automobiles, radios, televisions, that we can eat in restaurants like A & W? Is that what we mean solely by development, or do we mean by development that we are developing a better people – people with a conscience, people with a heart, people with the guts to stand up and defend their rights?

You know you clapped and maybe it sounds good. But do we really mean it? I would like you to answer this question for yourself because the argument here is very simple. After all, who will be harmed by the construction of the dams? How many are the Kalinga and Bontoc? They are primitive people, without any civilization, without education. When the dams are constructed there will be electricity in the entire Cagayan Valley, Isabela and other provinces; there will be irrigation; the harvest will increase; the national economy will prosper.

So I want you to ask yourselves. Is the Filipino to say, never mind if we kill or condemn one innocent man to save nine others, or is it more Filipino to say every man has a right to live in a way in which God has given him the right to live? Which are we going to vote for? I want you to consider this because upon these issues depend many of the other questions I asked you earlier this afternoon.

I hope you will see the connection between the situation in Kalinga-Bontoc and, for example the situation in Mindanao, or the situation of Ninoy Aquino, or our own situation vis-a-vis the American government. Behind all of them, there is one common issue: the right of every man to live as a human being in the way in which he wants to live so long as he does not harm anybody else. Behind that, that is the issue. Are we for that or not? The moment we talk about economics, the moment we talk about figures and statistics we seem to forget that behind every figure and every statistic is a living pulsating beating heart, a mind that thinks, a soul that feels, a person that loves. And the moment that we forget that, the moment we think of economics purely in terms of gross national product and per capita national income and how much percentage there has been and what increase in profits, the moment we think only of these terms, gentlemen and ladies, we are no longer being Filipinos. In fact, we are forgetting our own humanity.

I brought this problem to you because it is a very difficult problem. On the one hand, the government wants to push through this transaction: it has already contracted the people to build the dams; it's already starting to make the surveys. On the other hand, we have 15,000 families who are going to be uprooted and die. I don't know what to do. And it is not the only problem of that kind.

Let me read to you a similar problem that is happening in Bukidnon. Sugar is at the premium in the world market today. It will be for some years to come. So we produce more sugar. The logic is incontrovertible but it means a sugar central is going to be built in Bukidnon, in the municipality of Quezon. Ranches were being converted overnight into cane fields; some of these ranches were formerly occupied by Manobo tribesmen. Now, the Manobos are claiming them as ancestral domain encouraged by Presidential Decree 410. But they are told that the decree is in abeyance. Does this mean also that their rights to the land of their forefathers are in abeyance? Meanwhile, the land is converted into sugar fields all in the name of economic progress. The Manobos do not understand in the same way that the Bontoc and the Kalinga do not understand.

I have been reading from a letter of Bishop Francisco Claver of Malaybalay, Bukidnon, who is himself a Bontoc and who knows the problem. This is the way that Bishop Claver ended his letter, and frankly, this is the reason why I chose this subject for this afternoon. And I quote:

> The Manobo do not understand in the same way that the Bontoc and the Kalinga do not understand and some have already been killed because they cannot understand. But they are the Little People, the Manobo, the Bontoc, the Kalinga. They are expendable, their lack of understanding does not matter because the President knows best. Something is wrong somewhere, very wrong and the rest of the country is silent.[8]

Today, I have spoken to you of this problem of the Kalingas and the Bontocs and the Manobos because I could not remain silent. And I pray that you of the Thursday Club will not remain silent either – that you will stand up and say in every way you can, everywhere you can, to everyone you can: "My God, I don't care whether there is martial law or not but every man, woman and child who is a Filipino has the right to live as long as he harms nobody else." And I will stand with the Manobos and the Kalingas and the Bontocs, as I stand with every victim of injustice, because I insist that above everything else, we are human beings and we do have the right to live.

I leave the problems of our brothers, the Manobo, Kalinga and Bontoc, to you. Tonight please say a little prayer for our imprisoned brother Ninoy.

---

[8]Bishop Francisco F. Claver, S.J., "The Little People," in *The Signs of the Times,* Association of Major Religious Superiors of Men and Women, March 14, 1975, p. 15.

THE LEGALIZATION OF THE COMMUNIST PARTY

In the Philippines those who believe in communism are treated, not as citizens with human rights, but as "enemies of the state." They are a minority group whose rights must be protected no matter how unpopular their ideology. It is unjust to prosecute a person for his political beliefs. If a murder is committed by a communist, he should be prosecuted as a murderer, not as a communist murderer.

On December 26, 1984, the Convenors Group – whom most of you, I should like to think, consider to be a fairly sober and respectable group, excluding some members like myself – issued a declaration of unity which sets out the principles that they share, the goals that they seek, and the measures that they commit themselves to take. Of the thirty odd measures that the Convenor's Group described, three were singled out for rather strong criticism:

>> The pledge to remove all foreign military bases from Philippine soil and, hereafter, not to allow such bases to be established;[1]

>> The undertaking to diffuse the ownership of the principal means of production and equitably distribute income, both as a measure of justice and to promote development, combat poverty and ensure the rational use of resources;[2] and

>> The commitment to legalize the Communist Party of the Philippines.[3]

The first measure – the removal of U.S bases – was discussed here two months ago, I understand, by Vice President Pelaez and Senator Salonga. The second measure – the need to diffuse the ownership and distribute income equitably – need not be defended in this forum since it reflects Catholic Social Doctrine. It is the third measure – the legalization of the Communist Party – that I have been asked to discuss with you this morning. But to grasp the

(Lecture delivered before the Bishops-Businessmen's Conference of the Philippines, Makati Sports Club, April 19, 1985)

[1] Declaration of Unity, par. 3.6.

[2] Idem, par. 4.

[3] Idem, par. 6.

problem in its proper dimensions, let us take a quick glance at the history of the Communist Party in our country.

The first Communist Party in the Philippines – notice the preposition I use, in the Philippines, not of the Philippines, because it was called Partido Komunista *sa* Pilipinas – had a short but frenzied life. It was organized on August 26, 1930, at the Templo del Trabajo in Tondo by a group of about sixty representatives of various worker and peasant organizations; and was formally launched on the night of November 7, 1930, at a public meeting held at Plaza Moriones in Tondo. These are two dates that were chosen deliberately. August 26 because it is the anniversary of the Cry of Balintawak, and November 7 because it is the anniversary of the founding of the Communist Party in Russia. The head and secretary general of the first Communist Party was Crisanto Evangelista, who was the president of the Union Obrera de Impresores de Filipinas, the Printers Union, probably the most active union before World War II. The party made no attempt to hide itself. It set up an open headquarters at 8 Basa St., in Quiapo, and it published a newspaper called *Titis* ("Spark"). And during its first four months it held almost daily mass meetings in Manila and in the Central and Southern Tagalog provinces in order to expand and consolidate its membership. It also presented candidates in the 1931 elections, although none was elected.

Now the party at that time was not armed and had no armed force, unlike succeeding parties which had first of all the Hukbalahap and then the HMB or Hukbong Mapagpalaya ng Bayan as its armed force, and later, the New People's Army or NPA. The first Communist Party in 1930 had no army. Yet its activities, particularly its rather incendiary rhetoric, greatly alarmed the authorities. For those were the days of the great depression, with massive strikes in Iloilo and Negros, and of course the Tayug uprising which happened on January 10, 1931.

To compound the situation, Antonino D. Ora, a party leader, died on January 17, 1931, in an automobile accident in Nueva Ecija while in the custody of the Constabulary. The Manila Police at first banned any large demonstration during his funeral but later relented under pressure of public opinion. As a result, Ora's funeral attracted more than 50,000 workers, who, according to a later account, "marched throughout the streets of Manila with red flags and anti-imperialist slogans."[4] Apparently things have not changed much in the fifty-four years that have lapsed since then.

Soon after the Ora funeral, criminal charges for inciting to sedition were filed against party leaders in Manila and Nueva Ecija. The trial courts convicted them and the Supreme Court affirmed. You will find one, two, three, four, five cases reported in Volume 57 of the *Philippine Reports*.[5] Then on March 3, 1931, when the party was barely four months old, then Manila Mayor Tomas Earnshaw refused to permit it to hold public rallies. He had issued permits, he revoked them and refused to issue new permits. And the Supreme Court upheld him.

Seven months later on October 26, 1932, came the final blow. The Supreme Court ruled that the Partido Komunista sa Pilipinas was an illegal association which violated Article 188 of the Penal Code, now Article 147 of the Revised Penal Code, because "according to the constitution and by-laws of the Communist Party, the purpose of the party is to incite class struggle to overthrow the present government by peaceful means or armed revolution. Therefore the purpose of the party is to alter the social order and to commit the crimes of rebellion and sedition. An association having such an object must necessarily be illegal" And the Court sentenced twenty of the party's top leadership to eight years and one day of what was called, surprisingly, confinamiento, but which actually meant exile. That is, they were sentenced to a far flung island where they could move around freely within the island but not outside of it and always, under strict government control.

So, twelve days before its second birthday, the legal life of the Partido Komunista sa Pilipinas came to an end.

It was never legally resurrected. On December 31, 1936, four years later, President Quezon granted Evangelista and other leaders of the Communist Party conditional pardons. Two years later, in 1938 in October, he instructed local governments to allow the party to hold public meetings. But he did not mention the party expressly. He simply gave instructions to all local officials to grant public permits to anyone who asked for it regardless of party. And Quezon could not, of course, revoke the decision of the

---

[4] Alfredo B. Saulo, *Communism in the Philippines: An Introduction,* Manila: Ateneo Publications Office, 1969, pp. 23-25.

[5] These are: People v. Evangelista, 57 Phil., 355 (1932); People v. Capadocia, 57 Phil., 364 (1932); People v. Evangelista, 57 Phil., 372 (1932); People v. Feleo, 57 Phil., 451 (1932); and People v. Nabong, 57 Phil., 455 (1932).

Supreme Court, nor did he try to get the law on illegal association amended or changed. So technically, the Partido Komunista remained an illegal association.

Not being sure of how far the authorities would allow it to go, it kept a relatively low public profile, until November 7, 1938, the eighth anniversary of its founding. On that date in solemn ceremonies held at the Manila Grand Opera House, it presented itself again to the Filipino people, but this time with two differences. First, its constitution and by-laws contained no reference to armed revolution. Second, it was a merger of the Communist Party of the Philippines and the Socialist Party which had been founded by Pedro Abad Santos, and one of whose leaders is our resource person this morning, Ka Luis Taruc. And the new party had the name "Communist Party of the Philippines (Merger of Communist and Socialist Parties)."

Again this party was not armed and had no army. It presented candidates in the 1940 elections. But all the candidates ran under the name of the Socialist Party. And eight of them won in Pampanga, one of them, Casto Alejandrino.

When this party was born in 1938, war was in the wind. In 1939, World War II broke out and two years after that the Japanese invaded the Philippines. More than other organizations, the Communist party had foreseen these events, and had been urging a united front tactic to oppose the forthcoming – what they had foreseen – invasion. Their pleas went unheeded. Indeed, shortly after the Japanese bombed the Phlippines on December 8, the Communist Party sent a memorial to both President Quezon and Governor General Francis Sayre, urging a unity and the arming of the people in order to repel the invasion and pledging their loyalty to the Philippine and United States governments. At that time, of course, you remember, although we were a Commonwealth, we were still under the sovereignty of the United States of America. Some of us, like myself, believe we still are, but that's beside the point.

In any case, the point is that up to then the Communist Party offered no serious armed threat to the Philippine or U.S governments in this country. Yet it had been outlawed.

How did the Communist Party get its arms? When the American and Philippine forces retreated to Bataan and Corregidor, they opened the doors of their armories to arms they could not gather and take with them, and told the people, "Get!". And since the Communist Party and the Socialist Party, the merger, was prepared for this invasion, it was the one that took the best advantage of that situation. One must also say that the Hukbalahap, as a guerrilla force, was probably one of the most effective if not the most effective guerrilla force in the country during the Japanese occupation.

After the occupation, the American government and the American military refused to deal with the Hukbalahap as a recognized guerrilla force. In fact, it was only recently, if I am not mistaken, about two or three years ago that recognition of the services of the Hukbalahap during the war through an awarding of backpay, was given to the Hukbalahap. And that was by President Marcos about two or three years ago, I think. In any case, not only was there no recognition of their work, but landlords who, in many cases, had been displaced during the war by their tenants under the protection of the Huks, came back with civilian guards. In fact one of the great leaders of the Communist Party and one of the founders, Juan Feleo, was killed while he was being "protected" by four MPs (military police) *and while he was doing pacification work for the government.*

The result of all this was that the Communist Party of the Philippines and its army, the Hukbalahap, found that they would be committing practical suicide if they surrendered their arms to the government. And at the same time they came to the conclusion they could not expect justice from the government, and therefore entered into armed revolt against the government. The government was quick to act.

The Hukbalahap enjoyed some tremendous successes initially. At one point, they captured Camp Makabulos in Tarlac and they held Sta. Cruz, Laguna, overnight. That was the capital of Laguna province. But in 1950, in a massive raid conducted by military and police forces in the greater Manila area, almost the entire politburo of the Communist Party fell into government hands.

At that time, the only law that was applicable to the situation of the Huks was the Revised Penal Code on the matter of rebellion. At first the government sought to convict CPP-Huk leaders of rebellion complexed with murder and other serious crimes, in order to deprive them of bail. But the Supreme Court ruled that the crime of murder, killing, was part and parcel of a rebellion. You can't have a rebellion unless you start killing people. And therefore you could not be prosecuted separately for them as long as they had some connection with the rebellion. So that the maximum penalty for the rebellion became, if I am not mistaken, 12 years and one day.

In the meantime, top leaders of the Communist Party and the Hukbalahap fell into government hands. In 1957, Republic Act No. 1700, the Anti-Subversion Law, was passed, once again outlawing the Communist Party, this time by law. The reason for its passage was simply that, with the Anti-Subversion Law, the penalty for becoming a member of/or continuing to belong to the Communist Party was increased so that if you were a leader or took up arms against the government then you would become liable to death penalty. Since then the Republic Act 1700 has undergone several amendments. The latest amendments were supposedly dated in 1981.

I say "supposedly dated" because the date of the proclamation is January 16, 1981, but the first time that this came to light was on May 10, 1983, two years later. So obviously this must have been done some time in 1983 and antedated to 1981, just before martial law was lifted in name. And in this Presidential Decree 1835 it's very clearly stated that:

> The Communist Party of the Philippines is hereby declared to be an organized conspiracy for the purpose of overthrowing the Government of the Republic of the Philippines ... The said party and any other organization, association, political party or group of persons organized for the same purpose and their successors are hereby considered and declared subversive organizations. [Sec. 2]
> As used in this decree, the term "Communist Party of the Philippines" shall mean and include among others, the organizations now known as the Communist Party of the Philippines and its military arm, the New People's Army, and any such organizations/associations whose purposes are allied thereto. [Sec. 3]

Now this has two significant meanings. First, the original Republic Act 1700 *simply and categorically* referred to, and I quote:

> ... the "Communist Party of the Philippines" shall mean and include the organizations now known as the Communist Party of the Philippines and its military arm, the Hukbong Mapagpalaya ng Bayan, formerly known as HUKBALAHAPS, and any successors of such organizations. [Sec. 3]

In 1957, the Anti-Subversion Law referred to what we now know as the PKP, the Moscow-oriented wing of the Communist Party. In fact, in 1957 there was still no NPA, because the NPA was founded in 1969. Actually, the Communist Party of the Philippines, the one headed by Jose Maria Sison, was organized on

December 26, 1968. Again they chose a significant date – that was the 75th birthday of Mao-Tze-Tung. Why they should choose dates I do not know, but they have their own reasons, I suppose.

In any case, this was chosen and organized on December 26, the army, on March 29 of the following year. So at that time there was no CPP-NPA. The effect of this PD 1835 is to legalize the PKP. It is no longer now a subversive organization, But the CPP has, by express definition, become a subversive, outlawed organization.

Now what I have tried to bring out, throughout all of this brief look at the history of the Communist Party and of its outlawing, is simply this: The outlawing of the Communist Party reflected and was the product of the fear of government and the ruling class. Now fear is a wonderful motivator but it's a very poor guide to action. Fear makes you act, it does not guarantee you act correctly. On the contrary, very often under the push of fear, we act wrongly. And I believe that the Communist Party would not present the problems it does today had it not been because of the fear which outlawed it, first in 1932, and later, when the Japanese were expelled from this country, in the refusal of the government to deal with the Hukbalahap movement for what it was, an authentic people's guerrilla movement.

This is one reason why, we believe, that the time has come to legalize the Communist Party. But let me be clear on what I mean by legalization. Because a lot of people ask, "Are you advocating that we say that it is legal for a group to meet together and advocate the overthrow of government by force?" Of course not. What we are simply saying is that no one should be punished simply because he belongs to the Communist Party or believes in the Communist ideology. Which means, in practical concrete terms:

>> One, that we advocate the scrapping of Presidential Decree 1835 and all other earlier anti-subversion laws;

>> Second, an amendment of the law on illegal association so that it will not include as illegal, associations organized for political purposes *even when those political purposes may include violence.* Why? For the very simple reason: Political "criminals" can hardly be considered and are not considered by our society anyway, as criminals. Because our whole history as a people has been a continuous political struggle to attain and enforce our rights as a people. That struggle has often taken an armed form. Often it has not. But certainly we never equate, for example, a rebel with a murderer or with a thief.

What does this mean in concrete terms? Does this mean that we will allow the NPA to remain? No! If the Communist Party or members actually commit crimes they should be prosecuted for the crimes they commit. *But they should not be prosecuted for being communists.* In short, if a murder is committed by a communist, he will be prosecuted as a murderer but not as a communist murderer. That is essentially what we mean and advocate.

And when you look at it from that point of view, the whole question of whether or not the communists should be required to give up their arms becomes irrelevant. They don't have to give up their arms. If they want to give up their arms, fine, if they don't want to and continue to possess them illegally and get caught, they will be prosecuted for illegal possession of firearms. If they use those arms in order to commit rebellion or sedition, they will be prosecuted for rebellion or sedition. *But certainly they will not be prosecuted for being communists.*

We believe that there are other important moral and practical reasons for this position. Take one, for example, very practical reason. At the time that the Communist Party of the Philippines, the new one, the CPP-NPA, was formed, General Cerrudo, who was then the commander of the first PC Zone, said that there were seven Huk commanders under Commander Dante operating in Tarlac. This was in April of 1969, just at the organization of the NPA. There were 88 fully armed Huks in Tarlac, 192 young recruits, 140 combat supporters and 44,800 "mass base" or civilian supporters.

If you take a look at the armed strength, 88 is all that they had in 1969. Today the government admits that they have somewhere between 10,000 to 12,000 fully armed operational units of the NPA. All this time from 1969 up to now, they have been outlawed. Their leaders have been put into jail. Others have been killed. Many of their leaders, even today, go around with a price on their head – which is, I think, very immoral. How can you say "dead or alive" and pay so many thousands for so and so? Yet the government does it. But anyway, despite all this they have grown. So obviously outlawing them is not the answer.

Some other reason: If they have grown, and they have grown, then obviously they must be meeting a need of the people. If the NPAs and the CPP were not answering some need of our people, they could not have grown this big this quickly. Now we must find out what is that need and how they are meeting it, and how those of us who do not believe in their ideology can meet that need. One cannot do so if we continue to declare them outlaws. We cannot do so if we say, "You are criminals." How can we learn from criminals?

Many years ago, in 1969, Alfredo Saulo, who had himself been a member of the PKP, wrote a short history of communism in the Philippines. This was published by the Ateneo de Manila University Press. And he said:

> The outlawing of the CPP has placed the party not only beyond the reach of the law but, quite significantly, also beyond any reliable assessment of its actual strength, program of activities, leadership and even strategy and tactics in the present period of its revolutionary struggle. In short, any assessment of the CPP in its present underground state is pure speculation.
>
> But what certainly is not speculation is the fact that the moral position of the CPP, as the party that claims to offer the best workable alternative to the present social order, gains more strength with the government's failure to put an end to graft and corruption, the "credibility gap" in the executive and legislative departments, the wanton waste or misspending of public funds, the apparent existence of double standards of justice, one for the rich and one for the poor, the turtle-paced implementation of the land reform program, the continued rise in prices of prime commodities, the yearly school crisis, the seasonal water crisis, the traffic problem, the housing shortage, the social dislocation resulting from natural calamities ...., and the inability of both public and private sectors to generate enough job opportunities to relieve the acute unemployment.[6]

What we feel to be wrong with outlawing the Communist Party is that that is a symptom of the wrong remedy for the very serious social ills that afflict our country. When you outlaw a party, you tend to say, "Anything that that party does is wrong." So when the party takes a nationalist position, you say "Nationalism? That's communism." When the party takes a position that works for social justice, you say "Social justice? Better employment conditions/Communist 'yan." It gives us an excuse to forget that what they are fighting for are in many instances authentic grievances that must be remedied, not as a matter of preventing dissidence, *but as a matter of simple justice*.

And that brings me to the second point that I wanted to make this morning on why we are so keen on eliminating this outlawing

---

[6]Alfredo B. Saulo, op. cit., pp. 72-73.

of the Communist Party: Because as long as the Communist Party remains outlawed, then government will begin to look at its programs in an instrumental fashion, rather than in their ultimate value. What I mean concretely is this. Government very recently announced P1 billion in civic action under the administration of the military. Government is implementing now, beginning June, a National Service Law, which will require our children from the fourth grade up to high school to take up civic welfare service, law enforcement service or military training – all three forms under the ultimate control of the military. This steady encroachment of the military into our civilian life stems from the government view that all these acts are designed to stop the rebellion, to quell dissidence, to cut out the growth of the Communist Party.

My friends, it's not going to be civic action which is going to stop the growth of communism. What we need is social justice. And as long as we think in terms of civic action and education always as instruments simply to put down the Communist Party, then we are not doing what we should be doing, which is doing what is right because it is right and not because we are trying to put down another political ideology.

Several years ago, the Black Pope, Fr. Arrupe, the head of the Jesuit order in Rome, issued a letter to all the provincials of the Jesuit order, which was published in the newsletter of the Office for Human Development. And Fr. Arrupe very categorically said that he was opposed to using Marxist analysis, and he gave his reasons why. But then at the end he says:

> ... I would like to make four observations. Firstly, whatever the reservations with regard to Marxist analysis, we should always understand well and appreciate the reasons that make it an ideal of liberating mankind from domination and oppression, of doing the truth while condemning the ideologies that conceal it, of ending class divisions ...
> In the second place, ... Marxist analysis is not unique in being affected by ideological or philosophical presuppositions that have permeated its system. In particular, the type of social analysis used in the liberal world today implies an individualistic and materialistic vision of life that is destructive of Christian values and attitudes.[7]

---

[7]Father Pedro Arrupe, S.J., in a letter sent to all provincials, December 8, 1980.

Now the third and the fourth observations are what I think are the most critical to us.

> Thirdly, as regards Marxists themselves, we should remain fraternally open to dialogue with them. Moreover, true to the spirit of Gaudium et Spes [n. 21, para. 6], we ought not to refuse practical cooperation in concrete cases where the common good seems to call for it [cf. Mater et Magistra, IV].[8]

Now how can you maintain dialogue, how can you be open for "fraternal cooperation in concrete cases" as long as that party remains outlawed? And last:

> ... We should also firmly oppose the efforts of anyone who wishes to take advantage of our reservations about Marxist analysis in order to condemn as Marxist or communist, or at least to minimize esteem for, a commitment to justice and the cause of the poor, the defense of their rights against those who exploit them, the urging of legitimate claims. *Have we not often seen forms of anti-communism that are nothing more than means of concealing injustice?* In this respect as well, let us remain true to ourselves and not permit anyone to exploit our critical assessment of Marxism and Marxist analysis.[9]

In the same vein, I beg you, let us not allow our disbelief in, distrust, dislike or condemnation of communism, let us not allow that to be ever used by anyone for purposes of exploitation and injustice. And we can prevent that. One way, as a small step, simply by legalizing the Communist Party.

---

[8]Ibid.
[9]Ibid; emphasis added.

CHRISTIANS AND POLITICAL PRISONERS

This speech emphasizes that Christians throughout the world would do well to emulate the example of Task Force Detainees of the Philippines. In every nation of the world, Christians should exert every effort to see to it that all nations everywhere respect the rights of prisoners that have been set out in international covenants based on the Universal Declaration of Human Rights.

That there are political prisoners at all in any country in the world should be a challenge to all Christians everywhere to show our compassion: if we are not willing to share in their suffering, dare we call ourselves Christians?

Those who search for an authentic religious life today may find it in consecrating themselves to the noble cause of human rights.

In many countries of Asia, Africa, Eastern Europe, and Latin America, as in the Philippines, this is not the age of Aquarius but the age of political prisoners. Governments govern, not under the laws of reason, but under the laws of public emergency. As a result, in jails and prisons, in detention and rehabilitation centers, in military camps and concentration camps, all around the world, men and women – and sometimes even children and babies – languish behind bars or barbed wire.

Many have been arrested because they have violated criminal laws; but many simply because of their political views, and because they have opposed – some violently and some non-violently – whatever regime holds political power in their country.

A few political prisoners have been tried and convicted of rebellion, or sedition, or subversion, but most have not been tried at all; many of them, indeed, have not even been formally charged.

Where trials have been held, they have been held in secret or in absentia; and the courts that have sentenced them have usually been military courts.

It is hard for someone who has never been imprisoned to understand the degradation that detention imposes upon a man and his family, particularly on one who knows that he is not a criminal, and that he is being held simply because he has stood up to the powers that be. Brutal and inhuman treatment often break a prisoner's body or mind – or both. Even when he is not beaten up

---

(Possibly delivered to the UPSCA, University of the Philippines, October, 1975)

or tortured, but, on the contrary, is treated with humanity and with respect for his dignity, life behind bars or barbed wire remains such a psychic trauma that many political prisoners leave the prisons broken in spirit. For detention is more than stone walls, barbed wire and iron bars; guard towers and armed guards; jailer and jailed; and seemingly senseless rules and regulations. Detention is boredom and loneliness; loss of privacy and regimentation; frustration and impotence; periods of hope followed by hopelessness, like stormy waves that can drown a man.

The effect of detention on the family of political prisoners is often worse than on the prisoner himself. Few are the political prisoners who are independently wealthy. Most are the breadwinners for the family. Sometimes both father and mother are arrested, leaving their children helpless orphans, dependent upon the charity of relatives and friends who themselves are often afraid to help lest they too be suspected of subversion. The family does not know what is being done to the prisoner – sometimes not even where he is kept confined. In addition to their daily chores, the wife and children must now set aside some time and some money for transportation to visit the prisoner; some money to bring him some clothes, food, medicines, books (when these are allowed); and more money and time and efforts, if any can still be spared, to secure his release either through legal processes or through approaches to administrative officials who may order his release. Detention worsens pre-existing family problems and creates new ones. Where detention is prolonged, families can – and do – break up.

Fear of being identified with political prisoners alienates friends and even relatives. Sometimes prison regulations ban visits of all but wives and children, or fathers and mothers. Disappointment in people they thought were friends becomes an almost daily routine for most political prisoners. Yet there is hardly anything more important to any prisoner -- political or criminal -- than to know that he is still part of the world; that there are still people who care for him; that there is still something he can do, despite being in jail; that there is meaning in the suffering and humiliations he and his family are undergoing.

It is here that Christians can help. But should they? Should not Christians stay away from political prisoners? After all, haven't these prisoners violated their duties to society and lost their right to Christian sympathy? Haven't they tried to subvert society and -- in the case of communists -- even denied the very Christ that we Christians revere as God? Why should we help them? Wouldn't we be exposing ourselves to possible reprisals?

To ask these questions is itself to deny our Christian faith. Yet one should try to answer them for those who waver and those who misunderstand.

Briefly the answer is this: many political prisoners have not actually committed any criminal or subversive act -- many have been arrested on mere suspicion or on the pretext of a precautionary measure; a few, because of mistaken identity or on false charges that have arisen out of personal vendettas or because what they have done or were trying to do has been misunderstood.'

More important still, even if all who are detained are guilty of subversion -- and many are not -- Christians who would follow Christ must never forget that the Lord himself announced that his mission was "to bring the good news to the poor, to proclaim liberty to captives and ... to set the downtrodden free."[1] To emphasize the importance of helping prisoners, the Lord's description of the last judgment expressly mentions visits to prisoners as one of the acts of love that distinguish those blessed by the Father:

When the Son of Man comes in his glory, escorted by all the angels, then he will take his seat on his throne of glory. All the nations will be assembled before him and he will separate men one from another as the shepherd separates sheep from goats. He will place the sheep on his right hand and the goats on his left. Then the King will say to those on his right hand, "Come, you whom my Father has blessed, take for your heritage the kingdom prepared for you since the foundation of the world. For I was hungry and you gave me food; I was thirsty and you gave me drink; I was a stranger and you made me welcome; naked and you clothed me, sick and you visited me, in prison and you came to see me." Then the virtuous will say to him in reply, "Lord, when did we see you hungry and feed you; or thirsty and give you drink? When did we see you a stranger and make you welcome; naked and clothe you; sick or in prison and go to see you?" And the King will answer, "I tell you solemnly, in so far as you did this to one of the least of these brothers of mine, you did it to me.[2]

"Insofar as you did this to one of the least of these brothers of mine, you did it to me" -- this is the command and the promise that every Christian should have burned into his heart.

---

[1]Luke, 4:17-22.
[2]Matthew, 25:31-46

Of course, to help political prisoners and their families can incur official suspicion, if not invoke reprisals and harassment. But are we not, as Christians, to love one another with more than "just words or mere talk"; to be ready "to give up our lives for our brothers?"[3] Did not the Lord himself admonish us "Do not be afraid of those who kill the body and after that can do no more?"[4]

How can the Christian help best? Here the Church in the Philippines provides an example for the rest of the world. The Association of Major Religious Superiors in the Philippines has organized a group of religious and laity into a "Task Force Detainees of the Philippines" (TFDP) to provide spiritual and material consolation to political prisoners and their families. Nuns and priests visit detention centers, concentrating on those who have no one to visit them and on those who are sick. They have helped set up handicrafts to while away the time of prisoners. They have offered medical care and legal assistance to political prisoners and their families, and have provided the necessities of life to those who are poor or have become destitute with the imprisonment of the head of the family. They have exposed cases of brutality and torture, and striven for improvements in prison conditions. They have sought the release of prisoners unjustly detained.

The Philippines is, at least in Southeast Asia and perhaps in the world, the first country in which the Christian Churches have and are playing an active and organized role in extending Christian love to political prisoners and their families. The presence of our religious men and women in detention camps and centers has done much to ameliorate the conditions of political detention. Christians throughout the world would do well to emulate this example.

What are the objectives Christians should strive to attain? Ultimately, of course, the end to all political detention. But harsh realities make this an unrealistic immediate goal. For the present, perhaps, and without losing sight of this ultimate goal, Christians in every nation of the world should exert every effort to see to it that all nations everywhere respect the rights of prisoners that have been set out in international covenants based on the Universal Declaration of Human Rights.

These covenants, though unanimously adopted by the General Assembly of the United Nations, have not yet entered into force because the required number of nations have not yet ratified them

---

[3] 1 John 3:18, 16.
[4] Luke, 12:4.

formally. Nevertheless, they remain standards to be striven for; and in the Philippines, at least, form part of the law of the land.

Among these standards are:

First, that "in time of public emergency which threatens the life of the nation," the State may curtail civil and political rights only "to the extent strictly required by the exigencies of the situation,"[5] and, by necessary implication, only for the duration of the emergency.

Second, that in no case may the State curtail any of the following rights:[6]

(1) The right to life. "No one shall be arbitrarily deprived of life ... Sentence of death may be imposed only for the most serious crimes in accordance with the law in force at the time of the commission of the crime ... The penalty can only be carried out pursuant to a final judgment rendered by a competent court."[7]

(2) The right to bodily integrity. "No one shall be subjected to degrading treatment or punishment. In particular, no one shall be subjected, without his free consent, to medical or scientific experimentation."[8]

(3) Freedom from slavery and servitude. "No one shall be held in slavery ... No one shall be held in servitude."[9]

(4) The right to human dignity. "Everyone shall have the right to recognition everywhere as a person before the law."[10]

(5) Freedom of thought and religion. "Everyone shall have the right to freedom of thought, conscience and religion. Freedom to manifest one's religion or beliefs may be subject only to such limitations as are prescribed by law and are necessary to protect public safety, order, health or morals or the fundamental rights and freedom of others..."[11]

These requirements are spelled out in great detail in the Standard Minimum Rules for Treatment of Prisoners adopted on August 30, 1955, by the First United Nations Congress on the Prevention of Crimes and Treatment of Offenders, and approved and recommended to member States by the Economic and Social Council in Resolution 663 CI (XXIV) of July 31, 1957.

---

[5]International Covenant on Civil and Political Rights, Art. 4, par. 1.

[6]Idem, Art. 4, par. 2.

[7]Idem, Art. 6, pars. 1 and 2.

[8]Idem, Art. 7.

[9]Idem, Art. 8, pars. 1 and 2.

[10]Idem, Art. 16.

[11]Idem, Art. 18.68

In the Philippines, the Revised Administrative Code requires that "prisoners shall be treated with humanity. Juvenile prisoners shall be kept, if the jail will admit of it, in apartments separate from those containing prisoners of more than eighteen years of age; and the different sexes shall be kept apart. The visits of parents and friends who desire to exert a moral influence over prisoners shall at all reasonable times be permitted under proper regulations." No doubt similar provisions exist in the laws of other countries which have political prisoners.

The rules mentioned above apply to political prisoners detained under emergency conditions. What about their initial arrest?

After several seminars held in different parts of the world, a Committee created by the U.N. Commission on Human Rights adopted a set of Draft Principles on Freedom from Arbitrary Arrest and Detention which, as to cases of emergency, provide that:

Article 34: When an emergency which threatens the life of the nation exists and has been officially proclaimed and it becomes necessary to provide for special powers of arrest and detention, such powers shall be granted only for the duration of the emergency and to the extent strictly required by the exigencies of the situation. The conditions under which and the procedures according to which these powers may be exercised must be clearly defined by law.

Article 35: 1) Arrest and detention under emergency powers shall take place only upon written order from the competent authority indicating the reasons for the order and the facts in support thereof.

2) A copy of the order shall be given to the person at the time of his arrest and he shall be informed at the same time of his right to make a representation against the order and to have legal counsel.

Article 36: 1) The order of detention shall be submitted within twenty-four hours of the arrest to a competent court or other body established by law at least half of whose members are drawn from the judiciary for the purpose of deciding whether or not there is sufficient cause for the detention. The reviewing authority shall hear the detained person and his counsel. It shall be furnished with such information by the detaining authorities or other persons as it may require.

2) If the reviewing authority decides that there is sufficient cause for the detention, it may be continued subject to periodic examination by the reviewing authority.

3) If the reviewing authority decides that the detention is not justified, the order shall be revoked and the detained person released forthwith.

4) The reviewing authority shall inform the detained persons of all his rights and shall inquire into the treatment accorded to him in custody.

(Comment: This article requires the order of the detention to be reviewed by an independent body. The importance of this safeguard was stressed at various United Nations seminars. At the Baguio Seminar it was agreed that "close conformity to ordinary criminal procedure was desirable as a safeguard to liberty and that a citizen detained should be entitled to know the grounds for his detention, to be heard and to have his case reviewed from time to time." At the Wellington seminar there was general agreement that "if a country found it absolutely necessary to resort to detention without trial, it was essential to establish some tribunal (with at least one senior judicial officer as one of its members) charged with the duty of examining every case, in order to minimize the possibility of grave injustice.)

Article 37: Any person who has been detained under special powers shall have the right even after the termination of the emergency to obtain compensation from public funds for any material or moral damages which he may have suffered on account of any abuse of their powers by the authorities detaining him or of any excess or unreasonable exercise thereof.[12]

Though lip service is generally paid these provisions, they are not, in fact, followed by most countries that hold political prisoners. Certainly, they are not observed in the Philippines.

Christians everywhere should exert efforts to have their government adopt and faithfully implement these salutary requirements proposed by international bodies.

Karl Menninger, the noted American psychiatrist, has said: "I suspect that all the crimes committed by all the jailed criminals do not equal in total social damage that of the crimes committed against them."[13] And in a South Carolina jail, a prisoner wrote these heartrending words on the wall of his cell:

---

[12]Department of Economic and Social Affairs, *"Study of the Right of Everyone To Be Free From Arbitrary Arrest, Detention and Exile,"* New York: United Nations, 1964, pp. 215-216

[13]Karl Menninger, *The Crime of Punishment*, New York: The Viking Press, 1968, p. 28.

To the builders of this nitemare: Though you may never get to read these words, I pity you; for the cruelty of your minds have designed this hall; if men's buildings are a reflection of what they are, this one portrays the ugliness of all humanity. If only you had some compassion.

If this is true about jailed criminals, isn't it even more true of political prisoners -- who, no matter how misguided we may think they are, are impelled not so much by a desire to harm as to improve society?

That there are political prisoners at all in any country in the world should be a challenge to all Christians everywhere to show your compassion: if we are not willing to share in their suffering, dare we call ourselves Christians?

THE RULE OF LAW AND STATE VIOLENCE

Some of the causes of state violence can be traced to our culture. We should eliminate as many of them as we can. We should insist that government represent also the poor and the have-nots, giving priority to their needs.

Let us have a land that is free from bases and nuclear power, where we alone decide what is good for us and live in peace despite differences in belief and ideologies.

Man is born in violence. And the urge to react violently is in him until he dies. That is why he beats up or kills when his wishes are frustrated, or because of what he considers an insult (a dirty look for example), or for no reason at all that we can discern.

Yet, if resort to violence is natural in man, so are attempts to control it. Man wants to live, but he also wants to live well. Life is not worth living if he must live under the constant lash of fear. Violence is part of life, yes. But to tame violence is to civilize life.

That is why we have laws and government, courts and lawyers, and military and police. That is why, after World War II, Western lawyers came up with the doctrine of the rule of law. In layman's language, the rule of law is the rule of fair play, enforced by a government whose authority the people recognize as legitimate.

The doctrine did not escape criticism. It was, critics said, unable to solve basic issues of social justice, because it was itself a supporter of the status quo of the prevailing system of power and privilege. For the rule of law required that legal changes come only through recognized political processes; that government have a monopoly of force; and that any defiance of the law be dealt with firmly. In exchange, theoretically, governments were to use force only to prevent force from being used against the people, and only as a last resort.

The doctrine of the rule of law is not perfect. Yet it is another step to curb violence, and should be used to the extent possible to contain oppression and to force fiscals and judges and justices in a repressive regime to look at themselves squarely.

But what if governments use force against us, instead of for us?

(Paper read at the seminar-workshop on "State Violence" held by the Social Issues Committee of the Philippine Social Science Council, PSS Center, Diliman, Quezon City, May 8, 1986)

What if they use violence not as the last but as the first and continuous resort? Can the rule of the law then protect us? If not, can we meet violence with non-violence or should we, in the phrase so popular today, "meet force with force?"

First things first. Why do governments resort to state violence? In our society, the Philippines, state violence is not new. There were political detainees during the Spanish regime, during the U.S. regime, during the Japanese occupation, during "liberation," during "independence," during the Marcos regime, and at present. Torture, disappearances, extra-legal killings (salvaging), and hamletting were practiced then as they were practiced during the Marcos regime. Listen to Agoncillo:

> In Pulo and Malinta, Bulakan, where the Dominican estates were situated, the Spaniards massacred the people just to keep themselves busy. The poor people, peasants all, believing that they would be protected by the approaching soldiers, innocently walked to meet them and were shot down like dogs. Arrests were arbitrary and it was enough for a person to be suspected of being a Katipunan member or a sympathizer to be arrested and given the "works" by the Spanish inquisitors. In most cases, the accusations were utterly false and without any foundation whatsoever. The most common form of torture was to hang the accused by the hands, and then suddenly dropped to the ground. Another method of torture was the use of an electric machine, with its wires connected to the feet or hands of the accused. Yet another consisted of standing the victim barefoot on a hot brazier, or else the poor man was hanged by the hand, the feet barely touching the ground.[1]

What Agoncillo wrote has been written of the succeeding eras. And the reason is simple enough: we were a colonial society then. We are a neo-colonial society now. Then as now a foreign power allied with our elite ruled our lives. Then as now ours was an export economy, satisfying the wants of foreigners and the rich, rather than the needs of our people. Then as now the economy did not produce enough to meet both wants and needs, so the privileges of the wealthy and the powerful were threatened. Then as now, governments did not represent the poor and the have-nots. Then as now, using the tools of propaganda, elements in government wanted the military, the police and the people to believe that

---

[1] Teodoro A. Agoncillo, *The Revolt of the Masses,* Quezon City: University of the Philippines, 1956, p. 163.

anyone who opposed the present system is a communist or communist sympathizer, and he should be denied his legal rights, though his criticisms might be well-founded. Put these circumstances together, mix them well, and the product is state violence, the use of force to cow the people and coerce us into acquiescing to the iniquitous exactions of our"betters."

Take torture, a favorite weapon of state violence. Governments resort to torture not only to coerce confessions from detainees or to extract information that could lead to the arrest of dissidents or to punish detainees whom government assumes to be guilty, but also to fabricate "evidence" to discredit persons or organizations opposed to government, and to sow terror among the opposition and the people.

Or take disappearances. Governments resort to them not only to hide the effects of torture, but also to avoid charges of arbitrary arrest, to obviate the expense of prolonged detention and public trials, to confuse companions of the person who disappeared, to eliminate potential threats to government, and to spread fear among our people without creating martyrs.

Finally, take hamletting. Governments resort to it not only to punish entire communities they believe to be sympathetic to dissidents and prevent them from feeding, sheltering or funding them, but also to deter other communities from doing so.

What can we do to avoid a repetition of these atrocities? Clearly the rule of law as we know it was not enough. Politically powerful leaders interpreted the law as they pleased and the courts were subservient to them. That was the end of the rule of law. *Inter arma silent leges.* [In the clash of arms, the laws are silent.]

Human rights lawyers and activists tried to reverse the formula: *Inter leges silent arma.* [Among the laws, arms are silent.] But to no avail. At best they could produce dents in the Marcos system, but not breakthroughs. Law must find support in something outside law, just as justice can be judged only by values other than the value of justice.

What then are we to do? Or is there nothing that we can do? Our recent experiences teach us that we can do something about it.

We know that the causes -- or some of them -- of state violence lie in our culture. Let us eliminate as many of those causes as we can. Let us take advantage of the drafting of this new constitution to insist that government represent also the poor and the have-nots. Let us give priority to their needs. Let us have a land that is free from bases and from nuclear power. Let us have a country in which we, and not foreigners, decide what is good for us; and let us respect each other's beliefs and ideologies, regardless of how much we may disagree with them. Above all, let us expand our organizations and let us remain united. Against a united people, no force is strong enough to prevail. Not even state violence.

THE LAW AND MARTIAL LAW

When martial law was imposed, what happened to the law?

And so law in the land died. I grieve for it but I do not despair over it. I know, with a certainty no argument can turn, no wind can shake, that from its dust will rise a new and better law: more just, more human and more humane. When that will happen, I know not. That it will happen, I know.

Not blind faith nor romantic optimism inspires this conviction, nor yet a penchant for lost causes, but awareness of our people's past and the experience of their present. During the two years I was detained, I had a chance given to few to read and to imbibe, in the quiet of solitude, the history of our nation. And after my release nearly nine years ago, I have been privileged to work closely with little people, the plain men and women with little money and less schooling, but much wisdom and even more fortitude. I do not deify them: I am all too aware of their vices, their faults, their weaknesses and their shortcomings. But I have also felt their strength. I have seen them wake up every morning with hunger, pass the day with misery -- yet still go to bed with hope.

Tell me, for I have never come across it: at what period in our history did our people stop fighting oppression? Armed with little more than an enduring heart, an ear for music and an eye for beauty that betray a fascination with harmony, and a longing for justice without which there could be no harmony, they have for centuries, pursued a dream that will not die: the dream of a noble society. They have been -- they still are -- deceived and deprived, defeated and defamed. Yet they struggle on, however bumbling, mistaken or misguided their efforts may at times seem to us.

I pray that we, the men and women of the law, may join their quest and work at their side: for they labor for us also. But let us have no illusion that they need us. With us or without us, they will triumph. One day justice and its works will reign in our land. Never completely, but firmly enough to restore sanity into our society and decency into our life.

A NEW LEGAL ORDER

We need a new legal order that will lead to authentic democracy, where the people will decide on critical issues.

Let me stress two things before I begin. First, I shall speak as a Filipino and as a lawyer -- not as Chairman of the Presidential Committee on Human Rights. Second, I wish to thank all my friends in Bicol for the prayers and the help they gave me in my recent bouts with cancer. Thanks to their help -- and the mercy of God -- my health is fully restored.

Now let me begin:

Before February 25, 1986, the major problems of the Filipino people were food and freedom, jobs and justice.

They still are.

In 1983, more than half of our families -- 4.8 million or 51.2 per cent -- were not able to purchase the food they needed, let alone their other needs. And 1983 was a better year economically than 1985.

Every year, the number of unemployed and of underemployed has gone up -- despite the Marcos government's attempts to tamper with the figures. The problem is aggravated by low wages, although the productivity of labor remains high.

Our problems are compounded by gross social inequality. Take 1985 as an example. The year 1985 was a very poor year economically, in which our GNP (gross national product, the sum total of all goods and services that we produce) was 3.95 per cent lower than 1984, and our GNP per capita was 6.27 per cent lower. Yet even in 1985, we could have wiped out poverty and still have P7.7 billion left over for incentives, if our social institutions and structures allowed a more equal distribution of income.

With so many people out of jobs and so many families unable to buy the food they need, justice and freedom were -- and had to be -- denied to our people to keep the system going.

What are we lawyers going to do about it?

We may not agree on what causes the problems.

(Speech delivered to the BICOLANDIA --Bicol Concerned Lawyers for Nationalism, Democracy and Integrity Association -- at their Third Regional Conference and Induction Ceremonies, Aristocrat Hotel, Naga City, May 10, 1986)

Some say they were caused by the greed of Marcos, his family, and their cronies.

Others say this explanation is too simplistic: our major problems are caused by our under-development, particularly our under-industrialization and specially our lack of heavy industry. Our economy simply is not producing enough to feed our growing population. This, as much as human greed, produces political corruption.

Still others believe even that does not explain enough, for it does not explain why we are underdeveloped. They believe that our major problems are caused by following the same colonial policy of export-oriented growth, instead of growth based on meeting the basic needs of our people using our own raw materials and our own ingenuity. Export-oriented growth has led to low wages, dependence on imports and exports, especially on imported capital goods, a decline in net terms of trade, and a climb in our trade deficit. These, in turn, have resulted in decreases in the peso exchange rate, and increases in foreign debt and in reliance on foreign investment -- all of which produced a rise in the consumer price index and a fall in the purchasing power of the peso.

Yet others accept all these explanations, but add our social structures and institutions to these causes. They claim that our educational system is designed to discourage independent thought, and our laws are biased against the poor and the unlettered. They cite the land system, health system and tax system as glaring examples.

Whatever causes our problems, it seems clear to me that at least two things are needed if we are to solve them:

First, that what happened under Marcos should not happen again; and

Second, that government seriously attend to the problems of poverty, unemployment, underemployment, low wages, social injustice and foreign control.

In turn, to meet both conditions, we need at least two things:

First, our society must not be militarized. We should expose any violations of our rights, by the military, by the police, or by anyone else. We should oppose any attempt by any of them, or even a minority of them, to intimidate us into accepting or doing anything contrary to our principles.

Right now, for example, a minority of the military want us to forgive them for violating human rights. I do not agree. Perhaps it is my training as a lawyer that has taught me that *Fiat justitia ruat coelum* (Let justice be done though the heavens fall) -- and the heavens will not fall if justice is done to the victims and punishment meted out to the culprits who violated human rights. Our people feel the same way. They have mandated the new government to "pursue national reconciliation based on justice" [Proclamation No. 3, March 25, 1986, Sec. 1, (f)] -- and justice is more than forgiveness. In this, the Filipino people are not alone. The conscience of all mankind condemns violations of human rights. In the <u>Declaration on the Protection of All Persons from Being Subjected to Torture and other Cruel, Inhuman or Degrading Treatment or Punishment</u>, the General Assembly of the United Nations categorically said:

No state may permit or tolerate torture or other cruel, inhuman or degrading treatment or punishment. Exceptional circumstances such as a state of war or a threat of war, *internal political instability or any other public emergency* may *not* be invoked as a justification of torture or other cruel, inhuman or degrading treatment or punishment.

If there is no excuse for torture, there can be no excuse for rape, for disappearances, for salvaging, for massacres, or for other violations of human rights.

Second, we need a new legal order.

Please do not misunderstand me: the old legal order was not bad. It was just inadequate. In a developing country, it stood for the development of the politician, the middle class, the rich, and the foreigner, but not for the development of the poor.

It did not even stand for authentic democracy. Governments normally protect the interests of those with whom they communicate regularly. Governments ordinarily communicate with the rich, the middle class, and the representatives of foreign trading and manufacturing companies. It is not that governments are run by evil men. but that normally only the rich, the middle class and foreigners have the means to communicate regularly with government.

To have authentic democracy, then, government should also represent the interests of the poor, not just those of the middle class and the rich. Government needs restructuring to build permanent channels of two-way communications between the poor and the political elite. The Magsaysay 10-centavo telegram and the present government's ministry for the urban poor are steps in the right direction. But let us not forget that poverty is more rampant in the countryside than in the cities. More important, unless these mechanisms are institutionalized, they do not survive the administration that started them.

Representing the poor may thus require much more than building channels of communications with them. It may require that the method of representation be changed, so that the people will be represented not only on the basis of area as in the past, but also on the basis of sector and, within each sector, on the basis of income. Problems of implementation no doubt will arise. Into how many sectors shall we divide our population? Within each sector, how many income classes shall there be? How can we be sure that only those included in the same income classes vote for their sectoral representatives? How shall we apportion primary responsibility between the chamber elected on the basis of area and that elected on the basis of sector (like past constitutions that required the House of Representatives to initiate all appropriation acts and tax bills)? These are hard problems, but they are not beyond the capabilities of the people.

Representing the poor may also require that new structures be fashioned, structures to enlist the talents of citizens to identify, explain and solve national and local problems. My own experience is that people have far more creativity than we believe. For instance, one group I worked with produced the meta-legal tactic of having an entire barrio go to a government office to file just one paper; another group organized adjacent barrios to deny entry to those bent on burning their homes; a third group arranged to have their Holy Mass said on a raft in the river dividing the land they occupied, when they were denied access to the land's chapel. And better than us, the poor knew that their problems of lack of schools, health services, water and so forth could be solved more readily by building roads from poblacion to barrio than by building RP.-U.S. Bayanihan Schools or digging Magsaysay wells. Today we need barrio to barrio roads also. If we do not mechanize, to build the roads would provide jobs for our people. And once built, the roads would expand trade and industry.

To harness the talents of our people and more important to build structures for that purpose, are difficult problems. But they are not impossible. For instance, one can involve the people in the planning process from barangay to nation, instead of asking them to implement a plan already made. Of course, such a plan could be very different from that which a Makati-based technocrat could prepare. And instead of looking at exports for growth, the plan might look at satisfying the needs of the people, using Filipino ingenuity on Filipino resources. But since we are bent on having a democracy, should we not follow the people instead of the technocrats? Or are we bent on having only an elite democracy?

These changes should be accompanied by a change in our mentality. We must believe in ourselves, in our capacity to overcome hardship, in our ability to make the right decision. In short, we must have faith in the people, and not act like colonizers who know everything and distrust everyone, especially the people. So that, whenever a question impinges on the life of the people, it should be submitted to their judgment. It is on that judgment that we should rely, rather than on the judgment of individuals, no matter how honest, sincere and well-meaning they may be.

Equally important, we must view public office as a way to serve the people, not to profit at their expense. Unlike traditional politicians, we should not scramble for vacant positions nor use public office for private gain. Politics should not be a road for the political elite to become economic elite as well.

I do not like having to say this. It smacks too much of a "holier-than-thou" attitude -- and I have as many faults, if not more, than any of you. But it had to be said.

Let me sum up. Our political situation has changed. The challenge we face is to create a real democracy in our land. We can meet that challenge, we can succeed, only by being Filipinos, and letting no one -- civilian or military, Filipino or foreigner -- frighten us. Or decide for us.

If martial law has taught us anything it is this: against a united people, no human force will prevail. Against the will of our people, even guns of soldiers fall silent.

Let us remain united then. Together let us build a nation for our children, a nation that denies no one either food or freedom, jobs or justice.

NATIONALISM

II. NATIONALISM

What does Filipino nationalism mean? According to Pepe Diokno it is the determination to uphold the sovereignty of the Filipino people, the right of all Filipinos -- not of just a few and definitely not of foreigners -- to freely decide the destiny of the nation, what kind of government we should have and who should run it, what is the common good and how to attain it, how our society should be structured, the wealth of our land and seas used, developed and shared, and how our culture should be preserved and enhanced.

His range is broad; he moves from the historical causes of our past political and economic bondage to the present oppressions of being a neo-colony. He has an intelligent, practical solution for each problem, supported by a remarkable erudition combined with poignant experience. No one can surpass him in his sure and sharp grasp of the national condition. Even as he rejects violence, he insists that only social change, the elimination of gross inequalities and unjust structures, can save us.

In his pantheon of heroes, Rizal and Recto tower over the others in their nationalism, in the depth of their commitment to their country.

Despite the critical economic and political problems confronting the nation, Pepe Diokno maintains an unwavering faith in the people's ability to build a true, popular democracy.

A NATION FOR OUR CHILDREN

"A Nation for Our Children" was delivered late in 1984. At that time Pepe was deeply involved in trying to unify the opposition against the fascistic but failing regime of Ferdinand E. Marcos. This important and crucial task did not prevent him from delineating in near-lyrical language his dream of a nation for all Filipino children -- a just, humane and free society.

There is one dream that all Filipinos share: that our children may have a better life than we have had. So there is one vision that is distinctly Filipino: the vision to make this country, our country, a nation for our children.

A NOBLE nation, where homage is paid not to who a man is or what he owns, but to what he is and what he does.

A PROUD nation, where poverty chains no man to the plow, forces no woman to prostitute herself and condemns no child to scrounge among garbage.

A FREE nation, where men and women and children from all regions and with all kinds of talents may find truth and play and sing and laugh and dance and love without fear.

A JUST nation where whatever inequality exists is caused not by the way people act towards each other but by differences in natural talents; where poverty, ignorance, and hunger are attacked and every farmer has land that no one can grab from him; every breadwinner, a job that is satisfying and pays him enough to provide a decent standard of living; every family, a home from which it cannot be evicted; and everyone, a steadily improving quality of life.

An INDEPENDENT nation which rejects foreign dictation, depends on itself, thinks for itself, and decides for itself what the common good is, how it is to be attained, and how its costs and benefits are to be distributed.

An HONORABLE nation where public powers are used for the public good and not for the private gain of some Filipinos and some foreigners; where leaders speak not only well but truthfully and act honestly; a nation that is itself and seeks to live in peace and brotherhood with all other nations of the world.

(Delivered at a KAAKBAY-sponsored forum, St. Francis Theater, Mandaluyong, Metro Manila, October 12, 1984

Is this vision attainable? Or is it just an idle dream? If we base ourselves on today, we would be tempted to conclude that it is an idle dream. For our country today is in a mess. There is no other way to describe its condition.

Our economy is bankrupt. We cannot pay our foreign debt. Within the next two years, whether or not our foreign loans are restructured, prices and taxes will continue to rise. The peso will continue to fall. The domestic market will contract further. More workers will lose their jobs; more students will be forced to drop out of school. Hunger will spread, and disease will not be far behind. Crime will continue to stalk the streets even more menacingly. Anger, resentment, and frustration will escalate. Dissidence will propagate, and repression will intensify. The government has lost all credibility, yet it refuses to do the decent thing: return power to the people. Instead it continues to deny the people their basic rights and freedoms. And the calloused behavior of some of its leaders mocks and defies this cherished Filipino value.

Yet we must not give up our dream because of today. For if we look at ourselves, we have all the resources -- human and natural -- to become what we Filipinos choose to be. Our population is about 53 million, and that's the 17th largest potential domestic market in the world.

We are a literate people. Our adult literacy is 75 per cent, the 40th highest worldwide. Sixty-three per cent (63 per cent) of our young people in the 15-19 year age group are enrolled in secondary schools, which is about 50 per cent higher than the average for countries like ours. And 27 per cent of the 20-24 year age group are enrolled in colleges and universities which is twice the average of countries like ours and more than that of some developed countries like the United Kingdom, West Germany, Australia, France, Belgium, and Switzerland.

Our land area is 300,000 square kilometers, the sixty-third largest in the world. It is rich in natural resources. Less than half of our land has been systematically surveyed for mineral but commercial quantities obtained of the thirteen basic raw materials required by a modern industrial economy have already been discovered: bauxite, chromium, copper, iron ore, lead, manganese, nickel, phosphates, zinc, natural rubber among these. And we also have the human drive to develop these.

Encounters with nations which invaded and occupied us or traded with us have made us open to change and quick to adapt to it. Our people are ingenious and fast learners, competitive and achievement-oriented, rational and practical, and dedicated to freedom and independence. We are, let us not forget, the first Asian people who revolted against a western imperial power, Spain; the first who adopted a democratic republican constitution in Asia, the Malolos Constitution; the first to fight the first major war of the twentieth century against another western imperial power, the United States of America. Since 1972, we have suffered the brutal repression of martial rule, but freedom still burns bright in the hearts of most of us.

So there is no insurmountable barrier that could stop us from becoming what we want to be. Why then are we in this sorry condition? I think it is because we have forgotten one basic thing. We Filipinos are a variegated people. We live in seven thousand islands. We profess no less than five major religions. We pray in no fewer than seven native tongues. But all of us -- Muslim or Christian, Tagalog or Visayan or Ilocano or Kapampangan -- all of us are Filipinos not only because we are brothers in blood -- many of us are not -- but because we are all brothers in tears; not because we all share the same land -- many of us are landless -- but because we share the same dream. Whether we like it or not, we are one nation with one future, a future that will be as bright or as dark as we remain united or divided.

Sometimes -- as at present -- events obscure this truth. At other times, human selfishness tries to deny it. But the truth will not die. We are one nation with one future. Yet today that nation is sorely divided even on such seemingly uncontroversial questions like what to do with the Marcos government or how to deal with the U.S. government. Some -- I am one of them -- would want to change not only Marcos but the system he has implanted in our country. Others would want to change only Marcos. Others would not even want that. They would be happy with changing Imelda and Ver. And others would not even demand that, simply that Marcos give up Amendment 6 or the power to issue presidential detention actions or both.

On such a simple matter as the United States relations, some want statehood. Others want independence, and those who want independence do not all agree on what it means. Some believe in independence from every foreign government except the United States, the World Bank, and the International Monetary Fund (IMF). In fact, some of those who think this way seek U.S. government help to get Marcos out and put themselves in. Still others believe in independence from every foreign government which includes Russia, China, Japan besides the United States, the World Bank and the IMF. They want no U.S. intervention in our affairs not even to oust Marcos, and they want the U.S. bases out.

But some who think this way, or say they do, urge that U.S. issues be submerged for the time being. Let's finish with Marcos first, they say, and then let's take on the U.S. government.

Just as we are not agreed on what changes we want, we are not agreed on how to obtain those changes. Some believe that change can only come from within the Marcos system which is why they took part in the last elections. Others are convinced that change can only come about from outside that system which is why they boycotted the elections. Some think that only violence can bring about change which is why they joined the NPA, the MNLF or other guerrilla groups. Yet others think that non-violence can bring about change, and so they have joined militant, peaceful mass actions.

In this state of disunity, change could come about, but except by a stroke of luck, it would hardly be the change that any of us want. For change to be meaningful, it is important that we agree at least on the basic issues, i.e., (1) Do we want to change just Marcos, or do we also want to change the system; (2) Do we want to free ourselves from the dominant influence of the U.S. government, or do we want to continue under its control; (3) Do we want to return to the kind of society we had before martial law, or do we want to establish a better society, more just and more human.

If we can agree on the basics of these issues, even though we may disagree on some details, then disagreements on how we can achieve these goals would not be insoluble. As long as we pursue the same basic objectives, there should be no difficulty in coordinating the activities of those who wish to pursue these objectives by different means. Let me just give you an example of what I mean.

We have today what is commonly called the parliament of the streets, and the objective of this parliament is to get rid of the Marcos government as soon as possible. But we also have political parties that are gearing for the elections in 1986 and 1987. Surely there should be no basic contradiction between these different methods. We can pursue the parliament of the streets and hopefully change the government before 1987, preferably before 1986, preferably before 1985. But if we fail, what is to prevent us from using the other methods in order to change this government. The important thing is that we agree on what we want because if we do then the dilemmas that we face today would no longer be critical.

Take for example this possibility. Suppose that Mr. Marcos for one reason or another were to quit his office tonight. Do you think the opposition would be able to put one candidate for president and one candidate for vice-president to fight against whichever candidates Mr. Marcos and the KBL would put up within the next sixty days? In 1986 if there is no agreement to these basic objectives, will the opposition be putting up one candidate for the UNIDO, one candidate for PDP-LABAN, and one candidate for the LP, or more in the local elections as against the candidates of the KBL? And if so, what chance would the opposition have? And in 1987 if Marcos is still around to run, or even if he does not run -- if he sponsors a candidate -- would the opposition be able to put up one candidate, or will we be putting up four or five candidates to run against Mr. Marcos?

If we can agree, however, on all of these basic issues even if we don't agree on all the details, then it would be easier to get agreement on one candidate. Why? Because if all of us are agreed on what we want, then insistence upon running can only be the result of personal ambition. And no candidate will ever tell you that he has personal ambitions. In fact, they will all say: I don't want to run, but if the people want me, I will run.

And if we do agree on these basics, then does it really make much difference who is the candidate as long as we are all united and agreed on what is to be done? It may make some difference. Some candidates may be more competent than others. The mere fact that we are all agreed on these basics should not make it impossible to achieve these changes regardless of who is this candidate. And therefore if we can agree on these basics, then we should be able to achieve the first step in this long journey to a nation for our children, and that is, the step of regaining our freedom.

But to do that, as I have said, will take time. It will be difficult. Wounds have become very deep, I'm sorry to say. I arrived, as you know, about a week ago, and I have found out during this short week that between certain groups disagreements have become personal, and those are the most difficult to address. But I also wish you to know that efforts are being made, and will continue to be made, so that all these disagreements can be ironed out. We do not expect perfect unanimity, we do not expect total agreement on every detail, but we believe that we can all agree at least on these basics.

First, that we must change not only Mr. Marcos but the system he has implanted. We must return to a truly democratic government with an independent judiciary and a responsible Parliament. And more than that, we must bring government and the making of decisions closer to the people affected by those decisions.

Second, I feel that there should be -- and there will be -- no disagreement on the need to obtain our total liberation and freedom from American control. I say this because just the other day, there

was a short meeting between representatives of UNIDO and others -
- those who had taken part and those who had not taken part in the
last elections -- and on the matter of "let's start getting together,
let's talk and let's see if we can get some bases of agreement," one
of them said: "Tanny, do you remember two years ago we signed a
paper. Why don't we use that as the basis of the agreement?" And
Tanny said: "Fine. I don't remember what was in that paper we had
signed, but why don't you just send it over?" And it was sent over.
And the first two paragraphs of that agreement made it very plain
that every political force was committed to the proposition that the
Philippines must be controlled by Filipinos and that all foreign
bases must be removed from our country.

So I see no insurmountable difficulty there, and certainly I also
see very little difficulty with respect to the third agreement, i.e.,
that we use our freedom and our independence to improve the
quality of life of our people. Again we may disagree on how this is
to be done but on the objectives, I think we are all agreed. I think
that the second step in that long journey to attain a nation for our
children is simply this: that in order to improve the quality of life
of our people, what we have to do is really very simple -- do the
opposite of what Marcos has done for the last twelve years. I am
not being facetious. I am not trying to be witty. I'm trying to state
a fundamental truth.

Marcos has built his entire program on the principle of depending
upon the U.S. and Japan and getting all the loans that he could. We
must build our nation on the principle of depending on ourselves
and getting as loans only what we need, not what we can get.

Marcos has built his entire political system on gathering all
power unto himself and eliminating all checks and balances. We
must build our political system on respect for the sovereignty of
the people, on the establishment of adequate checks and balances,
and on empowering the people at the grassroots level.

Marcos has built his economic system on a policy of
overspending, export-orientation, low wages, recession,
unemployment, and poverty. We must build our economic system
on strengthening our domestic market by increasing the
productivity of our farmers and our workers and increasing their real
wages because without an increase in the real wages and the real
income of our workers and our farmers, it will not be possible for
us to industrialize. We will continue to be dependent on foreign
resources.

We must build our economy on removing disparities between
urban and rural areas so that whatever social services we supply our
rural areas -- health, education, water, power, roads -- must be of

the same quality and the same standards as the social services that we supply to our cities.

And we must build our economy on using every method that we know as soon as possible to restore the buying power of our workers, at the very least and as a first step, to what was their buying power in 1972. From 1972 to the present, the real wages, the purchasing power, of our workers has dropped by no less than 45 per cent across the board -- about 37 per cent for skilled workers and 48 per cent for unskilled workers. That has to be completely reversed. And our first objective must be to bring back their purchasing power at least to what it was in 1972 and then gradually increase it.

Marcos has built his entire social system on a system of falsehood, on a system of repressing creativity, and on creating in our people a feeling of impotence and helplessness. (I wonder how many of you have read Prof. Luisa Doronila's report on the textbooks that are being used in our public schools and the effects they are having on our children. When the children were asked what they preferred to be -- Filipinos, Americans, Japanese, etc. -- the lowest rank was gotten by those who wanted to be Filipinos. What are we doing to our children?) Our system must be the complete opposite. Our system must tell our children the truth. Our system must seek as much as it can to unleash their creativity.

I described to you when I began what I thought was the vision of most Filipinos of a nation for our children, and I know that for many of you, it may sound ideal. Yet reality is often much more beautiful than anything that we can conceive of. If we can but release the creative energy of our people, then we will have a nation full of hope and full of joy, full of life and full of love -- a nation that may not be a nation for our children but which will be a nation of our children.

PHILIPPINE NATIONALISM

"Philippine nationalism is more than patriotism. It is also the belief that, because the Philippines is our country, it is we who must have the power to direct its affairs, internal and external, for it is we who bear the responsibility for its future."

Thus the young senator defined Philippine nationalism *in an address before an American audience in 1968. It was a brilliant and clear exposition of the workings of U.S. imperialism. When he finished, there was no applause.*

No one who has visited my country has failed to be impressed -- and some have been shocked -- by the uninhibited freedom of our newspapers and radios: it is, someone has said, as if the libel law did not exist. This makes any disclaimer by the management of mass media unnecessary; nevertheless, no comments are aired over radio or television, without the warning that "the views to be expressed are those of the speaker, and do not necessarily reflect those of the management of this station." It also is unnecessary on this occasion for me to make any disclaimer; but let me be explicit: I do not speak for the Philippine Government, or the Senate, or even the Nacionalista Party, my party that is currently the majority party in my country; I speak only as a Filipino who believes he shares the hopes and the dreams, the aspirations and the determination of a good number of his people.

Since I received your invitation, I wondered how to begin telling you what must be said if we are to retain and to strengthen the ties of friendship that bind your nation and mine. Two days before I left Manila, I found the answer in an incident of the election for members of the board of directors in the village in which I live, Magallanes Village, a subdivision just off the Manila International Airport.

Under the rules of our homeowner's association, tenants with leases that are longer than one year have a voice and a vote on village affairs. Your government's Agency for International Development has rented a substantial number of houses for its staff, on two-year terms; so American residents take part in electing the members of the homeowner's association board of directors;

(Address before the New York Assembly, First Dinner Session, Westchester Country Club, New York, March 4, 1968)

and, as a matter of fact, we have generally had an American on the board. Our next election will be held in about ten days; for sometime now, the villagers have been going from home to home asking for votes or proxies for their favorite candidates. One of these candidates, who was nominated because he has been very active in church and social affairs, is a young man who is the president of a marketing firm that deals mostly with U.S.-made home appliances. His name is Michael Recto.

When Mike's friends talked to their American friends for Mike, they met a surprisingly cold reception. Puzzled, they tried to find out why; and finally they did. American residents thought that Mike was a son of the late Senator Claro M. Recto, the great Filipino nationalist; they feared that he shared his father's views, which they called "very anti-American."

The truth is that Mike is Don Claro's nephew, not his son -- but that doesn't really matter. In fact the incident as a whole is unimportant except for one thing: it is Philippine-American relations in miniature and it does throw into sharp relief what I believe is the basic problem that threatens our friendship -- the misunderstanding of the causes, the content and the thrust of Philippine nationalism.

From almost the very beginning that our two nations came into contact with each other, many of your people who make or influence policy have called Philippine nationalism "anti-American." Lately they have also described it as "communist inspired" and its leaders as "communists" or "leftists." And when they could not so describe a particular nationalist program, because it clearly ran counter to Marxist dogma, they have derided it as the tool of a few selfish Filipino interests seeking to attain by the laws of the State what they cannot achieve by the laws of economics. And so some of your leaders have never tired of warning us that, our nationalism must be "true" Philippine nationalism, not anti-Americanism; and that true nationalism demands "civic consciousness...self-sacrifice...and self-reliance;" and must be for the benefit of all Filipinos and not just a favored few.

I do not deny that, of late, Philippine nationalism has acquired a gloss of anti-Americanism; nor that, in the Philippines as elsewhere in Asia, communists have attempted to wrest the leadership of the nationalist movement away from those who believe in democracy. I do not deny, finally, that some Filipinos have profited more than others, over the short run, from economic policies that Philippine nationalism has espoused.

But what seems to have been overlooked or misunderstood or glossed over, is that Philippine nationalism is no more inherently anti-American, than American nationalism is inherently anti-Filipino; nor is its protection of Filipino capital any more selfishly motivated than is the protection that your government extends to what it believes to be the rights of American business in the Philippines inherently based on the greed of a few Americans. Inherently, Philippine nationalism is only pro-Filipino as American nationalism is pro-American; and like your nationalism, ours is inspired, not by any Marxist dogma but by the consciousness that we are one people, bound by common traditions, one land, one blood and one dream.

Moreover, Philippine nationalism is more than patriotism. It is also the belief that, because the Philippines is our country, it is we who must have the power to direct its affairs, internal and external, for it is we who bear the responsibility for its future. This belief combines with faith and determination: the faith that we can exercise that power as well as, if not better than, those who are not Filipinos; and the determination to use that power so that the blessings of our country will accrue to all our people, and not primarily to only some, nor to those who are not Filipinos. No one has expressed this better than a Filipino nationalist who advised us, before Dewey sailed into Manila Bay, so that he could not have been motivated by any anti-Americanism, that:

Look you always upon your countryman as something more than a neighbor. See in him the friend, the brother, or at the very least, the companion to whom you are bound by a single fate, by the same joys and sorrows, and by common aspirations and interests ... As long as the frontiers of nations exist ... to him alone should you unite in perfect solidarity of views and interests, in order to gather strength, not only to fight the common enemy, but also to attain all the goals of human existence.[1]

Let me give you some concrete examples to make clear what I have been trying to say. Most of you here today are concerned with what your former Ambassador to my country called "the economic content of our nationalism." It is this, I think, more than our protests over some of the terms of our bases agreement, that you consider anti-foreign, if not "anti-American," and also short-sightedly selfish. But the truth is that, from its inception

---

[1] Apolinario Mabini, "The True Decalogue," in *La Revolucion Filipina y Otros Escritos de Apolinario Mabini*, Maxim Kalaw ed., Vol. I, p. 103.

Philippine nationalism has had an economic content: for our first economic nationalist is the man we honor as the first Filipino -- Dr. Jose Rizal.

In mid-1892, Rizal was deported to Dapitan by the Spanish Government, on suspicion that he had been plotting against Spain. After two years of exile, in a letter to his friend Blumentritt, dated August 29, 1894, Rizal described how he had organized a consumers' cooperative in Dapitan to enable his countrymen to escape from the clutches of Chinese traders, and he complained that the Spanish military governor "though a good man, nevertheless favored the Chinese."[2] Rizal practiced what he preached. One year later, he wrote his mother: "I have vowed never to buy anything from the Chinese; so that sometimes I find myself in a fix. Now I have neither plates nor tumblers."[3]

Since Rizal was martyred before the United States purchased sovereignty over the Philippines for U.S. $20 million; since his writings contain no references to Marx or Engels or anything remotely resembling communist doctrines; and since history shows Rizal did not earn his living from business, it seems clear that Philippine economic nationalism was not, at its inception, anti-American, communist-inspired, or selfishly motivated.

"But," some may say, "Rizal's nationalism was directed against the overseas Chinese -- a common sentiment in Southeast Asia then as it is now. Surely the period of American sovereignty was different from Spanish sovereignty." Politically, yes; but economically, was it really different? No doubt, your governors were, as Rizal said of the Spanish military governor "good men." But by accident or by design, was not the result the same? Was not foreign capital favored over Filipino capital?

This is what the record shows for 1935, near the close of the American era in the Philippines: most of our imports were American consumer goods, which had been allowed to enter duty free into the Philippines since the Payne-Aldrich Act of 1909. As a result, the Philippines had little domestic industry and no capital goods manufacturing industry. What industry we did have was foreign-controlled: sugar centrals were mostly American and Spanish owned. Of the eight large coconut oil plants, two were American, two British, two Spanish, one Chinese and one Filipino. Of the ten factories supplying practically all the dessicated coconut exported to the United States, six were

---

[2]*Epistolario Rizalino*, Vol. V, Part 2, p. 669.
[3]*Epistolario Rizalino*, Vol. IV, p. 262.

American, two were British, one Chinese and one Japanese. None was Filipino. Of the investment in five cordage factories, 60 per cent was American and Chinese, only 40 per cent Filipino. Of cigar plants and tobacco plantations, 60 per cent were Spanish, the rest Swiss, American, Chinese and Filipino in that order. The three largest soap plants were, respectively, American, Swiss and Chinese. In lumber, U.S. $6 million of the total investment of U.S. $12.5 million were American; the rest, Filipino, Chinese, British and Spanish. And so on.

In 1935, as American sovereignty was about to end, we exported the same products that we had exported in 1896, when Spanish sovereignty was coming to an end. Under both flags our industry was under foreign control and mostly concerned with partial processing of agricultural export products. Free trade, it has been estimated, deprived the Philippine Government of some U.S. $1.75 billion. Even today, 1968, of the four oil refineries in the Philippines which supply 96 per cent of our energy requirements, Filipinos own only 25 per cent of one and 30 per cent of another. Is it any wonder then that Philippine nationalism still has an economic content? Is that content necessarily anti-foreign, or is it simply an expression of the determination of Filipinos that Filipinos should control the Philippine economy?

Let me say, in justice to both our countries, that the United States did try to promote "the happiness, peace and prosperity of the people of the Philippines;" most Filipinos realize this and are grateful. But almost as many also realize, as your professor Onorato of California State University at Fullerton has said, that it did so "only in the sense that ... (its) ... efforts were directed at producing a viable member of the American community;" but it failed to understand the need to change our economic and social structure to produce a viable Filipino independent nation. That is why that great Filipino President, Manuel Quezon, said that he preferred a government run like hell by Filipinos, to one run like heaven by Americans; that is also why, as first President of our Commonwealth, he insisted on social justice and a Filipino national language; and all of our Presidents thereafter have sought to effect social and economic reform to the extent that resources and practical means were available to achieve it.

This then was the result of the failure to understand our nationalism: you would make us over in your image; we insist upon our own. Perhaps, because of our desire not to displease, we have not articulated our insistence enough. Or perhaps our gratitude for what was done for our benefit misled you. But in any case the failure to understand that we have our own identity, that we approach problems in a manner you never would, has produced much of the tension between us. Until this is cleared up, more tension will arise.

Let me give another example of how Filipino economic nationalism has been misunderstood, and of the consequence of this misunderstanding. For this, let us go back to the Filipino who first explicitly stated the economic content of Philippine nationalism -- the lame Filipino lawyer, who was the first Chief Justice and the first Foreign Secretary of the first Philippine Republic of 1898, Apolinario Mabini. Mabini it was who first laid down the basic tenets of economic nationalism. "Economic life," he wrote, "is fundamental to every nation; a nation economically dependent on another cannot call itself independent in fact." And, as "the Filipino people desire a completely independent republic," he argued, "the nation cannot grant any privilege whatsoever to any foreign government to exploit our mines, or run our railroads, or other industries."

Mr. William Howard Taft, then Chairman of the Philippine Commission and first American civil governor of the Philippines, called Mabini "the most prominent irreconcilable among the Filipinos." Yet it was this same Mabini who prophesied that the United States "has been destined by providence to lead the regeneration of the world." In fact, Mabini submitted a "Plan for Independence," in which he urged that, if the United States were to grant immediate independence, "the Filipino people are ready to recognize and proclaim the United States as their liberator ... champion of oppressed nations;" give preferential treatment to American exports to the Philippines, until the Philippine Government could repay the U.S. $20 million which the United States had paid Spain for our country; and, under equal conditions, and in consideration of certain loans, give temporary preferential rights to American enterprises to exploit our mineral resources. Doesn't this sound surprisingly like parity? Still William Howard Taft said of Mabini that "Nothing he writes, nothing he says, but contains unjust insinuations against the American government and its good faith."

But Mabini was thinking only of promoting the welfare of the Philippines -- not of damaging the interests of the United States. In fact, what Mabini had offered for immediate independence in 1900 -- duty free entry of U.S. goods and temporary preferential treatment of U.S. investments in natural resources -- adumbrates parity and other provisions of the Bell Trade Agreement that your government imposed upon us in 1946 when, our cities in ruins, our fields abandoned, our economy ravaged by World War II, we could not refuse. Had Mabini's Plan for Independence been accepted, the United States would have earned our undying gratitude and respect; but it was not, and what was forced upon us 46 years later, has earned nothing but resentment, anger, and evasion. When men like Recto, Laurel and Tañada spoke out against it, they were smeared as Mabini had been, as anti-American and worse, as communists or tools of vested domestic interests. This I need not add has made many who could have contributed much of value to our dialogue reluctant to speak out their mind, to the detriment of the interests of both countries.

Two other examples of a failure to understand Philippine nationalism come to mind. One is the nationalization -- Filipinization would be more accurate -- of our retail trade. The application of this law to traders of other nationalities raised no hue and cry from the American business sector; but the moment that, in 1964, it was to be applied to American business interests, your chamber of commerce called the law, in effect, legalized robbery. And some of your government officials came to Manila to apply pressure. Yet the critics of this law do not mention the fact that, unlike other countries that have expropriated foreign business interests without just compensation or have long delayed compensation, our Filipinization of the retail trade law:

(1) permits every foreigner who was retailing as a sole proprietor at the time the law took effect, to continue to do so for the remainder of his natural life;

(2) gives every non-Philippine corporation ten years to liquidate the retail trade aspects of its business;

(3) as early as 1954, the Philippine Secretary of Justice defined what sales were to be considered retail, and this definition was not questioned by American business interests until ten years later, when the law was to be applied to them;

(4) the 100 per cent ownership requirement, that American business interests find oppressive, applies not only to American corporations but equally so to Filipino corporations so that, if American enterprises find it difficult to fulfill this requirement because their stock is traded on the stock exchange, so too do Filipino corporations whose stock is also traded on exchanges;

(5) finally, corporations controlled by other nationals -- including international corporations like Shell -- have adjusted to the law without undue hardship.

In short, the law does not seek to destroy American business but to promote Filipino control over the retail trade. The failure to understand this has caused -- and will continue to cause -- much tension.

Something quite similar is occurring with respect to the Philippine Investment Incentives Act. As the sponsor of the measure in the Senate and proponent of most of the provisions that have merited your criticism, if not condemnation, I hope you will allow me to repeat what I said to the Philippine chapter of the Federacion Internacional de Abogadas on how the philosophy of the law came to be what it is.

I began with an assumption that seems to me to be unassailable: that any Philippine policy on foreign direct investments had to be part of a policy on direct investments in general. Otherwise, we ran the risk of adopting policies that could run counter to each other, so that our economy might run, but go nowhere.

Given, then, that our policy on investments had to be one consistent policy, the question arose: How much investment do we need and where do we expect to get it? The answer of the Presidential Economic Staff was: "We need P16.9 billion in four years; 80 per cent must come from Philippine sources; 15 to 20 per cent from foreign capital." I checked with other sources; they gave me about the same answer. There simply is not enough direct foreign investment available to supply more than 20 per cent of our investment needs. Hence even if we Filipinos had been so devoid of a sense of responsibility and of dignity as to want to thrust upon foreigners the duty that is ours, we could not do so.

Well, then, if we had to raise 80 per cent to 85 per cent of our investment from Filipino capital, I concluded that we had to offer incentives that would appeal primarily to Filipino capital.

What does Filipino capital want?

The answer, in the terse phrase of Don Filemon Rodriguez, a former Chairman of our National Economic Council, is "profits and security." Fine, I thought. Foreign capital also wants profits and security. Thus far, there seemed to be no conflict of interest: for both Filipinos and foreigners seek lower costs, tax advantages, security of life and property, tariff protection, freedom from government competition and from expropriation, consistency in government policies.

But foreign capital seeks, in addition, guarantees of the right to remit profits and repatriate earnings; here their interests may clash with those of Filipino entrepreneurs who, in times of foreign exchange shortage, may need foreign exchange for raw materials or capital equipment. On the other hand, Filipino capital seeks another kind of security: freedom from foreign competition, not only through imported goods, but through foreign branches or foreign-controlled firms. This, of course, foreign capital opposes. But the Filipino capitalist believes that foreign companies have so much more knowhow, research facilities and capital, that they can drive a Filipino entrepreneur out of business. He may be right or wrong in his belief; but believe this way he does; so that unless he is given this security, the Filipino capitalist will not leave the safety of the land, which is protected from foreign competition, and venture into the lists of industry to do battle with giants.

Therefore, to induce the Filipino capitalist to venture into industry, I concluded that it is necessary to assure him that, in the areas he is likely to enter, no foreign-controlled firm would be allowed to compete with him on even terms; that there he would enjoy incentives that they would not. However, in areas into which he is unable or unwilling to go, there seemed to be no reason why foreign-controlled firms should not be welcomed and given incentives subject, of course, to two conditions:

   (a) That the area is not reserved for Filipinos by our Constitution and our laws; and

   (b) That the firms would transfer control to Filipinos within a period to be fixed by the Board of Investments that would be sufficient to enable foreign investors to recover their capital and make a good profit, but no longer than twenty years, extendible for another twenty years.

This is how the investment policy evolved; and I hope that you will understand that it responds not to a dislike for foreign capital but to the need to foment Philippine investment. I can only add that the first incentives bill -- entitled the "Foreign Incentives Act" -- was filed in 1954; since then, no less than fourteen other incentives measures were filed, but none became law because none was geared to the needs of Filipino investors. Indeed, had not our present law substantially complied with the principles of economic nationalism, I assure you, ladies and gentlemen, it would not have passed.

This brings me to the second point: Not only has Philippine nationalism been misunderstood or misrepresented, but its strength has been grossly underestimated, and dismissed as merely a creature of disaffected intellectuals or a greedy elite. This is wrong, believe me, my friends, it is wrong. So potent is Philippine nationalism that it has succeeded in substantially overcoming regional opposition to a national language; it is forcing through a land reform program; it resisted all investment incentives bills that did not give priority to Filipino investors; it has made the widespread use of terrorism at our polls impossible; by a vote of five to one, it has resisted attempts to alter our Constitution by increasing the membership of our House of Representatives and allowing Senators and Congressmen to run for the forthcoming Constitutional Convention without losing their seats; and it has created a uniquely Philippine religious sect whose members are so disciplined and united, that it has become a potent political, social and economic force.

Day by day, Philippine nationalism becomes more articulate. I need not dwell on the demonstrations before the American Embassy and the Manila Hotel during the Asian Summit meeting of 1966. But I think you should know that on February 8, 1967, leaders from all sectors of Philippine society banded together in what they have called "MAN -- the Movement for the Advancement of Nationalism." Among the resolutions they adopted at their first meeting were those calling for:

1. The abrogation of the Military Bases Treaty, Military Assistance Pact and the Mutual Defense Treaty with the United States, and the Manila Pact, and the eventual removal from Philippine soil of all foreign military bases;

2. The termination of all Philippine involvements in all American policies and adventures which are inimical not only to the sovereign status of our Republic but also tend to isolate the Filipino people from their fellow Asians;

3. The immediate adoption of a completely independent foreign policy based on equality and mutual respect;

4. Assertion and implementation of our laws prohibiting any foreign participation in any form in elections and other political activities.

x   x   x

2) The abrogation of unequal agreements including but not limited to the Bell Trade Act as amended by the Laurel-Langley Agreement with specific and particular reference to the parity and non-discrimination clauses embodied respectively in Articles 6 and 7 of the said agreement;

3) The abrogation of all agreements involving United States "aid," which are tied up with United States "advice" and other forms of restrictions and conditions which limit freedom of action and infringe our sovereignty.

These resolutions, one may say, are extreme; but they are not crackpot. In fact, the difference of opinion in my country on the points involving our existing treaties with your nation lies only in this: that while MAN demands abrogation, others prefer negotiation. Yet the sentiment is universal that the inequitable provisions of these agreements must go; and that great efforts must be exerted so that soon, if not now, conditions will improve in my country and the world to end all relations of dependence between our countries: military, economic, political or cultural.

If the United States runs counter to the force of Philippine nationalism, it will succeed only in convincing all Philippine nationalists, as some are now convinced, that there is no point in attempting any rational dialogue with you. Fortunately, not all are so convinced -- yet. But after parity, the bases agreement, the claim of United States ownership over our bases, the opposition to the creation of the Central Bank, the scuttling of Philippine applications for stabilization loans, the last minute opposition to the Filipinization of retail trade, and the use of diplomatic pressures on the Philippines to send troops to South Vietnam -- can one say that those who are convinced are entirely without reason?

If in days to come, your Government persists in the same course, Philippine nationalism will come to believe that it is truly the United States that is its major enemy; and in self-defense, aggravated by disenchantment, will commit itself to an irrevocable collision course against the United States: You or us.

There are ominous signs that this can happen.

In the recent consultations on the revision of the Laurel-Langley Agreement, your team has insisted not only upon a most favored nation clause but upon national treatment as well -- demands that run counter to Philippine aspirations to form a regional economic group in Southeast Asia, and to gain or retain control of every important segment of our economy. It is demands of similar nature that have delayed ratification of the Japanese treaty of friendship, commerce and navigation; and prompted the filing of six bills in the Philippine Congress -- three of which have already been approved -- to sterilize in advance the adverse consequences that are foreseen from these demands. Your team has also insisted upon the issue of vested rights in land and in franchises, concessions and licenses obtained during parity -- it is evident that these vestiges of parity will serve to aggravate what most Filipinos consider an intolerable imposition.

As I left Manila, your government's guidelines on foreign investment had prompted the filing of a bill, signed by Senators of all parties, banning the grant of loans to foreigners by government financial institutions and limiting the grant of loans to foreigners by private Philippine banks to no more than ten per cent of loanable funds.

The Philippine Chamber of Industries is discussing a resolution urging trade relations with the Communist bloc. The chairman of the House Committee on Foreign Affairs has demanded the removal of United States bases as a danger to Philippine security, and supported his demands with a litany of Philippine grievances. On the other hand, the House has just passed a bill authorizing the continued presence of Philippine troops in South Vietnam, after acrimonious debate that ended in a walkout by opponents of the bill and charges of muzzling. In the Senate, opposition to the bill gains ground -- if it passes at all, it will be by the slightest of margins.

These are current developments. How strongly your government adheres to its team's views on national treatment and the continuation after parity of rights acquired during parity; how acrimoniously your government reacts to the measures now being discussed at Manila on limiting bank credit to foreigners; on Philippine trade with the Eastern bloc; on opposition to retaining Philippine troops in South Vietnam -- these could well influence the course of Philippine-American relations more than any of us can foresee today.

For Philippine nationalism is today, as it has always been, the movement of the forces of change: our youth and our middle class. And it is becoming the articulate creed of our tenant and small farmers. Already, the point is being made with growing frequency that the peonage that characterizes our rural economy stems from the colonial system which concentrated our resources in the hands of the few, and led to the subsisting alliance between vested Filipino interests and foreign interests, whose combined economic power is so strong that they effectively influence your government and mine into maintaining the status quo.

American policy toward the Philippines is being explained in terms of the iniquitous landlord-tenant relation we call *Kasama* -- an unequal partnership, characterized by paternalism, usury, and dictation by landlord over tenant. In this analogy, of course, the United States is the landlord and the Philippines the tenant; and it gains strength because it is not an altogether invalid analogy.

Finally, the point is being made that only by emancipating our nation from this international system of peonage, can our tenant farmers break away from their domestic peonage. If this continues, and gains ground, I do not care to foretell whether there will remain any Philippine-American relation to speak about.

There are still, I think, elements in our friendship that must be preserved, if not for our mutual benefit, then for the benefit of mankind. I do not propose to tell you what the policy of your government should be to preserve these elements, anymore than I would accept your telling me what the policy of my government must be. I have pointed out the dangers that beset us. What you do about them is your business. But I can tell you the dream all Philippine nationalists share.

It is the dream to be the first former colony in Asia to achieve modernity, as it was the first to mount a revolution and the first to attain independence. It is the dream to join the modern world without sacrificing democracy to dictatorship, as others are doing; nor at the expense of the poor -- who have paid the price elsewhere -- but of those who reaped the benefits of colonialism and therefore can afford the cost of modernization. Philippine nationalism is determined to achieve this dream. It knows it must restructure the Philippine economy and Philippine society to do so. It knows it will be difficult and painful. All it asks of your people and your government is your understanding and, if you deem it worthwhile, your help to make the process faster, less painful; and if you do not deem it worthwhile, to leave us alone.

Let us do it as we believe it must be done, not as you would do it in our place. Let us make our mistakes, not suffer yours. For we are determined to make our dream a reality, cost what it may. Help us if you will; hinder us if you want -- one may speed, the other delay, but neither will stop us. With your help or despite your hindrance, Philippine nationalism will do the job. No one else can.

PHILIPPINE-AMERICAN
ECONOMIC RELATIONS

A lucid exposition of the severe disadvantages and sufferings of the Filipino people consequent to their neo-colonial economic relations with the U.S.

Let us, to begin with, agree on something. To discuss is to examine from a point of view and for some purpose. All else is idle talk. And this is not the time nor the occasion for idle talk. So I take it that, in asking me to discuss the economic relations between the Philippines and the United States, you wish me to examine those relations from the Filipino point of view for the purpose of changing them, if necessary, the better to attain Filipino objectives.

What are Filipino objectives?

Here we must not confuse the Filipino people with the Philippine government. The objectives of the two are not necessarily the same; and in the case of the current martial law regime, they are decidedly different. So let us disregard what the regime says, and more what it does, for the two occasionally coincide. Instead let us look as objectively as we can at the Philippine situation, for Filipino objectives arise out of the Filipino condition.

That condition can be summarized in four cruel paradoxes. We are a country independent but not sovereign, a state but not yet a nation, under a democratic constitution but an authoritarian government, living in a rich land filled with poor people.

Filipino objectives, then, are to transcend these paradoxes: to reclaim the sovereignty that will complete our independence; to forge the community that will convert our state into a nation; to recover the freedom that will make our government democratic both in law and in fact; and to share the riches of our land equitably among all the people that each may live a human life and enjoy the chance to bring his native talents to full flower.

One reason why these objectives have eluded us all these years is that none of the economic strategies we have pursued -- neither the

---

(Lecture delivered to the Junior Executive Club of the University of the Philippines, Diliman, Quezon City, September 2, 1980)

import substitution strategy of the 50's and 60's, nor the export orientation strategy of the 70's, nor the latest "basic needs" strategy -- none, I repeat, has addressed itself squarely to the basic weakness of our economy: its disarticulation, its lack of adequate linkages between different sectors.

Our colonial experience fragmented our economy and linked its three sectors more closely with the imperial economy than with each other. In a study of economic development in ten colonies, including the Philippines, Profs. Thomas B. Birnberg of Yale and Stephen A. Resnick of the University of Massachusetts at Amherst, summarized Philippine colonial development as follows:

> Philippines (1902-38). U.S. policy in the Philippines emphasized public works and other export-promoting expenditures, since a major U.S. objective was to expand its trade with the Philippines. This initial policy established a basic pattern: the Philippines used government expenditures to expand exports with an emphasis on education, communications, and transportation (especially highway construction)...

> As a result of these expenditures on infrastructure, agricultural output, particularly for export, increased rapidly...also U.S. trade policies facilitated an increase in Philippine exports. Until the 1930's these policies eliminated tariff and quota barriers, which increased U.S. demand for Philippine products, especially sugar. They also facilitated an increase of imports from the United States which acted as an incentive to further exports...

> ...Furthermore, Americans allowed the profits generated from the expansion of external trade to remain within the Philippines for reinvestment, especially in sugar centrals.[1]

The results of this type of development were:

> ...exports were developed to be sold to a developed country in exchange for imports of manufactures, and government expenditures were directed to facilitate and foster this international exchange ... Colonies served the political and

---

[1]Thomas B. Birnberg and Stephen A. Resnick, *Colonial Development -- An Econometric Study*, Yale University Press, 1975, pp. 62-64.

economic needs of the developed countries not only by providing assured sources of food and raw materials and markets for their manufactures, but also by providing profitable areas for foreign investment, greater control in response to economic and political rivalry among the countries of the developed world itself...

...the expansion of external trade fostered by the growth of capitalism in the developed world acted directly and indirectly to transform their agrarian economies by commercializing their lands, fragmenting their rural industry, and gradually producing social division of labor tied more to the impersonal world market forces of supply and demand relationships than to tradition or custom...The growth of the supply and demand, and the changes in the price of exports were...a function of income, price, and trade policies in the developed world, as well as a function of the accumulation of government capital in the colonial world...

These external and internal forces caused a reallocation of resources within the agrarian sector from a variety of non-agrarian tasks (rural industry) to increased specialization of export products. This reallocation of resources, and especially of labor, was accomplished under a variety of social organizations ranging from plantation labor to different tenure arrangements, and even to the development of wage labor in the agrarian sectors. Imports of manufactures from the developed world replaced the rural industry of the colonial world as organized industrial expansion fragmented the traditional unity of agricultural and industrial production based on the household. Corresponding to the shift of labor out of rural industry and into export production in the colonial world, there was a shift of labor out of agricultural production into manufacturing production in the developed world. Thus, an international division of labor emerged where changes in the developed and colonial world became duals of one another...[2]

This disarticulation, this lack of integration persists today. Even today, far too many of the products of our primary sector -- our fields, our mines, our forests and our waters -- do not enter into our industrial sector but are sent abroad; far too many of the materials and supplies, and almost all the machinery and spare parts used by our secondary sector -- our factories and our mills --

---

[2]Ibid, pp. 253-254.

come from abroad; and far too many of our people in the tertiary sector -- services -- expend their talents and their efforts for foreign firms abroad or foreign tourists at home. Our economy remains a puppet whose arms and hands are pulled by one set of strings, whose legs and feet are pulled by another, and whose head remains a wooden block.

The economic component of Filipino objectives, then, is to breathe life into this puppet, to create an integrated, self-directed economy, that consciously organizes, uses and develops Filipino resources and Filipino creative talent to supply the fundamental needs of all Filipinos and to continually improve the quality of Filipino life.

To avoid misunderstanding, let me hasten to add that this objective does not exclude foreign trade or international cooperation. What the Filipino people desire is autonomy, not autarchy; self-reliance and self-sufficiency, not isolation, though our people (although perhaps not our elite) are prepared to take such extreme steps if necessary. As the Coyococ Declaration, drafted by Lady Jackson (Barbara Ward) and adopted by the 1974 UNEP-UNCTAD symposium on "Patterns of Resource Use, Environment and Development Strategies," said:

Self-reliance at national levels may also imply a temporary detachment from the present (international) economic system; it is impossible to develop self-reliance through full participation in a system that perpetuates economic dependence...[3]

And last year Prof. Joan Robinson of Cambridge echoed those thoughts:

The decline in activity in the West spills over to the Third World in a decline in the volume of exports of primary commodities, while the prices of imports (including oil) continue to rise. At the same time, the burden of debt service is absorbing a growing proportion of what export earnings the primary commodities can provide.

---

[3]Guy F. Erb & Valeriana Kallab, ed., *The Coyococ Declaration: Beyond Dependency -- The Developing World Speaks Out*, New York: Praeger Publishers, 1975, p. 174.

The moral for the Third World is still the same: to shelter behind a poverty curtain and make use of their own potential productive resources to meet their own basic needs.[4]

Is the objective of a self-directed, self-reliant, self-sufficient Filipino economy attainable or is it merely a dream masquerading as a hope?

I believe that it is within our reach, and it is only the lack of determination by those who have held and hold power and their reluctance to make needed sacrifices that prevent us from grasping it. Look at the facts: natural resources, we have in enough quantities and enough varieties. Human resources, we have more than enough: our population is the seventeenth largest in the world; our people are 86 per cent literate; our workers and professionals are in demand in other countries of the world. Capital, we have: as the UP Law Center has found, we have been capitalizing foreign investments for years; and if the money salted abroad could be recovered and the leakages from corruption, smuggling, over-pricing, royalties and capital repatriation could be plugged, we would not need to borrow foreign funds. Technology we can buy or create ourselves. There are no insurmountable barriers, then, to achieve our economic objective.

Two eminent authorities share this view. Prof. Charles Wilber of the American University says:

Soviet-style development is possible only in countries having natural and human resources and the required market potential necessary for the development of large-scale, capital goods industries. Among countries possibly possessing these prerequisites are...the Philippines,...[5]

While Prof. Stephen Resnick has written:

This process of...(independent)...capitalistic development requires that a particular form of colonial rule or of external influence culminates in the political and economic emergence of a powerful native elite whose fortunes become historically tied to external trade and who at some specific point take

---

[4]Joan Robinson, *Aspects of Development and Underdevelopment*, London: Cambridge University Press, 1979, p. 142.

[5]Charles K. Wilber, *The Soviet Model and Underdeveloped Countries*, North Carolina: University of North Carolina Press, 1969, p. 14.

control of the state and by redirecting government expenditures and policies, create a favourable environment for the accumulation of industrial assets...the Philippines is one of the few countries which exemplifies the possibility of this type of capitalist development.[6]

If we have the potential to achieve either Soviet-style development or capitalist development, as these authorities say, how can we not have the potential to realize our own, Filipino-style development?

So, to evaluate the economic relations between the Philippines and the United States from the Filipino point of view -- and what other point of view can we take -- is to ask: Do these economic relations foster the creation of an integrated, self-directed, self-reliant, self-sufficient Filipino economy that uses Filipino resources to meet Filipino needs?

The answer to this question is a resounding "No."

Let us take up each component of those economic relations.

First, trade. Philippine-United States trade in 1979 was described by the Central Bank as follows:

Trade between the United States and the Philippines amounted to U.S. $2,786 million or 25.9 per cent of total external trade. It consisted of U.S. $1,402 million in imports from the U.S. representing 22.8 per cent of total imports and U.S. $1,384 million in Philippine exports equivalent to 30.1 per cent of total exports. Trade with this country, therefore, resulted in a U.S. $18 million deficit, a complete reversal of the U.S. $160 million surplus realized in 1978. The major purchases from the United States were cereals and cereal preparations, power generating machinery and equipment, general industrial machinery and equipment, and specialized machinery for particular industries. On the other hand, Philippine sales to the United States were composed mainly of semi-conductor devices, coconut oil and sugar.[7]

The pattern of trade was basically the same in previous years and it is clearly a neo-colonial pattern: the exchange of raw materials

---

[6]Stephen A. Resnick, "The Second Path to Capitalism: A Model of International Development," in *Journal of Contemporary Asia*, Vol. III, no. 2 (1973), p. 133.

[7]*Thirty-First Annual Report 1979*, Central Bank of the Philippines, p. 58.

and labor (for that is what semiconductor devices really consist of) for machinery. Because of the increase in coconut oil prices last year -- which was followed by a drop this year -- the terms of trade improved but still remained at 82 per cent of the 1972 terms. We are, in short, selling more products in 1979 to import the same quantity as in 1972. More important, the persistence of this pattern accentuates the disarticulated nature of our economy, and as coconut oil clearly illustrates, the ups and downs, boom or bust of substantial numbers of our people are determined, not by what their productivity is, but what foreign buyers are willing to pay for our products.

Next, aid. From 1946 to 1979, U.S. aid to the Philippines, including military aid, totalled U.S. $2.717 billion.[8] Beginning with 1976, the U.S. Congress decreed that foreign aid should be devoted "to help the poor majority...raise their living standards beyond subsistence levels." However, in October, 1979, the Center for International Policy, a non-governmental Washington based organization, published a report on U.S. aid to the Philippines from 1976 to 1978, entitled "Aid to the Philippines: Who Benefits?" with these findings:

1. Only 22 per cent of U.S. aid is reaching the needy.
2. This amounts to less than a penny per person per day.
3. As many as 78 per cent of preschool children are malnourished. Conditions for the poor have worsened since 1972. There are more desperately poor people in the Philippines today that at any time in its history.
4. The United States is responding to this urgent social and economic problem by increasing military aid by 138 percent.[9]

Where did the rest go? The paper answers:

The rest went for tobacco loans, insurance for a Bank of America branch office, military aid to a country that the Pentagon says faces no external threat, rural electrification priced out of reach of the rural poor, and balance-of-payments loans conditioned on the adoption of government policies that reduce real wages for the poor.[10]

_____

[8] *U.S. News and World Report*, March 31, 1980, p. 61.

[9] "Aid to the Philippines: Who Benefits?" *International Policy Report*, Vol. V, Publication Center for International Policy (1979), p. 1.

[10] Ibid, p. 2.

The pattern is not new. Pre-martial law aid, according to Prof. W. Scott Thompson of the Fletcher School of Law and Diplomacy, Tufts University, who is by no means a Marcos critic, had the following effects:

> The record is fairly clear. The United States almost exclusively allocated rewards to the Philippines in terms of strategic needs and perceptions of stability in the archipelago. In the 1960's, only when American needs were great -- as with the wish for at least symbolic support in the Vietnamese war -- was Philippine bargaining power great. The financial support rendered the Philippines in return was resented as much by the giver as by the recipient. A large aid program began anew only when it was perceived that President Marcos would make the internal changes deemed necessary to increase national coherence and stability, and martial law little affected -- indeed, it was postdated -- this judgment. Other than in communiques and July proclamations, the United States never paid much attention to the common adherence to democratic values. Although many American officials questioned the wisdom of the policy, Washington generally accepted martial law as a happier solution to Philippine problems than the old political system. The country team at the embassy, with some conspicuous exceptions, was enthusiastic about the regime and its results through early 1975. It is hard to find any negative component in Philippine-American relations that flowed from the institution of martial law. This is hardly surprising: in the duel between radical Philippine "nationalism" and the technocrat-military-American alliance, the latter had won.[11]

Describing the policy that produced these effects, Prof. Thompson says:

> The Americans had discovered the relative detachment of foreign policy and domestic affairs. They had discovered how modest was their ability to affect domestic affairs in other countries, and also that, as long as a foreign power inclined toward neither communism nor radical socialism, its own attachment to the United States would derive primarily from an

---

[11]W. Scott Thompson, *Unequal Partners,* Washington: Heath and Company, 1975, pp. 156-157.

identification of its own security and personal interests with it.[12]

and explains its application to the Philippines in these words:

In the Philippines, the dominant political elite had benefited from a vaguely radical anti-Americanism, because with it went an outflow of American investment which they, in their primary role as rich businessmen, could buy up. Technocrats emerged in the 1960s, partly because of the trends in Philippine education and partly because of Marcos' particular desires. They found themselves unable to administer the country efficiently because of the opposition to central control by these very powerful subsystemic elements, some of which were rivals of the state itself in power in certain areas. Marcos and his technocrats worked closely with the Americans, and used American aid...to strengthen their own control. Whether it was granted for purposes, ironically, of increasing "political development" under Title IX or of furthering decentralization (as AID officials so often said), its result was almost uniformly to reinforce the power of the state -- either in building up control and intelligence mechanisms through the armed forces, or in strengthening the bargaining power of Malacanang palace vis-a-vis traditional provincial political elites, by giving it more funds to disburse.[13]

Another American professor, Mr. Robert B. Stauffer, is less generous to both Marcos and the United States. He has called the process "the political economy of refeudalization." Whatever it may be, state-building or refeudalization, no one can seriously question that U.S. economic and military aid have not benefited the Filipino people and have not led to a better integrated, more autonomous Filipino economy, however much they may have benefited Marcos, his technocrats, the Philippine military and U.S. imperialist interests.

Third, U.S. direct investment. The value of U.S. direct investment in the Philippines is in excess of U.S. $2 billion. About 56 per cent of this investment is in manufacturing -- mostly in petroleum refining, food and beverage, transport equipment, cosmetics, and pharmaceuticals and chemicals, in all of which U.S.

---

[12]Ibid, pp. 157-158.
[13]Ibid, pp. 159-160.

transnationals predominate and all of which have a high import component. About 15 per cent of U.S. investment is in finance and insurance, where the average profit was 33.3 per cent per year from 1965-75. The rest were in mining, trade and services. Prof. Edberto M. Villegas of De La Salle University has found that, for every U.S. $1.00 invested into the Philippines, foreign investors borrowed the equivalent of U.S. $8.33 from Philippine sources to capitalize their investments; and the UP Law Center has disclosed that every U.S. $1.00 of direct investment generated U.S. $3.58 in profits, of which U.S. $2.00 have been repatriated, leaving U.S. $1.58 here to repeat the cycle of local borrowing, profit, repatriation, and reinvestment.

Clearly, U.S. investments have not promoted the integration of our economy nor supplied us with our basic needs. On the contrary, they have further deepened our dependence.

Thus far I have sought to analyze each component of our economic relations with the United States from an economic point of view. This is clearly an inadequate analysis because economic relations reflect not only economic policy but total policy.

This has been so from the time the United States subjugated our country. McKinley who, on May 18, 1898, instructed General Merritt:

> ...immediately upon his arrival in the islands, to publish a proclamation declaring that we come not to make war upon the people of the Philippines nor upon any party or faction among them, but to protect them in their homes, in their employments, and in their personal and religious rights."

and four months later instructed his Peace Commissioners to the Treaty of Paris that:

> Incidental to our tenure in the Philippines is the commercial opportunity to which American statesmanship can not be indifferent. It is just to use every legitimate means for the enlargement of American trade;...

How did commercial interests intrude into what was announced as a humane act of "benevolent assimilation?" Prof. Thomas J. McCormick of the University of Pittsburgh explains that:

> From the very beginning of the Spanish-American War, the McKinley administration intended to retain a foothold in the Philippines as an "American Hong Kong," a commercial

entrepot to the China market and a center of American military power. Formulation of this policy began seven months before hostilities with Spain...

x   x   x

Between June and October, business and government circles united vigorously around a policy of retaining all or part of the Philippines. Significantly, their rationale stressed the intrinsic economic worth of the islands far less than their strategic relationship to China -- both as a commercial entrepot and a political military lever...

...Led by the National Association of Manufacturers and the American Asiatic Association, many special business organizations urged retention of the Philippines "for the protection and furtherance of the commercial interests of our citizens in the Far East"...

Most of McKinley's close associates in the government (many of whom were themselves products of the business community) pressed similar views upon their chief. The redoubtable Mark Hanna, State Department economic expert Frederic Emory, the American Minister to China Charles Denby, his successor Edwin H. Conger, Comptroller of the Currency Charles C. Dawes, Assistant Secretary of the Treasury Frank A. Vanderlip, to name a few, all shared in general the conviction, (as Vanderlip stated) that an American-controlled Philippines would be "pickets of the Pacific, standing guard at the entrances to trade with the millions of China and Korea, French Indo-China, the Malay Peninsula, and the island of Indonesia.[14]

Albert J. Beveridge, the Senator from Indiana, said it more bluntly:

American factories are making more than the American people can use; American soil is producing more than they can consume. Fate has written our policy for us; the trade of the world must and shall be ours ... American law, American

---

[14]Thomas J. McCormick, "The Philippines Were Insular Stepping Stones to the Chinese Pot of Gold," *American Imperialism in 1898 The Quest for National Fulfillment* edited by Richard H. Miller, New York: John Wiley & Sons, 1970, pp. 129, 133-134.

order, American civilization, and the American flag will plant themselves on shores hitherto bloody and benighted, but by the agencies of God henceforth to be made beautiful and bright...

In the Pacific is the true field of our earliest operations. There Spain has an island empire, the Philippine Archipelago. It is poorly defended. Spain's best ships are on the Atlantic side. In the Pacific the United States has a powerful squadron. The Philippines are logically our first target.[15]

In essence, those are still the imperatives of U.S. policy towards the Philippines: to hold the Philippines as a military base; to exploit it as a market for American products; to use it as a stepping stone to the markets of China; and to "civilize" it by implanting the American way of life here, at first by education and by Christian missionaries, today by Peace Corps volunteers and mass media and advertising.

Since U.S. policy is so diametrically opposed to Filipino objectives, is it worthwhile to continue to maintain economic relations with the United States?

In the present form of those economic relations, no.

Is it possible to change those economic relations so that they will serve the interests of the Filipino people as a whole, rather than of some Filipinos only?

Yes.

How?

We cannot directly change U.S. policy towards the Philippines. That is true. But we can change Philippine policy towards the United States. And we can start by adopting a different economic development strategy, a strategy designed to integrate our economy, to place it firmly under Filipino control, to make it self-sustaining, and to direct it equitably so as to achieve a gradually improving quality of life for all Filipinos.

This is not the occasion to spell out such a strategy in its entirety -- nor would it be prudent to do so. But its essentials would include at least the following:

(1) Planning not only for growth of production, but for consumption and distribution, which means, in practice, determining the minimum standard of living that all Filipinos

---

[15]Richard O'Connors, *Pacific Destiny*, Little Brown & Co., 1969, pp. 269-270.

should enjoy, quantifying its basic components as much as is possible, determining what local resources can be used as basic materials for these basic components, and gearing production to meet these demands;

(2) Establishing an iron and steel industry as first priority using our extensive iron and coal mines, and leading to both a machine tools industry and capital goods industry that will make machines to make machines, the latter preferably for scaled-down miniaturized factories, rather than large-scale plants;

(3) Centralizing only capital intensive heavy industries, such as the iron and steel industry I have just mentioned, and dispersing consumer goods industries which should be composed of small scale family or cooperatively owned business, which utilize, in the language of Prof. A.K.N. Reddy of the Indian Institute of Science, "the technology of manufacture rather than machinofacture," technologies that are "energy-saving rather than energy-intensive," "capital-saving and employment-generating, rather than capital-intensive and labor-saving;"

(4) Raising the real wages of labor: Historically, rises in real wages have always preceded -- not followed -- economic development. Logically this has to be so. For without increases in real wages, workers cannot buy the products of industry; without sales, consumer goods industries cannot grow; and without growing consumer goods industries, capital goods industries could not be established;

(5) Undertaking a thoroughgoing land reform that will return agriculture to small scale, labor intensive farming, supported by security of tenure, guaranteed credit, and regular sales outlets, and reinforced by irrigation, electrification and communications (good roads, inexpensive transport) and technical research directed to land-saving and land-intensive cultivation;

(6) Socializing the financial system, which may or may not include nationalization, so that available monetary capital is used to advance -- not to frustrate -- the development plan;

(7) Plugging leaks from the economy such as waste, corruption, overpricing imports, luxury consumption, dollar salting, smuggling (both covert or open through U.S. bases), unemployment and under-employment;

(8) Emphasizing collective consumption by building small general public hospitals throughout the country rather than huge, expensive medical centers in urban Manila; medium and low cost housing instead of mansions; all-weather barrio roads instead of expressways; family run hostels instead of five star hotels; and limiting the consumption of public goods, such as free medical

care, free public education, and the like to the low income sector of society;

(9) Establishing new patterns of energy consumption such as the use of organic rather than fossil fuel fertilizers; public buses and mass transits rather than private cars; wood and coal for heating rather than petroleum products; and the like.

Several objections may be raised against these proposals. I shall attempt to meet the more important.

First, that the proposal to give priority to iron and steel is uneconomic because we could buy machines cheaper from the U.S., Japan or even the Peoples Republic of China. I am not certain that this is so, especially if social benefits and costs are added to economic benefits and costs. But assuming it to be so, can anything be more uneconomic than maintaining a standing army? Yet we do so, and will continue to do so. For the same reason, we must establish an iron and steel industry. It is more than an economic project -- it is the project that can bring our economic sectors together, and consequently is more than a matter of national security, it is a matter of national integration.

Another objection is that some proposals -- particularly the proposal to set up small-scale consumer goods factories -- violate the principle of economy of scale. I am not certain that this would be so in all cases (for example, clothing that changes styles with changes in fashion or some machine tools that are not susceptible to large production runs) but assuming that it were, would not the savings in transport and marketing costs made by locating these factories as close as possible to markets offset the advantages of economy of scale? And would not spin offs from such factories in the form of employment generation, encouragement for local growth of raw materials and the like also offset the disadvantages of small size?

The program I have outlined will involve basic changes in the structure of both production and of consumption. In these changed structures, aid will have no role to play, except perhaps on occasions of natural calamity, and even then only until our economy has not yet reached the integrated strength that would allow us to handle emergencies by ourselves. Trade will continue but its character will gradually change. Foreign investment will be subjected to common sense tests that will include, among others, these questions:

1. Does the economy need the product or service that foreign investment offers to produce?
2. If it does, can we not produce an equivalent product ourselves, using local raw materials and native capital?

3. If we can't, is there another method of getting the product --
   licensing for example?

Only if the investment passes these tests, will it be allowed.

In short, to change the nature of the economic relations between
the Philippines and the United States, we Filipinos must first
change the nature of our own economy. And to do that, our people
must regain their freedom and their sovereignty -- political power
must be lodged in the people in fact. For economy involves not
merely the exchange of goods but the exercise of power; and just as
concentrated power is politics, so politics is concentrated
economics.

Can the people regain their freedom and sovereignty?
Unfortunately, I cannot answer this question. But you can.

ECONOMICS AND SOCIAL CONSCIOUSNESS

"... Our economy is a Filipino economy, so that its goal should be to meet the needs of the Filipino people."

I am proud to be with you tonight and grateful for this chance to share some thoughts with you on the need to infuse economics with social consciousness. I am even more grateful for the hope you stir in me that one day, not too far away, we shall see a new generation of Filipino economists, who are more than mere technocrats, experts not only in means but also in ends, who seek not to fatten men's pocket books, but to enrich man's quality of life, who have clear minds -- and warm hearts as well.

God knows we Filipinos need men and women of this breed now more than ever before. A wise lawyer once said, "Technique without ideals is a menace; ideals without technique are a mess." To our sorrow, we Filipinos have experienced that mess and are facing that menace. Our economy was run by politicians and businessmen, and our people learned to regret it. Today our economy is run by technocrats and military men, and our people regret it even more. We need -- and our people hunger for -- an economy run by humans for humans.

What has gone wrong with our economy? Why is our economy still underdeveloped, after thirty-four years of independence and eight years of martial law, despite the abundance of our natural resources, the wealth of skills and talents of our people, the accumulation of capital over these years, and the size of our potential domestic market, the 17th largest in the world? Why are 78 per cent of our children malnourished, 1.5 million of them so severely that they have become mentally retarded? Why do less than 70 per cent of our families live at or below the poverty line? Why are at least 90 per cent of our workers paid less than subsistence wages?

Different answers have been given to these questions and there is some truth to all the answers.

One answer claims that policymakers have given too much importance to the problem of economic growth and not enough to

---

(Talk delivered before the Inter-School Business Association at the Tourism Pavilion, PICC, Manila, September 6, 1980)

the problem of economic development; that efforts are concentrated on increasing production to the neglect of improving distribution and equalizing consumption.

That is true. Our economy has grown at respectable rates, both before and during martial law; but poverty has grown even more rapidly. Economists seem to have forgotten that, although how much is produced is important, equally important are what is produced and who consumes it. Making guns and bullets, or artificially laying white sand beaches and raising the sea wall along Roxas Boulevard all increase GNP; but the poor cannot eat guns or bullets, white sand or bricks.

Another answer points to the export orientation of our economy as the culprit. That orientation, it is said, turns our economy upside down because, instead of organizing our resources, our manpower and our capital to meet our people's needs, we organize them to meet other people's demands. Besides, export orientation constrains the government to keep wages low; and since low wages require low prices for farm products, it also motivates the government to repress both urban and agricultural workers; and, in reciprocity for exports, to throw the door wide open to imports.

That is also true. Government is authoritarian; to put it plainly, dictatorial. It deliberately keeps our wage levels below those of neighboring countries, and it wantonly violates human rights. Our exports, of course, have grown, but our imports have grown even more rapidly. Misery has spread; inequality has become more pronounced. In truth, exports should not be regarded as the engine of economic development but as its results, as icing on a cake, not as baking powder.

A variant of the export orientation answer is that our economy has gone awry because international financial institutions -- the World Bank, the International Monetary Fund and the Asian Development Bank -- dictate Philippine economic policy. These financial institutions, it is argued, are interested only secondarily, if at all, in converting developing economies like ours into self-directed, self-sustaining, and self-sufficient economies. Their primary interest is to foster world trade. To do so, they insist on free trade, mindless of the historical facts, first, that nations benefit by free trade only after they have developed their own industries behind the protection of tariff walls, and, second, that it was precisely free trade between the Philippines and the United States that prevented the growth of manufacturing in our country during our colonial era; and heedless of the economic tendency of free trade to perpetuate the existing international division of labor and of wealth, and to doom developing nations, like us, to dependent development typified by component industrialization, at best, and to permanent underdevelopment at worst.

All that is true, too. The martial law government has, in fact, abdicated the making of economic policy to the World Bank and the IMF. One result is that even though we are so badly in need of foreign exchange that our foreign debt has soared to more than U.S. $11 billion, the Central Bank recently relaxed limitations on the importation of non-essentials and even luxuries.

Still another answer insists that the arrested growth of our manufacturing sector is the cause of the deplorable condition of our economy. Economic development, it is said, is not only growth but structural change and our economy has not changed structurally. As in our colonial days, today the three sectors of our economy -- the primary sector of agriculture, fishing, forestry and mining, the secondary sector of industry, and the tertiary sector of services -- have closer links with foreign economies than with each other; and the one development that could tie them together, a capital goods industry using domestic resources, has been largely ignored.

That, also, is true. After the spurt in industrialization of the 1950's, during which we adopted the import substitution model of development, and raised the contribution of our manufacturing sector from about 9 per cent to 20 per cent of GNP, manufacturing growth has been stunted, and its contribution to the national product has remained stagnant at about 24 per cent. Moreover, our manufacturing industry remains light, without the backbone of heavy, capital goods industry such as an iron and steel industry, despite the abundance of domestic iron ore, which we export, and the availability of coal.

Yet another answer stresses, as among the main causes of our economic ills, the waste and the corruption that make a mockery of economic planning and of laws intended to mitigate the rigors of an unregulated market. An economy, it is said, cannot develop if development strategies are changed prematurely, if plans are not implemented consistently, if meretricious exemptions to rules are granted, and if scarce resources are squandered or misappropriated.

There is truth to that, too. Over the years, our policymakers have changed development models, like their clothes, with every change of fashion. In the 1950's, following the Latin American example, they adopted the import substitution model I have referred to. Instead of pursuing this model to maturity, they abandoned it in the 1970's, lured by the example of Singapore, Taiwan and South Korea, and adopted its opposite: the export orientation model which was promoted by the World Bank and the Asian Development

Bank. Now that the folly of this model is becoming more and more evident, even to its most ardent supporters, they seek to shroud its failure with the new approach glamorized by the International Labor Office: the basic-needs model, which in our country has been given the catchy acronym BLISS and is being promoted with all the fanfare, skill -- and expense -- of a Madison Avenue advertising campaign for a new deodorant. Of the three models, unfortunately, only the first had the potential to launch a frontal attack on the fundamental weakness of our economy that I adverted to above -- its disarticulation, the lack of integration of our three sectors -- and this model was prematurely abandoned.

Equally important, the other models are not being implemented consistently. To cite a few examples: three years ago, aware that foreign investors borrowed the equivalent of U.S.$8.33 in local funds for every U.S. $1.00 that they brought into the country, the Central Bank decided to limit their local borrowings. However, the rules were riddled with exceptions; and the first exemptions were granted to subsidiaries of General Motors, Ford, Unilever, Procter and Gamble and the like, transnationals whose gross sales exceed our GNP. Every year the martial law government decrees increases in minimum wages and allowances but exempts export industries and distressed firms. As a result, less than 30 per cent of our workers receive the legal wage. Other rules are changed so rapidly and so whimsically that even so huge a corporation as Ayala and Company has recently complained that it cannot plan for more than six months at a time.

Each of the answers I have summarized emphasizes a different factor, but if we carry each answer one step further, all point to a common failing. Why have our policymakers concentrated on production and neglected distribution? Why have they adopted the policy of export orientation? Why have they abdicated the power to make economic policy? Why have there been no real efforts to establish a capital goods industry? Why are laws and plans and policies not implemented consistently?

The answer common to all these questions is the failure to understand that economics is social science and that the economy is for all, not just a few. Our policymakers appear to have overlooked these simple truths:

>> that our economy is a Filipino economy, so that its goal should be to meet the needs of the Filipino people;

>> that our economy cannot meet these needs and indeed cannot develop if workers are not paid enough to buy the goods the economy produces; and

>>   that the key to developing our economy is not how much foreign leans we can get, or foreign investments we can attract, or exports we can ship; the key is optimizing and using wisely and equitably what Adam Smith called the "surplus part of the produce" which is the excess of what our natural and human resources could produce given the present state of technology, over what our people must consume to stay healthy and productive.

Professor Dudley Dillard has graphically pointed this out:

> Productive use of the social surplus was the special virtue that enabled capitalism to outstrip all prior economic systems. Instead of building pyramids and cathedrals, those in command of the social surplus chose to invest in ships, warehouses, raw materials, finished goods and other material forms of wealth. The social surplus was thus converted into enlarged productive capacity.[1]

In our case, those who control the surplus part of the produce do not, it is true, build pyramids and cathedrals. These have gone out of fashion. Instead they build convention centers and five-star hotels -- and salt dollars abroad, accept kickbacks euphemistically called "commissions," overprice imports, and dissipate wealth in senseless extravagance.

In short, the reason why our economy has failed to develop is the failure of our policymakers to extract the potential surplus that our economy could produce, to allocate that surplus equitably to increase consumption for the poor and to investment, and to channel investible surplus into productive industries in the correct priority, that is, a priority that will ensure the integration, the autonomy and the self-sustaining capacity of our economy and enhance its ability to provide a gradually improving quality of life for all Filipinos.

There are two ways we can cure this defect: we can convince our policymakers to change their policies or we can change our policymakers. Either course requires public power; and that, of course, involves politics. So, in the end, the problem of economic development demands a political solution.

---

[1] Dudley Dillard, "Capitalism," in *The Political Economy of Development and Underdevelopment*, Charles K. Wilber, ed., New York: Random House, Inc., 1979, p. 70.

That should not surprise us. Economics is more than an exchange of goods; it is also an exercise of power. And just as concentrated power is politics, so politics is concentrated economics.

That, ultimately, is why we need economists who are more than economists:

>> economists who are socially conscious and politically aware;

>> economists who can distinguish structural problems from personal problems, who, for example, seek the solution to poverty, not in charity or alms giving but in structural change, because they see poverty as caused, not by defects in the character or training of the poor, but by the injustice of our social system;

>> economists whose standards transcend efficiency and "rationality" to include justice and equity, because for them economic problems are human problems, not merely technical problems.

The projects you are undertaking nourish the hope that you are the forerunners of this new breed of economists. Eight years ago, during the first day of my detention, I tried to cheer up fellow detainees by telling them how the economic historian, Charles Beard, condensed the lessons of history into four sentences. The first three were:

Whom the gods would destroy, they
first make mad with power.
The wheels of God grind slowly, but
they grind exceedingly small.
The bee fertilizes the flower that it
robs.

Eight years of martial law have taught us how true these three lessons are. But it is the fourth that is particularly relevant to this occasion. That fourth lesson is:

When it gets dark enough, you can see
the stars.

These days are dark, my friends, almost pitch black. But as I look upon you young men and women, I know that I see the stars that herald the not too distant dawn of a better, not a so-called new, society, but a Filipino society based on a just, human and humane Filipino economy.

WHAT THE PHILIPPINES EXPECTS OF FOREIGN INVESTORS

The terms and conditions of foreign investments in the Philippines are clearly delineated. They are informed by a sense of justice, friendship and fairness. There are ample rewards for the foreigner who decides to invest in the Philippines.

No Philippine policy has been criticized so severely -- or misunderstood and misrepresented so grossly -- as the policy on foreign investments laid down by Republic Act No. 5186, the Investment Incentives Act, and Republic Act No. 5455, the recently enacted law that defines the fields of business and investment for foreign capital in this country.

Criticism, we welcome. Distortion, we deplore. The former may lead to a better policy; the latter only harms both the Philippines and potential foreign investors: the Philippines, because it makes the pace of our economic development slower than it otherwise could be; foreign capital, because it frightens it into giving up, without any reason, the chance to earn substantial profits in a guaranteed and growing Philippine and Asian market.

I shall, therefore, seize the opportunity you have given me of speaking with you this afternoon to spell out, as clearly as I can, what Philippine policy on foreign investments is; what the Philippines offers foreign capital; and what it expects from foreign capital in return.

In any discussion of the Philippine economy, the role of American capital always looms large. This is not only a product of our past relationship of colony and colonial power, but of the sheer size, wealth and power of the present day American economy. For one thing, the United States takes in some 43 per cent of our exports and provides some 34 per cent of our imports. For another, the largest individual and corporate income taxpayers in the country, as a whole, are U.S. citizens and the corporations they own or control. Indeed, as the U.S. Ambassador told the Manila Junior Chamber of Commerce on November 19, 1968, American industry in the Philippines paid "almost 20 per cent of all taxes paid." I

(Speech before the Manila Sales Convention of HONIRON on January 20, 1969 at the Insular Life Auditorium)

shall, therefore, have a few words to say specially for American investors, actual and potential, in the spirit of the old Filipino proverb: *"pagsasamang matapat, pagsasamang maluwat"* - Frank talk makes fast friends.

To understand the Philippine policy on foreign investments, it is essential to understand our national objectives and aspirations. The first and foremost is to convert a basically agricultural economy, dependent upon the export of a few raw materials, into a self-sustaining industrial economy, exporting manufactured products. Only by this conversion, can we hope to catch up with the rest of the world and to create jobs and provide decent levels of living for our growing population. Our long struggle for independence and our sense of dignity made it imperative that we solve this problem ourselves and not thrust it upon others. To solve it, however, we must be sovereign in fact, as well as in law, in our land. But we have learned that it is impossible to divorce political power from economic power. We note this, not necessarily ascribing evil motives to wealth; but simply as a fact. To protect itself, economic power naturally seeks political power. So that, to be truly sovereign, Filipinos must have both political and economic control over the Philippines. Only then can we modernize our society, and see to it that the gains of modernity are not monopolized by only a favored few -- whether Filipinos or foreigners -- but are distributed among all Filipinos.

It is these objectives that the Philippine policy on foreign investments seeks to attain. Stripped to bare essentials, the policy is this:

(1) Over the years, by our Constitution and laws (some of which were enacted during the period of American sovereignty), certain areas have been reserved, for reasons of national security, for Filipinos: the ownership of private land; the acquisition, exploitation, development and utilization of public agricultural land and natural resources; the operation of public utilities, including domestic air transportation and commerce and coastwise shipping; banks and savings and loan associations; the retail trade; the rice and corn trade; and insurance adjusting.

(2) In these areas, foreigners may invest in up to 40 per cent of the capital stock of domestic corporations, except in coastwise shipping, where the maximum foreign share may not exceed 25 per cent; and in the retail trade and the rice and corn trade, where no foreign investment at all is allowed.

(3) In 1967, a government agency was created -- the Board of Investments -- that annually publishes a plan, called the Investments Priorities Plan, approved by the President, specifying

what existing industries should be expanded and what pioneer industries should be established, and by how many units of production in each of these areas -- called preferred non-pioneer and preferred pioneer areas, respectively -- should be increased.

(4) Enterprises engaged in any preferred area -- pioneer and non-pioneer -- enjoy substantial incentives in the form of extra tax deductions, tax credits and protection from foreign competition and from government competition. More incentives are offered pioneer than non-pioneer enterprises. And indicating the Philippine policy to set up a capital goods industry and export industries as early as possible, still more incentives are offered enterprises in these areas.

(5) Foreign capital is welcome to invest in up to 40 per cent of registered non-pioneer enterprises and up to 100 per cent of registered pioneer enterprises. However, foreign capital in pioneer enterprises must, within 20 years, attain 60 per cent Filipino ownership -- though this period may be extended for another 20 years if Filipino capital is not willing to buy its shares or some other cause exists that the Board of Investments may deem sufficient to extend the period.

(6) In areas not included in the annual investments priorities plan, foreign capital is welcome to invest -- without any condition other than registration for purposes of record -- in up to 30 per cent of the outstanding capital of an enterprise. When the share of foreign capital is or will be greater than 30 per cent, then prior authority from the Board of Investments is required. The Board, however, is instructed to grant this authority, unless the investment:

(a) would conflict with existing constitutional provisions and laws regulating the degree of required ownership by Philippine nationals in the enterprise; or

(b) would pose a clear and present danger of promoting monopolies or combinations in restraint of trade; or

(c) would be made in an enterprise engaged in an area adequately being exploited by Philippine nationals; or

(d) would conflict or be inconsistent with the investments priorities plan in force at the time the investment is sought to be made; or

(e) would not contribute to the sound and balanced development of the national economy on a self-sustaining basis.

In short, then, this is our policy on foreign investments: in areas that are designated by the Board of Investments as pioneer areas of investment in the annual investments plan, foreign capital is welcome and, even if it is the sole or controlling owner, it is granted substantial tax benefits, a guaranteed share of the market, and protection from competition by imports, including imports by the government. In areas designated as non-pioneer but preferred areas of investment, foreign capital is welcome to invest in up to 40 per cent of the voting stock of any enterprise, and accorded substantially the same privileges. In areas not designated either as preferred or as pioneer, no incentives are offered either foreign or Filipino capital; and foreign capital is welcome only if its investments would not duplicate existing investments and would help the balanced development of the Philippine economy.

Let me now try to clear up some of the more important misgivings about this policy and related issues that have been expressed by the U.S. Department of Commerce in the last issue of its magazine International Commerce for 1968, and by U.S. Ambassador G. Mennen Williams in a speech to the Manila Junior Chamber of Commerce on November 19, 1968.

First, is what the Commerce Department calls "uncertainties concerning the rights of American investments after the expiration of the Laurel-Langley agreement in 1974;" or, as Ambassador Williams says: "the duration of rights acquired by American investors under the 1946 and 1955 Agreements." Perhaps the best answer is that of Dr. Frank H. Golay, Professor of Economics and Asian Studies at Cornell University, who has studied intensively and written extensively about the Philippine economy. Dr. Golay calls this "a new spurious issue." In a paper prepared for The American Assembly session at Davao in 1966, Dr. Golay said:

> ... The issue of property rights established under the parity amendment is spurious for the simple reason that such rights are economically insignificant. Postwar American investment has moved into manufacturing and trade for reasons which have been explained above, and investment in the exploitation of natural resources and in public utilities has increased little, if at all. In addition, many prominent firms engaged in activities covered by "parity" are within striking distance of 60 per cent Filipino ownership originally specified in the Constitution.[1]

Spurious or not, the issue is now before the Philippine courts where it belongs. For it is essentially a legal issue; neither the President nor Congress can authoritatively settle it; only our Supreme Court can. And no one, I think, Filipino or foreigner who has had any experience in the Philippines can reasonably doubt the

---

[1] Frank H. Golay, ed., *The United States and the Philippines*, Englewood Cliffs, N.J.: Prentice-Hall, Inc., 1966, p.120.

integrity, impartiality, independence and sense of justice of our Supreme Court. Moreover, for whatever comfort it may give United States investors, the record shows that the Philippines has never expropriated -- much less confiscated -- any foreign investments at all; nor has it defaulted on any of its public international debts.

Second, the U.S. Commerce Department notes, as a factor that will discourage new foreign investments, "the growing areas of discretionary authority accorded Philippine governmental agencies." Yet, I cannot see how a developing nation, like the Philippines, can use its resources rationally and efficiently without planning; nor how plans can be made or implemented unless some agency is given discretionary authority. The point then, is not that discretionary authority exists; it is whether discretion can be exercised arbitrarily so as to impair acquired rights and thus make planning by private enterprise impossible. Our investment laws have foreseen and forestalled this as much as is humanly possible. Before it adopts its annual plan, the Board of Investments is required to hear and consult with the private sector; the plan is then submitted for study by the National Economic Council where the private sector is represented; thence it goes to the President for final action. But the President himself cannot change the plan adopted by the Board of Investments; he can only approve or disapprove it, in whole or in part. Once approved and published, the plan is final; and any enterprise registered under the plan acquires and retains all the incentives given it by the law even though, in subsequent plans, the areas of preferred and pioneer investments are changed. In any case, to forestall possible abuse of discretion by the Board of Investments recourse is given by law to the Courts. As for discretion exercised by government agencies other than the Board of Investments, the law specifically gives investors and enterprises in areas designated by the plan as preferred and pioneer, the right of recourse to the Board of Investments who will resolve all conflicts between investors and other government agencies regulating their business. Not only does the law require all these other agencies to implement the Board of Investments plan, but the decision of the Board of Investments binds these government agencies. It does not, however, bind the investor, who may go to Court if not satisfied with the Board of Investments decision. Finally, the law specifically directs that any doubts concerning the scope and application of incentives should be resolved in favor of the investors. With these safeguards, there is, I submit, no rational ground to fear "the growing area of discretionary authority accorded Philippine government agencies." After all, these agencies govern not only foreign but Filipino investors and enterprises as well. We could hardly have given them unbridled power to cut our own throats.

Third, Ambassador Williams notes that "the United States does not seek special privileges in the Philippines after 1974; it is interested in knowing, as clearly as possible, just what the treatment of Unites States investors is to be." Yet the answer, I think is perfectly clear: after 1974, the United States investors will have the same rights as other foreign investors -- certainly no less, but no more, either. And these rights are clearly and simply stated in Republic Act Nos. 5186 and 5455, which I have tried to summarize. At this point, may I express the hope that American investors will begin, even before 1974, to consider themselves simply as foreign investors -- not as United States investors with special privileges -- in this country. Continued insistence upon the right of national treatment given United States citizens under the Bell Trade Agreement and the Laurel-Langley Agreement serves only to strain relations between us. It was the first U.S. Civil Governor, William Howard Taft, who coined the phrase "The Philippines for the Filipinos." But so far, the phrase has meant "The Philippines for the Filipinos and the Americans." For as long as United States investors insist upon national treatment, so long will they be targets of our resentment, to our mutual detriment.

Fourth, the U.S. Department of Commerce bewails "tight controls over new foreign direct investments and portfolio investments in Filipino firms" (referring to Republic Act No. 5455), and "other bills providing for nationalization of the oil industry and restriction of domestic commercial bank credits to Filipino firms" -- all of which it describes as "indicative of the attitude of strong interest groups to foreign investments." Since I sponsored both the Investment Incentives Act and the law defining the fields of investment for foreign capital -- and since I authored the Oil Industry Commission bill and the bill that would Filipinize domestic bank credit -- I seem to be the villain of the piece and the spokesman "of strong interest groups." Let me say clearly that I represent no interest group at all, except the interest of the Filipino people to control our destiny. But that apart, let me say that:

(1) The Philippine Congress has no intention to nationalize or even Filipinize the oil industry. The bill that is pending in Congress which the President certified as urgent, seeks only to create an oil industry commission that will supervise the operations of the oil industry, fix maximum prices for petroleum products, and prevent monopolistic practices. When one considers that 96 per cent of the energy requirements of our country are

supplied by petroleum products, that the oil industry is predominantly foreign owned, controlled and operated, and that there is no law that would protect Filipino consumers from unwarranted shutdowns or unjustified price increases, is it unreasonable to seek to supervise the industry and fix its rates in the same manner that we supervise and fix the rates of the public utilities that depend upon the oil industry?

(2) As for the bill Filipinizing bank credit, the purpose is, not to scare away foreign investments, but to make clear that foreign investments should be adequate investments -- not merely minimum investments that depend upon and seek to take advantage of organized local credit to finance operations. The bill does not seek to ban totally the use of domestic bank credit by foreign investors. Statistics show that approximately 90 per cent of domestic bank deposits are Filipino deposits; the bill provides therefore that 90 per cent of the bank loanable funds should be reserved for loans to Filipino debtors, and the balance may be loaned to foreign firms. Instead of favoring a few Filipinos, the bill is designed to meet the problem of small Filipino enterprises whom President Marcos recently described as being "still shut off from conventional sources of financing at reasonable rate of interest."[2]

(3) As for Republic Act No. 5455, what the U.S. Commerce Department describes as "tight controls on new foreign direct investments and portfolio investments in Filipino firms" are merely these: that when the investment would be made in an area not specified as either preferred or pioneer by the Board of Investments, and would exceed 30 per cent of the capital of the enterprise, prior authority of the Board of Investments is required. That authority, however, as I have said, is to be freely given, unless the investment would violate Filipinization laws, create monopolies, subvert the investment plan, or constitute an uneconomic duplication of existing investments. Certainly, I find it difficult to see how anyone could find fault with those conditions. They are designed to make the investment plan effective; to give the Board of Investments power to insure the best economic use of scarce resources and to avoid waste of time, effort and capital. We Filipinos realize that, no matter what we did, we could never attract as much foreign investment as we might want. Over the last ten years, for example, with United States investors enjoying national treatment across the board in the Philippines, the

---

[2]Letter to Commerce Secretary Virata, *Manila Chronicle*, January 20, 1969, p. 20.

net new United States private direct investments have amounted to only U.S. $3 million dollars annually,[3] and have cost us an average of 6.5 per cent annually, which is higher than the interest rate on comparable international loans.[4] Since we cannot hope to get as much new investment as we want, Republic Act No. 5455 proposes to direct as much as we can get into these fields where they will do the most good. Surely, the rationality of this policy should, for potential foreign investments, be a plus rather than a minus factor in weighing the advisability of investing in the Philippines. It is always better to deal with a government that attacks its problems rationally rather than emotionally or corruptly.

What have we to offer foreign investors that we should seek to direct their investments into specified channels?

First, a growing economy. From 1955 to 1968, our net national product, at constant 1955 prices, almost doubled; from P7.624 billion to P14.928 billion, an increase of 95 per cent over 13 years. The average household income also increased from P1,471 per family in 1957 to P2,541 in 1965; and the market continues to grow.

Second, a labor force that is 72 per cent literate, and almost 40 per cent English speaking; and a growing body of trained supervisory and middle management personnel.

Third, a guaranteed share of the market if the investment is made in a preferred or pioneer area of investment: for every area has a measured capacity; each enterprise in the area has a registered capacity; once the measured capacity is filled, no new enterprise may be registered. In addition to tax deductions, credits and exemptions, pioneer enterprises are given post-operative tariff protection of up to 50 per cent upon registration, automatically effective upon the start of commercial operation. Preferred and pioneer enterprises may obtain the banning of competing foreign products, if dumped into this country, without the cumbersome procedures of the Customs Code. Even the government agencies are barred from importing competing products.

Fourth, subject only to the needs of the country for food and essential commodities, remittances of profits and interest payments, and repatriation of capital are guaranteed. And the staff of the Senate Committee on Economic Affairs are studying a bill that I propose to file in the coming session that would allow enterprises, Filipino and foreign, to retain a percentage of the

---

[3]*Manila Daily Bulletin,* December 21, 1968.
[4]*Manila Daily Bulletin,* December 24, 1968.

foreign exchange that they would earn by exporting new manufactured or processed products, free from any restrictions by our Central Bank, so long as they use the foreign exchange for purposes and in a manner that will not subvert the value of the peso.

Fifth, we offer a record of political stability in freedom that is unmatched in this part of the world, and I dare say unsurpassed by any other country developing or developed; a record of never having expropriated or confiscated any foreign investment, and never defaulting in any public international debt.

Finally, we offer an opportunity to make greater rates of profit than are generally possible in developed economies. In 1967, for example, the oil industry -- predominantly foreign -- earned almost 15 per cent on equity. And the largest income taxpayers, individual and corporate, are foreign investors and the enterprises they control.

In return for these advantages, we expect foreign investors and their enterprises to act as good neighbors, respecting our traditions and our culture, and above all our sense of the equality of all men in human dignity. In concrete terms, we would want foreign investments:

(1) To concentrate on pioneer areas of investment, particularly in developing a capital goods industry here and in producing finished goods from domestic raw materials for export that will provide foreign exchange and thus make it easier to remit profits and repatriate capital;

(2) To open their enterprises to Filipino investors, and particularly to the Filipinos who work in their firms by profit sharing schemes for labor that will enable labor to become a real partner in the enterprise;

(3) To adhere to the principle adopted by the United Nations of "equal pay for equal work;" and particularly for international firms, to adopt an international pay scale that will give Filipino employees sent to work abroad the same salaries and allowances enjoyed by all other expatriate employees;

(4) To adopt and implement a regular and methodical program to train Filipino laborers and employees in the technical and managerial skills that will enable them to take over jobs now being handled by foreigners;

(5) To bring in investments that are adequate to finance both the establishment and the operations of the enterprise, so as to free domestic bank credit for use primarily by Filipino enterprises, particularly those now shut off from this source of financing; however, no one would object to foreign enterprises tapping, for

equity investment, as yet unorganized sources of Philippine investment funds, as United States firms have done in Mexico.

Above all else, we expect that foreign investors will respect our national dream. Just as we Filipinos were the first colony in Asia to revolt against the Metropolitan power in 1896; the first to found a constitutional republic in this part of the world in 1899; the first to attain political independence by negotiation in 1946; the first to overcome subversion without using a single foreign soldier in 1950; the first to change wielders of power peacefully by ballots in 1946, 1953, 1961, and 1965 -- so too we Filipinos are determined to be the first colony in Asia to achieve modernization and economic independence, without sacrificing human dignity and freedom. So long as foreign capital respects and does not hinder us in achieving this dream, we welcome it as one of us.

RIZAL FOR TODAY

"... Your tasks as writers also remain the same ... What I ask of you is much simpler: to be great writers. Great in the sense in which Rizal spoke of the greatness of man: 'A man is great ... because he discerns what it (his generation) wants.' That ultimately is your job, to discern what our people want and say it so clearly so they themselves will see it, and seeing, gather their strength to achieve it."

Your invitation is a great honor -- and a great mystery.

The pen has played as vital a role as the sword in our nation's history. And no one has wielded the pen to greater effect than Dr. Jose P. Rizal. To be invited to deliver the Rizal lecture on this occasion is therefore a great honor which, I hasten to add, is richly undeserved.

For why you should think I might have something meaningful to say is an unfathomable mystery. I do not think you want my advice as a lawyer, since to talk about the law today -- except to mourn its passing -- is utter futility. Nor could you want my advice as a politician, since our country's ruler has called me "a discredited politician" and his chief apologist berates me for being "outside the mainstream of political life today." And, I am not a poet, essayist or novelist. Worse, I am a frustrated writer. At one time, I tried to live by the pen. But soon I found myself forced to turn to the more mundane -- and I must add, the more lucrative -- practice of law. I have always dreaded the task of putting my thoughts to paper as a woman who has undergone the experience quails at the pangs of childbirth. If at times I succumb it is only because of the pleasure of conception and the blessed relief of ridding myself at last of a burden that weighs heavy on my soul. And how can I advise you on conquering fear? My knees tremble as much -- and as often -- as yours do, and perhaps even more.

So I know I cannot meet your expectations. But I know that Rizal can. So tonight, with your permission, I propose to offer a layman's gloss on the message Rizal has for all of us who today work and play, laugh and cry, and live (or just exist) and die -- a gloss that, I hope, may have some meaning for writers trying to

(Lecture delivered at the PEN Conference, National Press Club, Manila, July 2, 1983)

write in a climate of fear, writers who, in Rizal's words, "feel their wings but find themselves in chains, choking for want of the air of freedom."[1]

Rizal's Success--
And Failure

Of Rizal, the poet Cecilio Apostol wrote -- I translate freely and somewhat clumsily --

> But if a bullet destroyed your cranium,
> Your ideas in turn destroyed an imperium.

Poetic hyperbole, perhaps, but not too much of an exaggeration. Long before our American colonizers chose Rizal as the model hero to offer to our youth, the great Mabini, whose title to nationalism cannot be questioned, had called him "the unforgettable Rizal, the most illustrious son of our nation, who had died content, knowing that his death gave birth to the most glorious era of our history."[2]

Rizal's writings did destroy an empire. But, to our sorrow, they failed to change our society.

Social Evils
Still Plague Us

The late Leon Maria Guerrero, perhaps the best English translator of Rizal, has stressed Rizal's "timelessness, or more precisely, (his) timeliness in another world and another age."[3] Guerrero is right. For there is scarcely a page of Rizal's writings that holds no lesson for us today. Almost a hundred years after he described the ills and vices of our society, they remain to plague us. The names of the characters have changed. The imperial power is different. The pace of life has quickened. And girls no longer choose, as Maria Clara did, the nunnery or death rather than an unwanted bridegroom. Yet as Rizal wrote in the unpublished foreword to the Fili, "man passes

---

[1]Jose P. Rizal, *El Filibusterismo,* translated by Leon Ma. Guerrero, Hongkong: Longmans, 1978, p. 193. References to the Noli Me Tangere (Noli) and El Filibusterismo (Fili) are to Guerrero's translations, but I have not always used his translation. At times, I have tried to make the quotations more faithful to the Spanish rendering of Rizal's thought.

[2]Apolinario Mabini, *La Revolucion Filipina,* Quezon City: Phoenix Press, Inc., Vol. 1, p. 102.

[3]Fili, p. xii.

away, but his vices remain -- and to attenuate or expose their effects is what the author aspires to do."[4] In exposing our vices he succeeded; in attenuating them, unfortunately, he failed.

Today, as we all know, we still need "a godfather for everything from baptism to burial, to get justice or a passport, or to exploit any industry whatsoever."[5] And when we cannot get a godfather we must be ready to pay -- unless, that is, we are "big people."

The Elite

Today, our elite is still peopled by Capitan Tiagos who endure everything, even cuckoldry, to retain their privileges; by Attorney Pastas who, to succeed, become friends of everyone, but specially of those in power; by Quirogas, the ubiquitous Chinese businessmen, who bear all insults with a smile as long as they are allowed to try their hand at all kinds of business and amass fortunes; by Dona Patrocinios whose major purpose in life is not to be surpassed in luxury by anyone, and Capitana Tinchangs who, loaded with diamonds, are "walking shop-windows;" by legislators who plot and maneuver, argue and debate only, in the end, to do what the friar orders because, sadly, they had "a puppet for a leader."[6]

Torture, Killing

The friar, of course, is gone. But other less visible, more anonymous -- yet equally vicious -- forces have taken his place. And the guardia civil, God save us, is still with us. At least, their methods are. Young men and young women are still arrested, as the medical student Basilio was, when they visit homes of friends who, unknown to them, are under surveillance or have been arrested. And I know of a young girl who, just as Juli gave herself to a friar to free Basilio, surrendered herself to a PC sergeant to save her father from further torture. The kind of interrogation and beating to death of detainees, described so vividly in the Noli, still happens frequently today. I have known of men forced to masturbate themselves, then hanged head down into a well; of men and women

---

[4]Jose P. Rizal, *El Filibusterismo,* Manila: Comision Nacional del Centenario de Jose Rizal, 1961, Appendix C.

[5]Fili, p. 239.

[6]Jose P. Rizal, *Noli Me Tangere,* translated by Leon Ma. Guerrero, Great Britain: Longmans, 1961, pp. 107-113.

subjected to repeated electric shocks and to sili ground into their eyes, nostrils and genitals; of men suffocated in plastic bags, tightly wound around their necks with plastic tape that leaves no marks; of so-called truth serum applied to such extent that one victim lost his sanity and has only partially recovered it -- and I could go on and on. The methods have become more sophisticated and more excruciating than in Rizal's day; but the abomination that is torture continues.

Language

So does the debate on language. The arguments of Simoun and Basilio are echoed in today's newspapers, the only difference being that it is not Spanish but English that is discussed. It is as if we have forgotten what Rizal taught us "that as long as a people keep their own language, they keep a pledge of their freedom."[7]

Loyalty to
Imperial Power

There are still many early Ibarras among us who believe that the good of the country lies in continued union with the imperial power, then Spain, now the United States;[8] and Isaganis who would willingly die for the imperial power and the Philippines against an alien foe "because, after all, ... we are bound to (it) by firm ties: the past, history, religion, language."[9] They apparently ignore Elias's pointed question: "Because we have received great benefits, is it a crime to protect ourselves from suffering great harm?"[10]

Government Officials
Favor Foreigners

From Dapitan on August 29, 1894 -- ninety years ago -- Rizal wrote Blumentritt:

I have founded a commercial company here. I have taught the poor inhabitants of Mindanao to unite themselves in order to trade, to the end that they may become independent and free

---

[7]Fili, p. 50.
[8]Noli, p. 313.
[9]Fili, p. 196.
[10]Noli, p. 313.

themselves from the Chinese and so be less exploited. But I have to talk long with the local governor who, despite being a good man, is nevertheless partial to the Chinese, and favors them over the inhabitants of Mindanao.[11]

Chinese traders are still with us. They have expanded into exporting, manufacturing, insurance and banking -- and they have been joined by transnational corporations. And today, government officials still favor foreign capital over Filipino welfare.

The recent devaluation of our peso is the latest example. The immediate beneficiaries are the banks -- most of which are owned by foreigners, including Filipino citizens who remain foreigners in all but name. From the start of the year, these banks bought dollars at rates averaging less than ₱10.00 to the dollar. Overnight, after devaluation, they are able to sell these dollars at ₱11.00 each. After the banks -- and before considering our workers and farmers -- the government looked after the oil companies. Two days ago it raised the price of all oil products by 32 centavos, despite the fact that, to retain the same profit of three centavos per liter which had earned the oil industry almost ₱400 million yearly in 1981 and in 1982, gasoline companies required at most an increase of 22 centavos. The government has not disclosed how much of the 32 centavo increase is added taxes. Let us assume that five centavos are new taxes. That would give the oil companies a net profit of at least eight centavos per liter, a total of almost a billion pesos per year for the entire industry -- plus another billion in windfall profits gained by selling at the new prices the inventories they bought at the old prices. Compared to these ₱2 billion in profits, the depredations of Dewey Dee were small -- and for these profits, you and I and our countrymen must pay, if not in money, in sweat and in pain.

Politicians in The Opposition

My friends, the politicians in the opposition -- God bless them -- debate whether to participate in the coming elections. They seem to have forgotten what Isagani told Atty. Pasta: "A people who detests its government should demand of it only one thing: that it give up power." Or what Simoun told Basilio: "They deny you representation in the parliament. Good for you! Even if you were

---

[11]Jose P. Rizal, *Epistolario Rizalino*, Manila: Bureau of Printing, 1938, Vol. 5, Part II, p. 669.

able to elect representatives of your own choosing, what could they do there but be drowned among so many voices, yet sanction by their presence the abuses and wrongs which may afterwards be committed?"[12]

Of our teachers today, as in Rizal's day, "neither learning nor zeal are expected...only resignation, self-abasement, and passivity." And this down-trodden sector of our society, charged with difficult tasks yet treated worse than Metro Manila aides, goes along for the same reasons Rizal's schoolmaster did: "God forgive me if I have betrayed my conscience and my reason, but I was born in this country, I must make a living in it, I have a mother to support, and I must go along..."[13]

Writers

And you writers, how many of you have suppressed the urge to write, or unable to do so, write like the scholar Tasio in hieroglyphics, "so no one can read what I write" except a future generation?[14] Tasio, at least, composed his hieroglyphics in Tagalog -- how many of us can write passably in our native tongue?

A Republic of the Greedy and the Needy

In short, we are what Rizal feared we would become: "a republic of the greedy and the needy,"[15] "a nation without freedom, everything in us borrowed, even our defects,"[16] many among us "feeling privately ashamed...but remaining publicly silent...wrapped up in our selfishness, begging with our eyes for a share of the booty."[17]

An Astonishing People Under An Incredible Government

We are "submissive and patient subjects who thrive on disillusionment and hope."[18] And well we might. We have tried

---

[12]Fili, p. 51.
[13]Noli, p. 98.
[14]Noli, p. 152.
[15]Fili, p. 49.
[16]Ibid.
[17]Fili, p. 297.
[18]Fili, p. 250.

everything -- except the right things. And, of course, nothing has worked. In politics, we tried democracy and then dictatorship, armed struggle and non-violent confrontation, only to witness inefficiency, favoritism, corruption and injustice become intensified. In economics, we started with import substitution only to turn to export promotion, shifting from economic nationalism to dependence on foreign loans, investments and dictation -- yet our currency has been devalued, our financial system has teetered, poverty has spread, inequality has deepened, and the quality of our life has deteriorated.

So today we are still a state that is not quite a nation, independent but not sovereign, with a democratic constitution but an autocratic government, a poor people inhabiting a country rich in natural resources and human talent, a small nation, weak and without enemies, that willingly offers itself as a sacrificial target for nuclear destruction to protect one super-power from another. Truly we are, as Rizal said, "an astonishing people under an incredible government."[19] And still we hope, still we pray for a Messiah, a deliverer!

Rizal Shows
The Way

Yet Rizal had shown us what we should do. When the early Ibarra, as today so many of our elite do, pinned his hopes on education, arguing that "we shall find our way by the light of knowledge," Elias replied, freedom first: "Without freedom there is no light."[20] And "a man is free," as Simoun said, only "as long as he thinks for himself...hope only in yourselves and in your own efforts...Develop an independent, not a colonial, mentality."[21]

That is a first step, but it is not enough. We must also defend the rights of our countrymen: "There are no possible distinctions or exceptions: there is only the fact of a violation of rights, and any honest man who does not take the side of the victim makes himself an accomplice to the crime..."[22] As Lt. Guevara told Ibarra, "Here one cannot be honest without having gone to jail."[23]

In truth, we must do more. We must unite ourselves with the people. Listen to Elias again: "By ourselves we are nothing. But

---

[19]Fili, p. 50.
[20]Noli, p. 320.
[21]Fili, p. 51.
[22]Fili, p. 251.
[23]Noli, p. 21.

take up the cause of the people, join them, do not turn a deaf ear to their voice, give an example to the rich, give us an idea of what it is to have a country."[24] Can writers -- or anyone else -- hope for better advice than this?

Rizal Vindicated --
But Not By Us

It took the rest of the world eighty years to learn the lesson Rizal had tried to teach us -- but which we have yet to apply. In 1975, at Karachi, Pakistan, about a hundred of the world's most distinguished development experts came together to found the Third World Forum. Their hope was to formulate third world concepts and strategies of development. One of the men behind the forum, the Pakistani economist Mahbub Ul Haq, pointed to three basic principles that must guide the Third World if development is to be meaningful and human. Rizal had tried to teach us these principles almost a century ago.

1. "The poor and the weak always get exploited unless they get organized," said Ul Haq. *"Ang isa-isang tingting ay madaling baliin, nguni't mahirap ang isang bigkis na walis,"* Rizal taught the women of Malolos.[25]

2. "No exploitation can continue for long except with the tacit cooperation of the exploited," said Ul Haq. "There are no tyrants where there are no slaves," Rizal told us.

3. "Our national independence is neither complete nor meaningful unless political liberation if followed by economic and intellectual liberation," said Ul Haq. *"Taong walang sariling isip ay taong walang pagkatao; ang bulag na tagasunod sa isip ng iba, ay parang hayop na sunod-sunod sa tali,"* Rizal wrote.[26]

A Cavalier Way
To Treat A Hero

If Rizal showed us the way nearly a century ago -- and he did -- why are we still lost? I can think of only three possible reasons: either we have not read him, or having read him, have not

---

[24]Noli, p. 320.

[25]It is easy to break one stick, but not a whole broom.

[26]A person with no mind of his own is not human; the blind man who follows the ideas of others is like the animal who follows the leash.

understood him, or having understood him, ignore him. What a cavalier way to treat our national hero!

We Are Still
A Colonial Society

I cannot believe that this cavalier treatment is due to a genetic defect in us. There is, I am persuaded, something in our environment, something in our society that causes it. That something, I suggest, is that, despite 37 years of independence, we remain a colonial society: colonial in our dependence on foreign markets and foreign arms; colonial in our ways of struggling, using delay and evasion, instead of confrontation; colonial in deprecating what is indigenous in our culture; colonial in our view of the world as controlled by two super-powers, to one or the other of which we must cling or perish; colonial in our subservience to ideas and ideologies of west and east; colonial in our distrust of our creative powers and the strength and the will of our people.

Tasks Remain
The Same

So our tasks as Filipinos remain the same as they were in Rizal's day: regain our freedom as individuals, assert our sovereignty as a people, and use our freedom and our sovereignty to create a just society. And your tasks as writers also remain the same. For, as Rizal said, "the struggle must commence in the field of ideas before it can descend into the arena of action."[27] Do not misunderstand me. I do not ask you to lead, or to teach, and much less to agitate our people for this or that cause or credo. What I ask of you is much simpler: to be great writers. Great in the sense in which Rizal spoke of the greatness of man: "A man is great, not because he goes ahead of his generation, which is in any case impossible, but because he discerns what it wants."[28] That ultimately is your job: to discern what our people want and say it clearly so that they themselves will see it, and seeing, gather their strength to achieve it.

---

[27]Noli, p. 320.
[28]Fili, p. 53.

Writers' Task
Dangerous and Difficult

It is a dangerous and difficult job you must undertake. You face the same risks Rizal did: harassment by interrogation and libel suits -- which some of you have already experienced -- arrest and detention -- which others among you have undergone -- torture perhaps, even disappearance and extra-legal execution. You may not have to face a firing squad; but you may end up just as dead. These things -- don't deceive yourselves -- are happening today with great frequency. Just yesterday, distraught parents came to me because their son had disappeared in Oroquieta, Misamis Occidental, since May 26. He wanted to go to Saudi Arabia to work and decided to earn some money to fix his papers by hawking paintings in Mindanao. But he is a Tagalog; and by that fact alone, suspected of being an NPA. The Oroquieta military arrested him. They admit this, but claim they released him after a few hours. Yet the young man has not gone home, has not been heard from, and the paintings he had yet to sell were still where he had deposited them. That is only one of many similar cases brought to me -- and there are others where the relatives of those who have disappeared are too frightened to seek help.

The Omnipotent PCO

If you are arrested by virtue of a judicial warrant of arrest, count yourself lucky: you may at least put up bail and gain temporary freedom. But if you are arrested by virtue of a Presidential Commitment Order or PCO, then give up all hopes of getting relief from our Courts. Our Supreme Court has said that it will not look into your arrest, and that you must stay in prison until the President finds the time to order your release himself. The reason for this, according to the Court, is that the President has suspended the privilege of the writ of habeas corpus, the ancient writ of liberty, and by suspending it, has taken "absolute command." So the people "can only trust and pray" that he will do no wrong. Because he is in absolute command, the President may order any person arrested not only because that person has committed a crime, but also because he might commit a crime. Once so arrested, the President need not release him even if the Courts acquit him, or the fiscal refuses to prosecute him, or if found guilty even after he should have served his sentence. And such cases have happened.

In April, 1982, a young artist was arrested when he called on a friend. The Quezon City Fiscal found no evidence and dropped the charges against him. The Supreme Court ordered him released. But because he was held under a PCO, the Colonel having custody of him refused to release him -- and despite the Supreme Court order, he had to wait in jail for more than two months, until Mr. Marcos returned from visiting his friend Mr. Reagan and found time to act on his papers.

In Bicol, another young man held under a PCO was acquitted by the Courts for lack of evidence. The military refused to release him, so he went on a hunger strike. Nevertheless, he languished in jail for some months, despite a habeas corpus petition filed with the Supreme Court, until Mr. Marcos found himself in the mood to order his release.

And in Camp Crame, several young people, among them a young lady, are still detained although they have served their sentence. They had pleaded guilty because the prosecutors had promised to release them after their plea since they had been detained longer than their possible maximum sentence. After their plea, the prosecution reneged on its promise. Despite an appeal to the Supreme Court, they are still detained today.

So our liberty today is in the hands of one man: the President and not only our liberty, but our life itself: for the Supreme Court has ruled that it cannot review even killings if the President has ordered them. He enjoys, in short, a license to kill.

Damn the Risks

How, you may well ask, can we take those risks? In today's climate of fear, how can we afford to face those dangers?

The answer, I suggest, is that it is precisely because of the climate of fear that we cannot afford not to face those dangers. We must damn the risks; and in a sense emulating our moslem juramentados, say what must be said, and suffer the consequences. The alternative is to be, in Rizal's words, "always running after butterflies and flowers,"[29] to die not only "without seeing the dawn break over our country,"[30] but knowing that we have held back the dawn. Writers can lay down their pens and tear up their manuscripts -- but I know of no human -- and writers are nothing if they are not human -- who can completely silence his conscience.

---

[29] Fili, p. 49.
[30] Noli, p. 402.

Writers' Task
More Difficult

If your task is as dangerous as was Rizal's, it is more difficult for at least two reasons. One is that today the enemy is not as concrete, nor as obvious as the friar was. Behind those that we see as oppressors today are impersonal, faceless forces: transnational corporations, international financial institutions, and foreign governments, particularly the government of the United States. In Rizal's day we could pinpoint the root of our malaise: external colonialism. Today we suffer from both external and internal colonialism, the external hidden behind the internal, but operating it like a program running a computer.

The second difficulty lies in the clash of ideology that characterizes our situation. In Rizal's time, the conflict was clear-cut: self-determination against imperialism. That issue remains, but it is clouded by the contest between capitalism and communism, and the struggle between democracy and autocracy.

What to Do

I have no advice to give you on how you might settle these conflicts nor on which side you should range yourself. That is a matter each of us must decide for himself. I can only hope that we do not become blinded by labels or dogmas, but try to see reality whole, and decide according to what we see would be best for our people. We are not blind, mindless chess pieces moved about by higher powers, whether of history or of God. We are men and women and in some measure masters of our fate -- and answerable, at least to our conscience, for what we make of it.

Nor, having made your choice, can I suggest which paths you should follow to achieve your goals: satire or criticism, tract or expose, the novel or the essay or the poem. That depends on what your talents are and where your bent lies.

But I do have one request -- which you are free to disregard: please emulate our friend and master of ceremonies Ponciano Peralta Pineda, and use a language our people understand not only with their minds but with their souls. Use tagalog, kapampangan, sugbuhanon, hiligaynon or any other of our languages. But please write for the people, not for the elite, the people of whom Elias said:

The people do not complain because they have no voice; they do not move because they are in a stupor; and you say that they

do not suffer because you have not seen how their hearts bleed. But some day you will see and hear! ...[31]
Help us all see and hear people -- not some day, but today.

---

[31]Noli, p. 157.

CLARO M. RECTO

During his life Recto's nationalism was criticized as unrealistic and visionary. It was even unpopular. Today that nationalism is so cogent and so relevant that it bears repeating, studying and applying to the problems that confront us as a nation.

"The true believer of Recto owes it to himself to come out of the shell in which he has hibernated during the last two years and a half, and speak out against the desecration of our democratic institutions."

Your presence in this hall today to listen to a short discourse on Claro Mayo Recto is a tribute to the man in more ways than one. It speaks well of your courage of conviction and intellectual integrity -- both of which are traits that Recto himself exemplified and without which his teachings would have sounded hollow.

Your courage of conviction is emphasized by your mere presence here. That the speaker is virtually a pariah in the so-called "New Society" has not discouraged your attendance. And the intellectual integrity that has become a tradition in the UP community is etched clearly by your interest in a discourse on a man who has long been dead and who, under ordinary circumstances, would not have had any relevance, specially in times of stress such as these are.

Yet this is precisely where Recto's merit lies. Although he would have gone to his Maker fifteen years ago come October, the legacy he left behind is more relevant than ever and has assumed greater cogency and meaning.

His thoughts and words were already relevant in his time, but the men and women of his generation were not prepared to comprehend him. His relevance remains undimmed in this generation. It remains to be seen, however, if the contemporary Filipino is ready to listen to him; and listening, to understand him.

Recto's legacy is multi-faceted, but they all have a common denominator. And this common denominator is nationalism.

In the minds of many, not as much now as in the past, "nationalism" is a dirty word. Just as Hitler's blackshirted soldier was ready to draw a gun at the sound of the word "kultur," "nationalism," or any aspect of it, arouses a feeling of hostility in the mind of one who cannot understand what it is all about.

(Delivered at the University of the Philippines, 1975)

There was a time when all one had to do, if he wanted to smear the character and reputation of another, was to call the latter a "nationalist." This was possible because, through incessant propaganda, "nationalism" came to be equated with "communism" -- another word which was something no one was expected to touch with a ten-foot pole.

Recto, however, stood up against all this and held aloft the banner of nationalism. He ignored attempts to denigrate him by small minds which could hardly comprehend even the most insignificant thought that passed through his. Uncowed by the spectre of unpopularity that awaited those who espoused losing causes, he carried on the struggle to make "nationalism" respectable and, finally, desirable.

Belonging to the party in power at the height of his political career, it would have been easy for him to rationalize his adherence to institutions and policies which rankled his conscience. Many of his colleagues then followed, as many of our leaders now are following, the easy path to political expediency. Not Recto. His intellectual integrity would not permit him to abandon conviction in the interest of opportunism.

In the pursuit of his convictions, he gave no quarter and asked for none. He did not hesitate to take on, before the last global war, Roxas, Osmena or Laurel. Nor did he, in later years, spare Quirino, Magsaysay, Romulo, or even the leaders of his own party when by sparing them he would thereby compromise his cherished values. He possessed a courage of conviction that recognized no formidable foe.

When he battled Magsaysay at the height of the latter's popularity and when he ran for President in 1957, the odds he faced were insurmountable. The dice were clearly loaded against him. Many could not resist the temptation of likening him to the Castillian knight giving battle to the windmills, and his closest friends advised him so. But Recto was not to be dismayed. He knew he was on the right path; and he was aware that he had a mission to perform.

He criss-crossed the country, went up and down the archipelago, with only one obsession: to enlighten the people on the issues that affected their future and those of their children. It was as if he knew that he was talking not only to the present but also to the future. In one of his speeches, he said:

I place in your hands ... this message to the Filipino youth from one whose only authority is a firm conviction and a lifelong experience, and who, in his declining years, still loves to plant trees, knowing that he will never sit in their shade, happy in the thought with Tasio, the Philosopher, that some day, in a distant future, one may say of him and the nationalists of his generation: "There were those who kept vigil in the night of our forefathers." (No todos dormian en la noche de nuestros abuelos.)[1]

With the clinical thoroughness of the compleat trial advocate that he was, he patiently and with clarity explained to everyone who was willing to listen that nationalism was not something to be abhorred or feared; rather, because it simply meant love of one's country, it was something to be nurtured in the heart of every Filipino.

In the context of the issues current at the time, nationalism dictated that the Philippines refuse involvement in the war in Indo-China; that the country seek friendship among its immediate neighbors, even if, under the Cold War complex, they happened to be on the other side of the fence; that the trappings of political independence do not by themselves make a country independent unless it likewise manages to toss off the yoke of economic imperialism; that the Philippines abandon a foreign policy characterized by unabashed mendicancy; that, after all is said and done, nationalism signified self-reliance, standing up on one's own feet.

On the mendicant foreign policy, Recto said:

... Our foreign policy was conducted from the very beginning, and is being pursued, in the erroneous assumption of an identity of American and Filipino interests, or more correctly, of the desirability, and even the necessity, of subordinating our interests to those of America...[2]

He advised his countrymen to "awake from the daydreams of adolescence, and cease to imagine ourselves as the saviors of a world in distress, riding out on fanciful adventures for which we have neither heart nor strength, while we neglect the care of our

---

[1]Claro M. Recto, "Nationalism and our Historic Past," *The Recto Reader* edited by Renato Constantino, Manila: Recto Memorial Foundation, 1965, p. xiii.

[2]Claro M. Recto, "Our Mendicant Foreign Policy." Address before the University of the Philippines graduating class, April 17, 1951.

own concerns."[3] And he added: "In the pursuit of this dazzling mirage, we may lose sight of our own national interests, and inebriated with grandiose visions of chimerical achievements, unwittingly surrender the vital realities to which we should hold fast."[4]

It is an advice that should have long been heeded during his time; more heeded these days.

Claro Mayo Recto's admonition for the Philippines to "make no enemies where we can make no friends"[5] is as valid today as it was yesterday.

His thoughts about issues current in his time that are still current up to this time are as illuminating now as they were then. Take, for instance, his views on the constitution: to him, "a constitution is only as good as the men who enforce it, and the men who obey and respect it."[6]

> The free and ordered life of our nation depends upon the preservation of the Constitution. Without its orderly processes and guarantees, its discerning allocation of government authority, and its calculated system of checks and balances, it would be difficult, not to say impossible, for our people to choose a truly representative government, or having chosen it and entrusted it with power, to protect themselves from its deterioration into an irresponsible and tyrannical oligarchy.[7]

He saw the Constitution of 1935 -- the constitution which was drafted by a convention of which he was the president -- as an "inviolable sanctuary for our rights and liberties,"[8] provided that it be

> ... (e)nforced, obeyed and interpreted, in the pristine spirit in which it was promulgated, by a people dedicated to the ideal of

---

[3]Claro M. Recto, "The Administration's Sabotage of Japanese Reparations," in *The Recto Reader*, p. 81.

[4]Ibid.

[5]Claro M. Recto, "Our Mendicant Foreign Policy," op. cit.

[6]Claro M. Recto, "Our Constitutional Crisis," in *The Recto Reader*, p. 133.

[7]Claro M. Recto, "The Future of the Constitution," in *The Recto Reader*, ibid.

[8]Claro M. Recto, "Our Constitutional Crisis," in *The Recto Reader*, p. 131.

self-government and human freedom which they so long pursued and saw at last within their grasp....[9]

In a speech he delivered on February 16, 1952, it seems as if he had telescoped the years ahead of him and he foretold, while talking about the 1935 Constitution, a coming "constitutional crisis":

> But it has not been so enforced, obeyed and interpreted. Its best intentions have been perverted, its balanced machinery upset, its mandates defied and ignored, its most basic guarantes violated by men who have interpreted it in the false light of their own political convenience.
> We could not reasonably foresee that the very men charged with upholding and defending the Constitution would be the very first to violate and prostitute it.[10]

Notwithstanding such observations, he never faltered in his reliance on the Constitution for the protection of the people's rights.

Recto's devotion to civil liberties was something that no one doubted. Of the constitutional freedoms, he was most partial to the right to free speech and expression. However, to him, freedom of speech was only a beginning,

> ... For freedom of speech means more than freedom to criticize. It must have a purpose; it must serve some end; it is not an end in itself. Such a purpose can be no other than to enable us to govern ourselves wisely and well, expressing our grievances that they may be redressed, and our desires for justice, peace, order, and prosperity, that they may be satisfied. Freedom of speech is calculated to help the people select those among them best suited to achieve these great national objectives, under God and the Constitution.[11]

Freedom of speech was of such importance to him that he was ready to defend the exercise of it even by "those with whom we disagree, of those whose concepts of society and political authority

---

[9]Ibid.

[10]Ibid.

[11]Claro M. Recto, "The Paradoxes of our Democracy," in *The Recto Reader*, p. 117.

we violently resist."[12] Thus he took the cudgels for Communists who were facing charges of fighting the state, at a time when many of his brothers in the law profession were willing to see them deprived of their liberties, since, anyway, they were Communists.

When President Quirino suspended the writ of habeas corpus in 1951, he came out in violent opposition to it. But he chided his countrymen, specially the press, for their timidity or complacency. He said:

I wish to point out that the suspension of the writ of habeas corpus has revealed another serious paradox in our democracy. We have seen that, although freedom of speech and freedom of the press may not be curtailed, the administration can, and may, and does, oftener than not, ignore and flout public opinion; but here we have a case where, possessing freedom of speech and freedom of the press, the people and the press fail to use them for their own protection! Surely this failure is even more ominous for democracy than the defiance and callousness of arrogant administration. When citizens fail to demand the restoration of one of the most essential constitutional guarantees, when the newspapers waste their power and their freedoms and allow such a vital issue to slide quietly into obscurity and oblivion, either through inadvertence or through timidity or complacency, then indeed we are faced with a grave breakdown of democracy, where ancient liberties may be lost by disuse and abandonment, and where the Constitution is ignored and suffered to degenerate into a powerless formality by the very citizens it was designed to protect and shield.[13]

He admonished his countrymen not to take our democracy for granted. He recalled that

... (i)n the 1930's the German people, in their millions, haunted by fear of Communism, desperately eager for security, infinitely weary of destitution and unemployment, cast aside the Weimar Constitution and gave absolute power to a

---

[12]Claro M. Recto, "The Future of the Constitution," in *The Recto Reader*, p. 118.

[13]Claro M. Recto, "The Paradoxes of our Democracy," in *The Recto Reader*, p. 119.

dictator, with all the disastrous consequences of such an injudicious choice...[14]

When, therefore, somebody asks what Claro Mayo Recto would have done if he were alive today, he does not indulge in an empty or futile exercise. For surely, Recto has the answer to that question.

For Recto was well ahead of his time. His contemporaries in his generation did not understand him. But his influence among the young of his time was immeasurable. The time has come for yesterday's young, who is today's citizen, to proclaim that Recto's teachings were not in vain.

For two and a half years, we have been living under a euphemism known as "smiling martial law," which, in fact, is nothing but a wolf in sheep's clothing. The truth remains that a dictatorship has supplanted the republicanism proclaimed by Recto's 1935 Constitution. The true believer in Recto owes it to himself to come out of the shell in which he has hibernated during the last two years and a half, and speak out against the desecration of our democratic institutions.

The opportunity presents itself in the next few days, when the Filipino people will be treated -- as they were twice treated last year -- to a farcical spectacle that the so-called New Society has been pleased to call the referendum.

I do not pretend to know what those in the government under the so-called New Society hope to achieve by this deception, but I believe they know that they are fooling no one. They are aware of the fact that everyone regards this referendum as one grand joke. For who can ever take seriously a project to make the people, under a regime of martial law, to express what they really feel and to unburden their conscience? Who can ever trust that the results would be correctly counted and reported when the body charged with such task flaunts its efficiency at puppetry?

To ask those questions is to give the reasons why a lot of well-meaning citizens, who include the heirs of the Recto brand of nationalism, have decided not to participate in the February 27 zarzuela. They cannot bring themselves to take part in a travesty of democracy.

---

[14]Claro M. Recto, "The Future of the Constitution," in *The Recto Reader,* p. 118.

"We cannot leave to others the defense of our rights," Recto told us. "We must do it ourselves."[15]

Allow me to end my short talk by sharing with you the following warning from Recto's pen that bears repeating and repeating:

> ... neither in the toils of the day nor in the vigils of the night can the sentinels of the Constitution relax their vigilance. Let us, therefore, all be wary and stand upon our arms, lest, by culpable tolerance or by criminal negligence, our country should in some desolate future become a desert of liberty, wherein only the massive ruins of our republic shall remain, magnificent but tragic monuments of the past, in whose desecrated labyrinths our descendants, by then the forlorn bondsmen of some corrupt despot, shall in vain endeavor to decipher the language of the Constitution inscribed, as in forgotten hieroglyphs, on the sarcophagus of our lost freedoms.[16]

[15]Claro M. Recto, "Address at the Namfrel Symposium," in *The Recto Reader*, p. 124.

[16]Claro M. Recto, "The Future of the Constitution," in *The Recto Reader*, pp. 132-133.

AFTER MARCOS, WHAT?

Given the national turbulence after the Aquino assassination, the departure of Marcos from the highest office was merely a matter of time. EDSA I justified this prediction.

Different scenarios are outlined for the aftermath -- whoever the successor government is, it must deal with the basic problems of Philippine society -- "the inequality of its social system, the maldevelopment of its economy, and the dominant influence of the U.S..."

Again this prediction has come true. Even a government with "good intentions" like the Aquino government is finding it extremely difficult to resolve these problems.

The post-Marcos era has begun. It began on August 21, 1983, when an assassin's bullet shattered the skull of Senator Benigno S. Aquino. That bullet, we now know, did more than kill the leader of the opposition. It also shattered the regime of President Ferdinand E. Marcos. What we witness today are its death throes.

True, Marcos still occupies the presidential palace. But his control over men and events has dwindled. The assassination of Senator Aquino touched everyone. It destroyed the apathy and fear that had immobilized so many, particularly among the affluent. It united people of all social classes for the first time since martial law was declared. It evoked from all -- the rich, the poor and the middle class -- an unprecedented outpouring of grief for the fallen leader, shame over their past submissiveness, and outrage at the government that, if it had not itself perpetrated the crime, had, by its neglect permitted it. After the initial shock had passed, grief, shame and outrage hardened into an unrelenting demand for change.

The demand has come at a time when Marcos is peculiarly vulnerable. His health is failing. The economy is a shambles, the result of bad policies, badly implemented. His inept handling of the Aquino assassination and the arrogance with which it was carried out, destroyed his credibility, the little credibility he still had, both at home and abroad. Local capital fled the country. Foreign investments stopped. Foreign creditors refused to grant new loans

---

(Address delivered at the FLAG Annual Conference, Cebu, September 9, 1983)

or roll over old ones. He has had to sue for a suspension of payments, to devalue the currency twice in three months, depreciating its value by more than 50 per cent from the start of the year, and to install a rigid system of controls. As a result, inflation has leaped, layoffs have increased, workers and employees in government and industry have become more restless, consumers angry and militant.

The United States Government, his staunchest ally, has begun to waver in its support for him. President Reagan canceled a state visit that Marcos had worked hard to get and needed badly to prop up his regime. The U.S. House of Representatives, by a nearly unanimous vote, has imposed two new conditions for continuing to support him: an impartial probe of the Aquino assassination and the holding of free and fair elections. These are conditions Marcos cannot hope to fulfill honestly without risking further loss of control.

Politicians and businessmen whose loyalty Marcos believed he could count on are beginning to desert him, if not turn against him. Persons close to him have been barred when they have appeared or their names have been mentioned in public gatherings. Marcos himself does not -- or cannot -- leave his palace and mix with the people.

In short, the once feared dictator has been reduced to little more than a lame-duck president. He is still fighting to hold on, but his options are limited by the economic crisis and the political milieu. His political end is now seen as inevitable, as merely a matter of time. Politicians and pundits worry more about what would happen when he finally does go, than about what he might do next.

And well they might. For while we know he will go, we cannot know for certain how he will go -- or when. Will he die from natural causes before his term ends in 1987? Will he be assassinated? Will he resign soon, either of his own volition or under pressure? Will he be defeated in next year's parliamentary election? Will he be ousted by a coup d'etat or overthrown by a revolution?

All these scenarios are possible.

But two seem more probable: death from natural causes or resignation under pressure. Assassination seems unlikely because Marcos rarely ventures outside the palace grounds, and is at all times protected by tight security measures; assassination seems remote.

A coup d'etat is equally remote because Marcos does enjoy the personal loyalty of his generals all of whom owe their appointments to him, and because both General Ver, who controls the Presidential Security Command, and General Ramos, who heads the Constabulary and Integrated National Police, are related by blood to him.

The chances are also slim that the opposition could wrest the majority of the seats from the Marcos party, the Kilusang Bagong Lipunan, in the parliamentary elections set for May, 1984. Given Marcos' power over the purse and over the military, the natural desire of his party's candidates to retain their seats, their combined control over the electoral system and the officials who administer it, the opposition would have to be more united, better organized and better funded to win the elections than to force the Marcos government to resign.

With respect to the probability of a successful revolution, two rebellions have been going on for more than ten years: one led by the MNLF, the other by the CCP. The first appears to be waning. The second is gaining ground. But its own leaders admit it will take several years more -- some say at least ten years -- before the revolution could gather such force as to become a real threat to the regime.

What would happen if Marcos were to die soon? So many things could happen, it is foolhardy to try to foretell what would.

If the Marcos constitution were followed, the Executive Committee chaired by the Prime Minister would exercise the powers of the President; hold a free and fair election to fill the unexpired portion of Marcos' term; and turn over the government to the newly elected President. But the demand of the business community that the office of Vice President be created and filled indicates that they do not believe this procedure workable. And with reason. There is no certainty as to who would be Prime Minister at the time Marcos goes. Even if the financial crisis dictates that Virata continue as Prime Minister, Mrs. Marcos, supported as she would be by Gen. Ver, could count on more votes in the Executive Committee than Virata could. If conditions make an election propitious, she would probably become a candidate. If conditions are not propitious, martial law could again be declared or enforced without a formal declaration, and government by the Executive Committee prolonged. Fair and free elections would be remote, chaos and disorder imminent.

Perhaps the one fairly certain result of Marcos' death is that the country would become even more unstable and volatile than it is today. Deprived of Marcos' firm hand, latent rivalries would surface within and among the three components of his political machine: the Kilusang Bagong Lipunan (KBL), the technocrats, and the military. Would-be successors to Marcos' throne -- either from his own party or the opposition -- will jostle each other for positional advantage, or for survival; form cliques and alliances, and seek the support of factions within the military and some even the support of the United States Government. How reasonable is this assumption? Or phrased differently, how likely is it that the military will not attempt to seize power for itself and govern the country with the assistance of the technocrats following the Brazilian model?

Let me now try to recapitulate my thoughts. However Marcos leaves the political scene, whoever succeeds him, whatever role technocrats and military play in the transition and afterwards, the successor government cannot ignore the basic problems of Philippine society: the inequality of its social system, the maldeveloment of its economy, and the dominant influence of the United States, which together have bred poverty, injustice and the rebellions of Moslems, and of the dispossessed.

THE CHANGING POLITICAL SITUATION:
A CHALLENGE

*Through the phenomenal EDSA revolution we won our freedom
from a hated dictatorship. But now we must ask ourselves: are we
moving to a real democracy?*

Diokno's answer is unequivocal:

*"The challenge we face is to create a real democracy in our land.
We can meet that challenge. We can succeed, only by being
Filipino, and letting no one -- civilian or military, Filipino or
foreigner -- frighten us. If martial law has taught us anything it is
this: against a united people no human force will prevail. Against
the will of our people, even the guns of the soldiers fall silent. Let
us remain united, and together let us build a nation for our children,
which rations neither food nor freedom nor jobs nor justice."*

We Filipinos are often described as a nation passing from
authoritarianism to democracy. That we kicked out a dictator is
true.

But are we moving to a real democracy?

Today, not every Filipino can bring his native talents to full
flower. Not every citizen can take part in decisions that affect his
life. After fourteen years of martial law, that situation is to be
expected -- and deplored.

But are we now moving in the right direction?

Or are we moving to a democracy like the one we had before
martial law, a democracy that is really the dictatorship of a class
dependent on a foreign power? Do we want our politicians to
belong -- or use their offices to belong -- to the higher income
class, and to represent that class and the foreigners who control it?
Shall the political elite protect the economic elite most of the
time, and only marginally the poor who make up the vast majority
of our people?

That is the challenge we face today.

(Speech for the UP College of Medicine Faculty Association,
Science Hall, Philippine General Hospital, on April 16, 1986. Due
to conflicts in scheduling, it was not delivered.)

It is a challenge that we Filipinos -- not Americans, Japanese, Chinese or Russians -- but we Filipinos must meet. And for at least two reasons:

First, we are proud to be Filipinos. That pride will not allow anyone else to make so important a choice. We and we alone must choose between a real democracy and an ersatz democracy, between going ahead all the way or stopping where we had been before.

Second, whatever be our choice, we must live with it. Even if foreigners chose for us, we must still live with their choice. Of course, we can err -- but so can they. If we err, let us pay for it. But let us not pay for another's error.

It goes without saying that we Filipinos want a real democracy. What should we do now to make our democracy real? Soon we shall be asked to approve a new constitution. What should it provide to make sure we enjoy freedom, independence, and social justice?

Whatever else authentic democracy may require, it does need at least two conditions in the Philippine setting:

First, that what happened under Marcos should not happen again; and

Second, that government seriously attend to the problems of poverty, unemployment, underemployment, low wages, social injustice and foreign control.

If we are to meet both conditions, our society must not be militarized. We should expose any violations of our rights, by the military, by the police, or by anyone else. We should oppose any attempt by any of them, or even a minority of them, to intimidate us into accepting or doing anything contrary to our principles.

Right now, for example, a minority of the military want us to forgive them for violating human rights. I do not agree. Perhaps it is my training as a lawyer that has taught me that *"Fiat justitia ruat coelum"* (Let justice be done though the heavens fall) -- and the heavens will not fall if justice is done to the victims and punishment meted out to the culprits who violated human rights. Our people feel the same way. They have mandated the new government to "pursue national reconciliation based on justice" (Proclamation No. 3, March 25, 1986, Sec. 1, (f)) -- and justice is more than forgiveness. In this, the Filipino people are not alone. The conscience of all mankind condemns violations of human rights. In the Declaration on the Protection of All Persons from Being Subjected to Torture and other Cruel, Inhuman or Degrading Treatment or Punishment, the General Assembly of the United Nations categorically said:

No State may permit or tolerate torture or other cruel, inhuman or degrading treatment or punishment. Exceptional circumstances such as a state of war or a threat of war, internal political instability or any other public emergency may not be invoked as a justification of torture or other cruel, inhuman or degrading treatment or punishment.

Recently, Vice President and Minister of Foreign Affairs Laurel recommended that the Philippines sign the Convention Against Torture and Other Cruel, Inhuman or Degrading Treatment or Punishment which incorporates the same principles.

Another thing we should be doing today is strengthening the hand of our President.

We should be strengthening the President, first of all, because the people placed her in power, and she has many wily opponents. I do not refer only to the KBL, many of whom would probably be satisfied with public jobs and perquisites. I refer to all forces -- political parties, cause-oriented groups, the military, the bureaucracy, some segments of the Church, and the U.S. government -- each of which is trying to gain as much power for itself as possible by making the President its pawn if that can be done. It is normal that they should try -- it is also normal that the people should oppose them.

There is a more important reason why the people should strengthen the President: she is our best hope to come closer to the society we want. We can never become what we want to be if traditional politicians run the government. But the President is only half traditional. She comes from a traditional political family, but she herself depends on no political party. She is not above compromise when necessary, but she has a mind of her own. She stands between the old and the new, and the composition of her cabinet shows it.

How do we strengthen the fresh force that is in her, and keep down the old?

That depends on many factors that differ from person to person and group to group. But this much we can all do: we can weaken her enemies by not supporting them, by letting them know it is the President, not they, whom the people put into power, and the people will see to it that she completes at least her term. For example, an issue raised against the President now is that she has appointed local officials who should be elected. But these officials have already served the term to which they were elected under the Marcos regime; and there is nothing to prevent them, if they are supported by the people of their locality, from running again and getting elected under the new constitution. In the meantime, if the government is to run smoothly, the President must appoint officers-in-charge who will follow the orders and instructions of the central government without reservations and of whom she has no doubt, however much doubt others may have of their popularity.

Above all, we can strengthen the President by pointing out what she is doing that is wrong. I think we weaken her if we support everything she does even when we do not agree with what she is doing. Yes-men are not compatible with democracy. People expect our President and public officials to make mistakes -- but of course, to correct them as soon as they are convinced that they have erred. How can they know they have erred, if we do not tell them so?

So much for what we should be doing now. What about the new constitution, what provisions should it include to build a real democracy in our land?

For that, we need a new legal order.

Please do not misunderstand me: the old legal order was not bad. It was just inadequate. In a developing country, it stood for the development of the politician, the middle class, the rich, and the foreigner, but not for the development of the poor.

It did not even stand for authentic democracy. Governments normally protect the interests of those with whom they communicate regularly. Governments ordinarily communicate with the rich and the middle class: the successful businessman and professional, the large land-or-fishpond-owner, the monied fisherman, organized ethnic associations (like the American Chamber of Commerce), the Church, the bureaucratic elite, the military, and the representatives of foreign trading and manufacturing companies. It is not that governments are run by evil men, but that normally only the rich, the middle class and foreigners have the means to communicate regularly with government.

To have authentic democracy, then, government should also represent the interests of the poor, not just those of the middle class and the rich. Government needs restructuring to build permanent channels of two-way communications between the poor and the political elite. The Magsaysay ten-centavo telegram and the present government's ministry for the urban poor are steps in the right direction. But let us not forget that poverty is more rampant in the countryside than in the cities..

Representing the poor may require much more than building channels of communications with them. It may require that the method of representation be changed, so that the people will be represented not only on the basis of area as in the past, but also on the basis of sector and, within each sector, on the basis of income. Problems of implementation no doubt will arise. Into how many sectors shall we divide our population? Within each sector, how many income classes shall there be? How can we be sure that only those included in the same income classes vote for their sectoral representatives? How shall we apportion primary responsibility between the chamber elected on the basis of area and that elected on the basis of sector (like past constitutions that required the House of Representatives to initiate all appropriation acts and tax bills)? These are hard problems, but they are not beyond the capabilities of the people.

Representing the poor may also require that new structures be fashioned, structures to enlist the talents of plain citizens to identify, explain and solve national and local problems. My own experience is that people have far more creativity than we believe. For instance, one group I worked with produced the meta-legal tactic of having an entire barrio go to a government office to file just one paper; another group organized adjacent barrios to deny entry to those bent on burning their homes; a third group arranged to have Holy Mass said on a raft in the river dividing the land they occupied, when they were denied access to the land's chapel. And better than us, the poor knew that their problems of lack of schools, health services, water and so forth could be solved more readily by building roads from poblacion to barrio than by building R.P.-U.S. Bayanihan Schools or digging Magsaysay wells. Today we need barrio to barrio roads also.

To harness the talents of our people, and more important, to build structures for that purpose, are difficult problems. But they are not impossible. For instance, one can involve them in the planning process from barangay to nation, instead of asking them to implement a plan already made. Of course, such a plan could be very different from that which a Makati-based technocrat would prepare. And instead of looking at exports for growth, the plan might look at satisfying the needs of the people, using Filipino ingenuity on Filipino resources. But in a democracy, should we not follow the people instead of the technocrats?

One more thing is needed: a change in our mentality. We must believe in ourselves, in our capacity to overcome hardship, in our ability to make the right decision. In short, we must have faith in the people, and not act like colonizers who know everything and distrust everyone, especially the people. So that, whenever a question impinges on the life of the people, it should be submitted to their judgment. It is on that judgment that we should rely, rather than on the judgment of individuals, no matter how honest, sincere and well-meaning they may be. That is why I believe that the drafters of the new constitution should be elected, not appointed.

Equally important, we must view public office as a way to serve the people, not to profit at their expense. Unlike traditional politicians, we should not scramble for vacant positions nor use public office for private gain. Politics should not be a road for the political elite to become economic elite as well.

To these questions, the framers of our new constitution should also attend. Specifying when an issue must be submitted to a plebiscite, and when it may be, can take care of the first question. The second I leave to you, since I have been an appointed and an elected official myself and find a "holier-than-thou" attitude rather distasteful. I have said what I did only because it had to be said.

Let me sum up. Our political situation has changed. The challenge we face is to create a real democracy in our land. We can meet that challenge, we can succeed, only by being Filipinos, and letting no one -- civilian or military, Filipino or foreigner -- frighten us. If martial law taught us anything it is this: against a united people, no human force will prevail. Against the will of our people, even the guns of the soldiers fall silent. Let us remain united, and together let us build a nation for our children, which rations neither food nor freedom nor jobs nor justice.

SOVEREIGNTY

III. PHILIPPINE SOVEREIGNTY

More than anything else, the U.S. military bases offended Pepe Diokno's sense of nation. In many speeches delivered on different occasions he excoriated those responsible for the R.P.-U.S. Agreement on the military bases. Today no one doubts that the bases threaten us with total extinction, diminish our sovereignty, and hinder our development.

Through careful research Diokno proved that this agreement was not only immoral, but illegal. It was never submitted to the Filipino people for approval.

This is an original and brilliant contribution to the legal history of Philippine-American relations. Diokno was tireless in pointing this out in his crusade to remove the bases from our country through peaceful means. The U.N. Charter of Economic Rights and Duties of States and the Declaration on the New International Economic Order also point out the need to wipe out all remnants of colonialism like foreign military bases.

Today (1987) the legality of the U.S. military bases has become moot because the Constitution provides that:

After the expiration in 1991 of the Agreement between the Republic of the Philippines and the United States of America concerning military bases, foreign military bases, troops or facilities shall not be allowed in the Philippines except under a treaty duly concurred in by the Senate, and when the Congress so requires, ratified by a majority of the votes cast by the people in a national referendum held for that purpose, and recognized as a treaty by the other contracting State. [Article XVIII, Section 25]

This provision implicitly legalizes the RP-US agreement on the bases but it is silent on the urgent need to remove them from Philippine territory. However, there is a ray of hope in another constitutional provision: "The Philippines, consistent with the national interest, adopts and pursues a policy of freedom from nuclear weapons in its territory." [Art. II, Sec. 8]

SOVEREIGNTY AND DEMOCRACY

These are days of trial and trouble. Few Filipinos are happy with our country's condition, and most are fearful for its future. With good reason: we have applied every prescribed solution, but our problems have grown more intractable, our situation more critical. To develop our economy, we adopted import substitution then were induced to shift to export promotion -- yet our currency further depreciated, our financial system tottered, poverty spread, inequality deepened, and our standards of living deteriorated. We cherished democracy as a political system, but later bowed to authoritarianism -- only to witness inefficiency, cronyism, corruption, injustice and violence intensify. We embraced the culture of the West and when we tried to return to our roots, we discovered we had lost our identity.

Now the people know -- even if our technocrats do not -- that there are no ready-made answers to our problems. We are unique. There is no precedent we can use, no example from the West or the East we can copy. We must follow our own star, propelled by our own needs, piloted by our own thoughts, illumined by our own vision.

Because we know this, we are torn between urgency and impotence by the crisis that batters our nation. It is the people -- particularly the middle- and low-income groups -- who pay in pain and in blood for the crisis. And however it is resolved, and resolved it will be -- whether the economy goes bankrupt or stays afloat, whether the present government continues in power or is dislodged by a blatantly military government or one hidden behind a civilian facade -- it will still be the people of the middle- and low-income classes who will pay in more pain and more blood. Something must be done -- and done now.

Yet we feel we can do nothing. Some of us, because we do not know what to do. Others, because we are not certain that what we are doing will have any real, lasting effect. And all of us because, to a lesser or greater degree, we are still afraid, though we realize that the situation thrives on fear.

(Keynote address at the KAAKBAY Founding Congress, March 19, 1983)

If we could get together with others who think and feel as we do, we would conquer some of our fears. And we could also articulate a vision of our country that would provide a direction for our individual efforts, and assurance that what each of us is doing is meaningful.

But getting together implies organization, and many of us have balked at joining organizations. Something about them, or about us, or about the times, has made us hesitate. Perhaps it is disagreement with their methods or their goals, or disenchantment with their leaders, or our intellectual pride, or the belief that the time was not right. Whatever the cause, the result has been that many voices are not heard or are heard only feebly, and valuable contributions of talent, resourcefulness and industriousness remain untapped, contributions our people need now more than ever before.

How could these contributions be tapped? That was the question a small group of men and women asked themselves. They were a motley group, in many ways like you who are here: professors and professionals, theorists and activists, young and not so young -- and, like you, fiercely jealous of their independence. It did not take the group long to realize what the answer was: organize the unorganizables.

That would require an organization they themselves would want to join. And that meant a social movement, not a political party, focusing on issues, not elections, pursuing a vision, not lusting after power. A movement principled yet not dogmatic, wielding the weapons of persuasion not coercion, appealing to the nobility of the Filipino soul instead of to its selfishness. A movement positive rather than negative, that would oppose, yes, but also propose, and anticipate more than react.

Was that an idle dream, a Quixotic adventure? Cynics might think so but your response in coming here and the response of many others who could not come gives them the lie. If such a movement be madness, it is none the less the lunacy that preserves our sanity, the idealism that sustains our realism by evoking the best within us.

Thus was the Movement for Philippine Sovereignty and Democracy (KAAKBAY) conceived. Today, it is born. Tomorrow, it will be what our vision and our fortitude make of it.

If the past and the present teach us anything, it is this:

First, that unless our people are freed to work and create, to speak and decide -- that is, unless there is democracy -- and unless the nation is freed to be itself, to set its own goals and choose the means to achieve them -- that is, unless the nation is sovereign -- our country will never be what it can become.

And second, that freedom and independence, though indispensable, are insufficient: only a steadfast course of intelligent, dedicated nationalism can guarantee our survival, propel our development, and transform our society.

To install democracy, to assert sovereignty, then use that democracy and sovereignty to build a noble society -- these are the tasks that history has thrust upon our people. To contribute to accomplishing these tasks is the job that we have, by forming this movement, taken upon ourselves.

Lest we be misunderstood, let me stress the point that the purpose of our movement is to contribute, not to monopolize. We are under no illusion that we alone can do the tasks of our people, nor do we suffer from the delusion that we have been called to lead our people. Ours is the humble role -- yet no less important for being that -- to voice the unspoken hopes of our people, to help them clarify and shape their vision, to unearth and expose the truths that are hidden from them, and working with other groups of like mind, to add strength, however puny it might be, to the valiant struggles of our people against exploitation and manipulation.

Even this is a forbidding role. But we are fortified by the faith that inspired Mabini: the faith that it is in Asia that the future of the world will be decided and that, in deciding that future, our nation is destined to play a vital part.

How shall the movement discharge its role, and within the movement, what role shall each of us play? Those are questions for you to discuss in our working groups and for all of us to decide together when we meet later in plenary. But perhaps you might wish to consider some suggestions. Let me hasten to add that I offer them, not to curtail your freedom, but to expedite our task, for the time left us is short and to gather us together is not easy.

The forces arrayed against us are many and powerful, while we are yet few and weak. True, in any struggle, it is the strength of mind and of will, not of force or numbers, that is decisive. But fortitude is most effective when it is tinged with prudence. So let us think big, but let our movement start small, undertaking clear cut and simple issues first, and larger issues as we gather strength. Let our movement raise no issue until we have marshaled the facts and have better alternatives to offer than those we assail. Above all, let not our movement be deterred by the magnitude of our task, but speak out clearly and forcefully, confident that, if we make sense, our people will listen though the powerful refuse to hear.

Our movement is broad and there is verge enough in it for each of us to contribute what he can within the limitations that family and professional obligations impose on us all. Yet there are two things that I suggest we can all do. We can seek out our friends who are of like mind and heart and vision, and enlist their help and cooperation. And within our circles, we can meet with others, find out what issues are particularly urgent, what facts are known, what others should be gathered, and what the solution is or where it may be sought -- then let our movement know, that we may act.

If you find merit in these suggestions, may I ask that, in our working groups, we devote time to identifying issues, and classifying them into those the movement should take up immediately, in the medium-term and in the long-term?

The time for me to talk is over. The time for you to start work begins. We have embarked on a task that is difficult, but also exciting and full of hope and of promise. Let us prove ourselves worthy of it. We cannot do more -- let us not do less.

PEOPLE'S RIGHTS AND
FOREIGN MILITARY BASES

*No nationalist before Jose W. Diokno had ever argued that the
Military Bases Agreement was illegal from its very inception.*
*In this landmark lecture, Diokno makes this point convincingly.
Only by the removal of the bases can the sovereignty of the
Philippines be assured.*

This afternoon I would like to take up with you the subject of
people's rights and foreign military bases.

Thirty-one years ago another great Filipino lawyer, Claro M.
Recto, warned us of the dangers of nuclear war and painted a vivid
picture of the destruction that such a war would wreak upon
Manila:

> the radioactive waters of the Pasig...the broken arches of the
> Quezon Bridge...shattered tenements and poisoned
> fields...brutalized and monstrously deformed survivors
> scrambling with stunted limbs in the infected debris of their
> liberated cities...[1]

To many Filipinos who heard him that danger seemed remote
then. Today it is no longer so.

The policies of the Reagan administration, particularly its
decision to produce the neutron bomb and to adopt limited nuclear
war as part of its foreign policy, and the actuations of the Soviet
Union, particularly the intrusion by its airplanes into Philippine
skies, have made more and more of us Filipinos realize not only
that the possibility of nuclear war is real and frightfully close, but
worse, that when that war comes, our land and our people will be
among its first victims. Not because we pose any threat to the
Soviet Union, but because there are military bases of the United
States in our land.

(Address delivered on the occasion of the Gregorio M. Araneta
Foundation Memorial Lecture, College of Law, Ateneo de Manila
University, January 23, 1982)

[1]Claro M. Recto, "Our Mendicant Foreign Policy," in *The Recto
Reader,* edited by Renato Constantino, Manila: Recto Memorial
Foundation, 1965, p. 93.

Whether to permit those bases to remain is therefore an urgent and vital question. How we answer it could well lead to our survival or our extinction.

The military, economic and political arguments on both sides of this question are well known. They are important. They bear repetition. But I shall resist the temptation to gild the lily. Instead I would like to explore with you this afternoon this question from an entirely different angle -- the angle of its legality. To ask and to seek to answer the question: How valid in law is the Philippine-U.S. Military Bases Agreement?

This question is important for three reasons. First, until we determine that the agreement is legally valid, we need not concern ourselves with questions of whether it is foolish or wise. Second, if we determine that the agreement is illegal, then we need not wait until the end of the term of the agreement to insist that U.S. bases be dismantled immediately. Third, if we determine that the agreement is illegal, we need not worry about its being extended by Marcos.

To answer this question let us briefly review the facts that led up to it.

The question of military bases came up for the first time when on January 17, 1933, overriding President Hoover's veto, the U.S. Congress approved the Hare-Hawes-Cutting Bill. That bill contained this provision on U.S. bases, namely, that the United States receive "upon final withdrawal of sovereignty from the Philippine Islands such land or other purposes which has heretofore been designated for military and other purposes or as they be redesignated by the President of the United States within two years after the date of independence."

The clear meaning of the provision was that not only all existing military and naval bases at the time of independence would continue to be such after independence, but that the President of the United States unilaterally could designate additional military bases in the country.

The Hare-Hawes-Cutting Bill surprisingly also contained a provision requesting the President of the United States to seek the perpetual neutralization of the Philippines after independence. But as an American political commentator remarked, he could not see the sense of that provision with the military bases reserve because "you cannot neutralize a fort."

That bill required that it be accepted by the Philippine Legislature. On October 17, 1933, the Philippine Legislature, using very polite language, "declined to accept" the bill. And one of the reasons why it did so was "that the bases provisions were inconsistent with true independence, violate the national dignity and are subject to misunderstanding."[2] Shortly after that, President Quezon sailed to the United States, spoke with President Roosevelt and obtained a new independence bill.

Quezon in his memoir recalls his conversation with Roosevelt on the matter of the bases and says "that President Roosevelt agreed with me that the maintenance of American military reservations after independence would make the granting of independence a farce and that the Philippines should have a say in the establishment of naval reservations and refueling stations in the archipelago."[3]

And so, when the new independence bill was approved, on March 24, 1934, the provision on bases had completely changed. Under the provisions of the Tydings-McDuffie Act, the United States agreed that it would surrender sovereignty and all rights of control over all military reservations existing in the Philippines except for such naval reservations and refueling stations as within two years after independence the President of the United States and the President of the Philippines would agree upon.

That bill also contained, this time with a lot more reason, the provision on perpetual neutralization of the Philippines.

The Philippine Congress accepted this Tydings-McDuffie Law. And here is the interesting part about the law. The law required the Philippine Legislature to call a Constitutional Convention. It required that the Constitutional Convention adopt a Constitution that would conform with the provisions of the Tydings-McDuffie Bill. And further, it required that this Constitution would be submitted to the Filipino people and that the vote of the people on the Constitution would also be an expression of their will for or against independence. So that when the people voted on the Constitution, they were voting on whether they wanted independence under the terms and conditions of the Tydings-McDuffie Bill or not. This condition was actually printed on the face of the official ballot. Of course, the people overwhelmingly voted to accept independence as provided for in the Tydings-McDuffie law. In fact, and this is something else that has been insufficiently stressed, the Tydings-McDuffie law became a part of the Constitution because in Ordinance 3 of the 1935 Constitution, all the provisions of the Tydings-McDuffie law were incorporated in the Constitution.

---

[2]Philippine Legislature, Concurrent Resolution No. 46, October 17, 1933.

[3]Manuel L. Quezon, *The Good Fight*, New York: D. Appleton-Century, 1946, p. 147.

So five years later, in 1939, there were a few amendments to the Tydings-McDuffie Act. These amendments consisted only of the trade relations between the Commonwealth government of the Philippines and the United States Government, and the rights of the U.S. Government to have property for diplomatic and consular establishments. These were not very important amendments, yet by provisions of the Amendatory Act of the United States the Philippine Constitution had to be amended again. So that these amendments had to be accepted by the people before they could become law. And in fact, they were submitted and accepted by the people on August 7, 1938.

The provisions on military bases suffered no change. Then came World War II. As you all know, the Japanese occupied the Philippines. The Commonwealth government was evacuated to the United States and on October 7, 1943, the Imperial Japanese Government recognized an independent Philippine Republic.

To counteract this, on June 29, 1944, the U.S. Congress adopted two resolutions. The more important one, Resolution No. 93, expressed the "determination of the United States Government to drive the treacherous invading Japanese from the Philippine Islands as an independent and self-governing nation" and authorized the President of the United States to advance the date of independence from July 4, 1946, to an earlier date. But the quid pro quo was something else. For this same resolution provided categorically "that the President of the United States after negotiations with the President of the Commonwealth of the Philippines is hereby authorized by such means as he may find appropriate to withhold or to acquire or to retain such bases, necessary appurtenances to such bases and the rights incident thereto in addition to any provided for by the Tydings-McDuffie Act as he may deem necessary for the mutual protection of the Philippine Islands and of the United States."

Now the effect of this amendment, as President Roosevelt said categorically, was "on the problem of bases...The present Organic Act permitted acquisition only of naval bases and fueling stations ... The measure approved today will permit the acquisition of air and land bases in addition to naval bases and fueling stations."

Now we must remember that this particular Resolution was adopted on June 29, 1944, at a time when the Philippines was physically under the control of the Imperial Army of Japan. The Philippine Commonwealth Government in the United States was an exile government and President Quezon, the head of the government, was a sick man who was to die one month and two days later.

In any case this Resolution was never submitted to the Filipino people for approval.

On October 20, 1944, the United States forces landed at Leyte. On January 9, 1945, they landed at Lingayen and on February 3 they entered Manila. On February 27, the United States Army turned over the government of the Philippines to President Osmena, who had succeeded to the presidency after the death of President Quezon. And on June 9, 1945, President Osmena called the pre-war Philippine Congress to a special session. This was not a Congress that was newly elected. It was the Congress that had held office at the time of the outbreak of World War II. On July 28, that Congress adopted Joint Resolution No. 4 which accepted the Resolution of June 29 of the United States Congress, and authorized the Philippine President to enter into negotiations with the President of the United States on U.S. bases.

Although it was quite clearly an amendment of the Tydings-McDuffie Act, the resolution of the Philippine Congress was not submitted to the people for approval. Indeed, worse than being an amendment, it in effect was going back to the position very similar to the Hare-Hawes-Cutting portion which had been rejected earlier by the Philippine Legislature.

In any case, armed with these two resolutions -- the Resolutions of June 29, 1944 and the Resolution of July 28, 1945 -- the Governments of the Philippines and of the United States entered into the bases agreement on March 14, 1947.

On March 17, President Roxas submitted that bases agreement to the Philippine Legislature for ratification and on March 26, it was ratified by the Philippine Legislature. The U.S. Government never submitted the agreement to ratification by the U.S. Senate, treating it as simply an executive agreement that requires no senatorial or congressional ratification.

Since 1947 the agreement has been amended several times. The most important amendments were those of 1959, when American military base areas were returned to the Philippines, the most prominent of which were Sangley Point and Olongapo City; the revision of the article on criminal jurisdiction in 1965; the shortening of the term of the bases from 99 years to 25 years in 1966; and, of course, the 1979 amendments.[4]

None of these amendments was submitted to the Philippine Congress for ratification. This is understandable in the case of the earlier amendments, since they were all improvements on the

---

[4]The Bases Agreement was renegotiated in 1983/84, and is up for another renegotiation soon.

original agreement. But in the case of the amendments of 1979, the obligations imposed upon the Philippines were materially revised. For in the agreement approved in 1979 between Mr. Marcos and Vice President Mondale, the Philippines agreed to give the United States unhampered control over military operations involving its forces in the Philippines, unimpeded access to and from the bases, and, something that was not mentioned in the newspapers here but is in the text of the agreement, recognizes the right of the American base commander to take part in security activities outside the base area.

In any case, in exchange for these concessions, the Philippines was given a promise of U.S. $500 million in military aid for the next five years, the "privilege" of flying the Philippine flag alone, and having a Philippine commander as nominal commander of the bases.

Now these are the facts concerning the bases. What law governs it? I submit to you that in the light of these facts, the military bases agreement is not only illegal today but it was illegal at its very inception. So that there never was a valid, lawful agreement between the Philippines and the United States on military bases.

Why do I say this? First, a review of the history of the Tydings-McDuffie law makes it crystal clear that both from the Philippine and American points of view, that law was a solemn compact between not just the Philippine Legislature and the American Government, but between the Filipino people and the American Government. And therefore that solemn compact could not be changed in any way without the express approval of the Filipino people. As I mentioned earlier, even on such a minor matter as a change of conditions of trade and the right to own diplomatic properties, it was required that the Filipino people approve the change. And the Filipino people incorporated the entire agreement in their Constitution. How could that agreement be subsequently changed without the approval of the Filipino people?

That approval has never been given. In fact, it is my opinion that it was deliberately not asked for. Why? Because, at just about the time that the United States and the Philippines were negotiating the U.S. military bases agreement, there was being conducted in this country the tremendously acrid and acrimonious debate on the parity amendments. And the parity amendments were approved in a plebiscite on March 11, 1947. It was on March 14, 1947 -- three days later -- that the military bases agreement was signed. Obviously it was too risky to have to go through another debate and another plebiscite on the U.S. military bases agreement.

Of course, from the strictly legal point of view, the agreement is basically very, very simple. The Tydings-McDuffie law was part of the Philippine Constitution by virtue of Ordinance 3. The change in the law to enable the military bases agreement to be approved was a change of the Constitution. Therefore, for it to be valid, it should have been submitted to the people for approval. Of course, I understand, that it will be argued that the Ordinance which incorporated the Tydings-McDuffie law lapsed when Philippine independence was recognized on July 4, 1946. So that when the bases agreement was entered into nine months later in 1947, that Ordinance was no longer a part of the Constitution and, therefore, there was no need to secure the approval of the people. The answer to that is that the Ordinance did not automatically lapse on the declaration of independence on July 4, 1946. Because the Ordinance incorporated all the sections of the Tydings-McDuffie law, including sections that were going to take effect only after independence. Therefore that Ordinance could not have possibly lapsed upon independence, since it included sections that were to take effect after independence. And it is precisely those sections that were violated by the bases agreement.

Let us assume that the Ordinance lapses. Does that save the agreement? No. Why? Because by its very terms the agreement was negotiated under the authority of the two resolutions I have mentioned earlier of June 29, 1944, and July 28, 1945. Both of these resolutions were approved during the time when the ordinance was unquestionably in effect. None of these resolutions was ever approved by the people. Therefore these resolutions were, in themselves, invalid. They gave no authority to the negotiators to negotiate. And a formal treaty negotiated by persons without authority has no greater legal value than an ordinary contract negotiated by agents without powers of attorney.

But let us assume further and say that they did not need authority to negotiate. Does that save the agreement. No. Why? Simply because the bases agreement, and for that matter any base agreement, is, legally speaking, in the nature of a servitude or an easement on sovereignty. For those of you who are not lawyers, or not law students, let me explain by an example: typical of an easement or servitude is what is known as a right of way. I cannot stop other people from crossing through a portion of the property I own because it is subject to an easement of right of way. Now a foreign military base on land or in the air is an easement because while it does not deprive the country of its sovereignty it limits the exercise by that country of its rights of sovereignty. Under municipal law, the only way that you can create an easement on private property is by the consent of the owner or by law, so also in international law, the only way that you can create a servitude on sovereignty is by the consent of the sovereign or by international law. But there is no international law that requires any country to give a foreign military power bases within its own country. Therefore the only way that you can create a servitude of a military base is by consent of the sovereign power in the country granting the base.

Who has the sovereign power in this country? From the time of the Malolos Constitution it has been recognized, even during the Japanese war, even during the dark days of martial law which still continues, no matter how much in fact that sovereignty may have been denied, in law, the sovereignty rests or always will rest, in the people of the Philippines. And it is therefore only the people of the Philippines who by voluntary act of their own can create a servitude on their sovereignty.

It is not the Philippine Legislature. It is not the President. Neither of these is sovereign. They merely exercise some of the aspects of sovereignty that the Constitution has delegated to them. But neither the Philippine Legislature nor the Congress nor the President nor the Supreme Court is sovereign. The sovereign is the people. When therefore we speak of foreign bases and recognize that there are limitations on sovereignty, it seems to me to be, from a legal point of view, perfectly clear that only the people can approve of the grant of these bases.

But let us assume that I am wrong. Let us assume that the bases were originally valid. Are they still valid today? I submit to you that they are not. The reason is that just as in municipal law, acts which are not forbidden are valid, but once a law is passed forbidding those acts they become invalid, so, too, international agreements that may initially have been valid become invalid when international law passes or accepts as generally accepted, principles that invalidate those agreements.

After the adoption of the military bases agreement, it became a generally accepted principle of international law not only that the people have a right to survive as a people, but that a people have the right of self-determination and that a people as people have the right to development. You find these principles repeated time and time again in all the different actions and resolutions and declarations of the General Assembly of the United Nations. Nowhere are they expressed with greater clarity than in the Charter of Economic Rights and Duties of States, approved in 1974, Section 16 of which categorically states that it is the right and the duty of every state individually and collectively to eliminate all traces of colonialism, neo-colonialism, foreign domination and occupation and all the social consequences thereof as essential for development. And it seems to me perfectly plain as a question of fact that American military bases in this country fall within the vestiges of colonialism, with the actual weapons of neo-colonialism that prevent the development of this country. And therefore it is the right and the duty of the Philippines to dismantle those bases.

But, you may say, okay, that's international law. How does that affect the Philippines? Well, the answer is that under Philippine law, as incidentally under the law of Britain and of the United States, the generally accepted principles of international law are part of the law of the country. And the Philippines, to compound the situation, voted in favor of the Charter of Economic Rights and Duties of States. And therefore it is bound by the statement of rights and duties of states in that charter.

Now I'm sure that some of you will think, well if as you say, the presence of bases in this country violates the Charter of Economic Rights and Duties of States and therefore makes those bases illegal, then the bases in Japan of the United States, the bases in England, in Spain and in the NATO countries are also illegal. Is that your position? No. And for a very simple reason. The bases of the United States in this country fall within the prohibition of the Charter of Economic Rights and Duties of States because those bases are vestiges of colonialism. But neither Japan, nor Spain, nor England, nor the other NATO countries have ever been colonies of the United States. I do not say that those other bases agreements are valid. I only say that it does not follow that because Philippine bases are invalid under the Charter of Economic Rights and Duties of States, all military bases are thereby invalid. That does not follow. And I am limiting myself to the Philippine bases.

So summarizing then, the Philippine military bases agreement with the United States is invalid and was invalid from its very inception because it has never been approved by the Filipino people and because it has run afoul of the generally accepted principles of international law which are part of the law of the land. And this is specially true of the 1979 amendments because, as Ambassador Newsom candidly admitted, "when the new administration came in (referring to Carter's) they decided that rather than go back to try to pick up things where they had been left in 1976, they would make an effort by dealing directly with President Marcos in order to narrow down the issues we could be discussing in any further negotiations to those which Marcos personally considered politically important."[5]

In other words, from the American point of view -- and by their own admission, their negotiations in 1979 were not negotiations with respect to the Filipino people, they were negotiations with Marcos on what Marcos personally thought politically important. And quite obviously, this renders the entire proceedings totally null and void.

But of course, the question remains. True, that's illegal, what can we do about it? Marcos is in power. He is very close to the Americans. In fact, without American support it is doubtful that he could continue to be in power for minutes longer. But do you expect him to do this? Of course not. But I have brought out this question because, first, I believe that Mr. Marcos is not going to be here forever. And it is important that any successor government realize that this agreement is not valid; that if it wants to continue with this agreement, it will do so in violation of the basic Charter of the Filipino people.

And I have done so also because I wanted to stress people's rights. When we speak of human rights, we always tend to think exclusively of personal or individual rights, like the right not to be tortured, or the right to speak out. Very rarely, if ever, do we think of people's rights as I have just pointed out. The right to sovereignty. The right to survival. The right to development. And it is the violation of these people's rights that makes it so easy to violate personal rights with impunity. To give you just one example, in addition to the example of the bases, the sovereignty of the people demands that the people elect the government. But have we been able to elect a government since martial law? Isn't that precisely what makes it so easy to grab and capture people without warrants, torture them, detain them without justification and unofficially murder them?

There is a fundamental difference between individual rights and people's rights. And that difference is that in the case of personal rights, we can exercise them individually. Whereas in the case of people's rights, while we exercise them individually, it is only the sum total of our collective exercise that has legal significance. Unfortunately, our law has been very, very lax in finding remedies for violations of people's rights.

---

[5]Hearings on the Review of the Policy Decision to Withdraw United States Ground Forces from Korea, Washington D.C., U.S. Government Printing Office, 1978, p. 42.

One example: supposing that there is an election for mayor, and the election result is fraudulent. Yes, the mayor can protest, but supposing the mayor has been bought out by the other party, or has been threatened and doesn't want to protest, is it only the mayor's rights that are violated or is it the sovereignty of the people itself? Yet what remedy do the people have in such a case? Or take the case of a plebiscite on a constitutional amendment, where there is fraud in the plebiscite. There are no candidates. What remedy do the people have under the existing law? Yet all of them are violations of the right of the people.

I bring this up now, although I know the present government will do nothing about it, because it is the only hope that you, specially you young people, will ponder on these questions and try to amplify the concept of remedies in our law so that we will have remedies not only for violations of personal rights but for violations of people's rights. So that we will not be forced, as we are now being forced, to resort to the ultimate recourse -- revolution -- in order to defend our people's rights.

So, we can say of Don Gregorio Araneta what was said of Don Claro Mayo Recto, in one of his speeches quoting from Rizal, that not everyone slept during the darkness of the night. If we would want to be worthy of his example, if we would want to emulate his dedication to law, we can do no better than to devote ourselves, even though we are still in the darkness of the night, to finding remedies so that when dawn comes, we will be prepared.

And we will be able to lift our heads high and show the world that we have not been afraid, and we have looked forward, and that we are meeting the future face to face knowing that it will be the future that we want and not the future that some other nations have designed for us.

FOREIGN MILITARY BASES
AND THE THIRD WORLD

The U.S. military bases do not avert attack, they invite it.They do not ensure the survival of nations, they threaten their destruction.

The bases are not instruments of defense, but of aggression.

They hinder our national development because their very presence violates our sovereignty and creates insuperable socio-economic problems, viz, prostitution, gambling, inordinate consumerism. Therefore the U.S. military bases must go.

Foreign military bases pose more - and more difficult - problems in the Third World than in the First World. In developed nations like Japan, Greece, Spain (I mention these countries because we have participants from them in this conference), foreign military bases pose two distinct but related problems in this nuclear age:

First, do the bases ensure the survival of nations or increase the risks of their extinction?

Second, are they instruments of defense or attack?

Foreign military bases pose these two problems also in developing countries like the Philippines - but to an intensified degree. For Third World countries have less means of controlling foreign bases in their land.

In addition, foreign military bases pose another equally pressing and immediate problem:

Third, do they help or hinder our development, our struggle to free ourselves from internal exploitation and domination, our quest for a more just and humane society which respects the life, rights and dignity of every man, woman, and child and, by seeking to eliminate poverty and social inequity, allows all to bring their native talents to full flower and to laugh and cry, dance and sing, live and love with freedom and without fear?

The Philippine experience provides clear-cut answers to these three questions: for ours is a country caught in the grip of U.S. military bases.

On our plains, we have the largest U.S. air base outside the United States: Clark Air Base. On our shores, we host the largest

(Delivered at the 1983 International Conference for General Disarmament, World Peace, and Removal of All Foreign Military Bases, Quezon City, October 24-26, 1983)

U.S. Naval logistics support base in the Western Pacific: Subic Naval Base. On our mountains, we shelter a highly sophisticated U.S. communications system which is locked into both the satellite tracking system and the global military and naval communications system of the United States.

Although the U.S. government will neither admit nor deny it, the bases store tactical nuclear weapons. The primary function of the bases is to provide logistics support; and since U.S. nuclear armed warships call regularly at Subic, and all airplanes stationed at both Subic and Clark are nuclear capable, it would be extremely naive to assume that the bases would not store the tactical nuclear weapons these warships and airplanes need. Indeed, since March 10, 1978, Instructions No. C.8020.1A have been in effect in Subic prescribing procedures to follow in case of "nuclear material accidents or significant events." In an interview on January 24, 1982, the Philippine Chief of Staff said:

> ... we have an agreement with the United States that they will report to us any entry of nuclear weapons into Clark or Subic. But sometimes they don't do it.[1]

And since the June 11, 1983 revision of the Philippines-United States Bases Agreement requires prior consultation between the two governments, only about the installation of inter-continental ballistics missiles in the bases, the U.S. is free to install short- and medium-range nuclear weapons _ a freedom it would certainly exercise.

Across the China Sea, almost directly opposite the U.S. bases in the Philippines, stand the Vietnamese naval base at Cam Ranh Bay and the air base at Danang. These bases, ironically, were built by the United States. Today, the Vietnamese government allows the Soviet Union to use them. I do not have reliable information about the extent of control or the strength of the weaponry that the Soviet Union has in these bases, but I think it safe to assume that the control is not as pervasive nor the weapons as powerful as those of the United States in Clark and Subic. However, it is also safe to assume that the Soviet Union will try – as any other country in its place would – to achieve parity or at least enough control and strength to neutralize the U.S. bases in the Philippines. Already it is reported that Soviet warplanes have penetrated Philippine air space and Soviet missiles are aimed at the

---

[1]*Observer*, Vol. 1, No. 39, January 24, 1982, p. 10.

Philippines.

Obviously, the rationale for the Soviet posture is not that the Philippines is its enemy, or that the Philippines has committed any act of aggression against it or threatens it in any way. The rationale is simply that the presence of U.S. military bases makes the Philippines a legitimate – in fact, a primary – target in case of war between the super-powers: for the U.S. has in the past used the bases to support its interventions in Korea, the Quemoy-Matsu area, and Vietnam.

That is the tragedy of the Philippines and other Third World countries: that because we have allowed foreign military bases into our land, we have put ourselves in grave danger of being destroyed in wars we have neither made nor chosen.

So far, we have escaped disaster. But there is no guarantee that we will continue to do so. The next time the U.S. uses its bases here to intervene elsewhere, there could be retaliation that could trigger nuclear war.

The probability of nuclear war increases not only with increased tension between the super-powers or with the spread of war mentality – the inclination to solve political problems by military means – among the leaders of the U.S. and the U.S.S.R. The mere increase in nuclear weapons increases the probability of nuclear war. Scientists at the Stockholm International Peace Research Institute, at Harvard University and at the Massachusetts Institute of Technology have predicted that, unless the arms race is halted, nuclear war will become inevitable before this century ends – and that is less than seventeen years away.

The Philippine experience, then, provides a clear and categorical answer to the first question posed above: foreign military bases do not deter aggression, they invite it. They do not ensure the survival of nations; they threaten their destruction.

The Philippine answer to the second question is equally forthright: the bases are not instruments of defense, but of attack. U.S. bases in my country are not here to defend either the Philippines or the United States. They are here to project U.S. power in Asia and the Middle East.

To grasp this, let us turn back the pages of history about 50 years to the beginning of the problem of U.S. bases in my country.

The Philippines, as you know, was first a colony of Spain and later of the United States. By 1933, for reasons I need not go into, the United States became anxious to lessen its obligations towards the Philippines, and decided to begin the process of recognizing Philippine independence. That year, the United States Congress passed an act known as the Hare-Hawes-Cutting Act recognizing Philippine independence after a ten-year period as a semi-independent Commonwealth. But the Hare-Hawes-Cutting Act contained a provision which allowed the United States to retain such military and naval bases in the Philippines as the American President might unilaterally determine. When the bill was submitted to the Philippine Congress for approval, the Philippine Congress rejected it. One reason for the rejection of the bill was that "the military, naval and other reservations provided for in the said act are inconsistent with our independence, violate our dignity, and are subject to misunderstandings."[2]

So in the next year, 1934, the United States Congress enacted a new Independence Act for the Philippines: the Tydings-McDuffie Law. The new act provided that the United States would not retain any military bases whatsoever in the Philippines. It could, however, retain naval reservations and refueling stations for two years after independence. After that period, unless the Philippine government agreed to allow the naval bases to stay, even those bases would have to go. The Tyding-McDuffie Act was accepted by the Philippine Congress.

Moreover, it was made part of the Philippine Constitution which was approved overwhelmingly by the people. That Constitution, by the way, also renounced war as an instrument of national policy, adopted the generally accepted principles of international law as part of the law of the land, and pledged to work with all nations of the world for peace, equality and international justice.

So the question of U.S. military bases in the Philippines was, it seemed, settled. There would be no bases after independence.

Unfortunately World War II came before independence.

The Japanese Imperial Army invaded the Philippines. Despite American bases (for we were still an American colony), the Japanese army conquered the Philippines in less than four months and occupied the country from 1942 to 1945. But Japan never won the loyalty of the Filipino people. In an effort to do so, the Japanese army of occupation decided to create a so-called Philippine Republic in October, 1943. The "Republic was to be manned by leaders who had collaborated with Japan: for shortly after the war had broken out, the elected Philippine President, Manuel L. Quezon, and Vice-President, Sergio Osmeña, were evacuated to the United States and became, in effect, a government in exile.

---

[2]Philippine Legislature, Concurrent Resolution No. 46, October 17, 1933.

The creation of the Japanese-sponsored "Philippine Republic" worried the government of the U.S. and the Philippine Government-in-exile. Would the people accept such a government and give it their loyalty? This was complicated by another problem: the terms of office of the President and Vice-President in exile were about to expire.

To solve both problems, U.S. Senator Milard Tydings, one of the authors of the Philippine Independence Act, presented three Resolutions to the United States Senate:

> Resolution No. 93, which permitted the President of the United States to advance the date of Philippine Independence, but at the same time authorized him to acquire military and air bases in addition to naval bases in the country; Resolution No. 94, which created a rehabilitation commission to study the damages inflicted by the war on the Philippines and to propose legislation to the United States government on how to repair those damages; and
>
> Resolution No. 95, which extended the term of office of President Quezon and Vice President Osmeña, and continued the life of the Philippine government in exile.

On November 10, 1943, the last resolution was approved, and on November 15, President Quezon and company took new oaths of office for their renewed terms. The other two resolutions remained unacted upon until June 29, 1944.

The date is significant. By that date, the Allies had landed in Normandy, the U.S. had occupied Saipan, and it was evident that the Axis powers had lost the war, and their unconditional surrender was merely a matter of time. With their defeat, there remained no external threat to the Philippines. Yet on that date, the resolution authorizing the U.S. President to acquire military bases in the Philippines was approved on the pretext that they provided defense for the Phillipines.

At first blush, the Resolution was impeccable for it required the U.S. President to negotiate with the Philippine government (or President) to acquire the bases. But this was mere show. The reality was that Philippine officials were blatantly told that unless the U.S. were granted military bases, the U.S. government would not recognize Philippine independence nor grant reparations for war-caused damages. In a letter of then Secretary of State Edward J. Stettinius to President Truman, dated April 19, 1945 the Secretary said:

> ... *the question of Philippine independence is conditioned on satisfactory arrangements for bases.* (emphasis ours)

A month later, as a condition for granting desperately needed emergency aid to the Philippines, Philippine President Sergio Osmeña was required to sign a brief two-page agreement with President Truman entitled "Preliminary Statement of General Principles Pertaining to the United States Military and Naval Base System in the Philippines." This agreement was to tie the Philippine government until a final agreement could be drawn up and signed. It provided, among other things: "pending development of detailed plan, the United States will retain all sites which were held by the United States Army as military reservations on 7 December 1941 and by the United States Navy, and will be accorded rights to sites on the localities shown in the attached appendix," which listed all the new bases which have been created upon the landing of the American forces in this country. It provided further, in paragraph 9, that "consideration will be given to Filipino participation in United States Bases and vice-versa as indicated by the military situation." So, in our country, we were not entitled to participate in American bases. The U.S. would simply consider that matter.

And finally, the agreement provided, in paragraph 10, "No nation other than the United States or the Philippines is to be permitted to establish or make use of any bases in the Philippines without prior agreement of both the United States and the Philippine government." [3] So that we were tied hand and foot to the United States. We could not offer any other nation the same privileges of having military bases in our land that the United States exacted as a condition for our independence.

U.S. insistence on retaining military bases in the Philippines at a time when the Philippines had no external enemy and the U.S. had become the strongest military power in the world makes any rationale of mutual defense or national security suspect. What then was the real reason for and the main purpose of these bases? Documents provided at that time by the U.S. military establishment give us the answer.

---

[3]Preliminary Statement of General Principles Pertaining to the United States Military and Naval Base System in the Philippines to be Used as a Basis for Detailed Discussions and Staff Studies, Appendix A, declassified confidential security information prepared by the U.S. Office of Philippine and South East Asian Affairs.

In a paper dated April 23, 1945, the Strategy section, operation division, U.S. War Department General Staff said:

> ... the major portions of the world's supply of certain important strategic materials are located within this area [referring to South East Asia]], each of which is of utmost importance to the industrial and commercial interests of the United States.[4]

Japan's forced withdrawal from the region together with the development of China and possibly the East Indies "would expand this area to one of the future's great possibilities for investment and development." So, the Chief of Staff, Joint Chiefs of Staff, reported to President Truman: "the United States bases in the Philippines should be considered not merely as outposts but as springboards from which United States armed forces may be projected."[5]

This still remains the major purpose of these bases today. In an interview published in the Washington Times this year, Major General Kenneth D. Burns, Commander of the 13th Air Force stationed at Clark Air Base, said:

> United States trade with the Western Pacific allies exceeds in Dollar terms our trade with our European allies. Along with the 7th Fleet, our air forces out here provided the punch to protect our trade initiatives and economic interests.

And Rear Admiral Dickinson M. Smith, Commander of the United States naval forces in the Philippines, said:

> It would be difficult to over-estimate the importance of this base [Subic] to our fleet operations. This is the primary supply point for the Diego Garcia base and thus for our operations in the Indian Ocean.

The answer of Philippine experience, then, to the questions posed to all nations by foreign bases, is that foreign bases are not instruments of defense but of attack; they are intended not to deter aggression but to project armed power and secure advantages in

---

[4]As quoted by Steven R. Shalom in The United States and The Philippines, Philadelphia: Institute for the Study of Human Issues, 1981, p. 60.

[5]Ibid.

trade and investment.

As I have said, there is a third, and for us, an equally important question: do foreign bases help or hinder development of the host country? If development means – as I submit that it does – not merely that a society grows but that it transforms itself, not just that the people enjoy a higher standard of living but a better quality of life with all that that implies, then the experience of the Philippines with U.S. military bases shows that foreign bases hold back, they do not push development.

This has been so for several reasons. All foreign military bases imply a diminution of the sovereignty of the host country. This was made crystal clear, with respect to the Philippines, by George Kennan.

First, once bases are established, a force, an inertia arises against removing them.

As Dr. Falk mentioned this morning, George Kennan, the architect of U.S. foreign policy in the immediate postwar years, conservative but not particularly hawk-like, advocated a foreign policy that would assure the United States control of access to the vast resources of the world. With respect to the Philippines, that policy implied, as Kennan said in a letter to then Secretary of State Marshall, that the United States should "permit Philippine independence but in such a way as to assure that the archipelago remained a bulwark of American security in the Pacific region."[6] In lay language, allow the Philippines to be independent of every nation except the United States. Because as that very perceptive American Senator, Senator Fulbright said:

Is it not inevitable that because of our presence there [referring to the Philippines] and with this purpose we will always use our influence for the preservation of the status quo? We will always resist any serious change in political or social structure of the Philippine government. A policy which is very likely to be, in the long run, a detriment to the people of the Philippines. Wherever we have any kind of interest, why, we support the existing political and social structures, we will always be a representative of the status quo, always in the position of preventing any change which, in effect, probably would mean improvement, when the present situation is not satisfactory, which it is not in most of those cases.

[6]Ibid., p. 61.

Then he added: "And therefore, those who challenge the regime are always considered to be threats."[7]

These were very prophetic words stated in 1969. Prior to 1969, the record of American intervention in Philippine politics is well known. They had intervened in every Presidential election. Books by Americans belonging to the CIA indicate the extent of how they had attempted to subvert the candidacies of known Philippine nationalists such as the late and great Filipino nationalist, Don Claro M. Recto. They have trained our military and it is a fact to which the former United States Attorney General Ramsey Clark referred when he came here to the Philippines. He managed to visit a military safehouse where it had been alleged that a considerable amount of torture had been done. And he was surprised to learn that one of the things that the officers he interviewed were very proud that they had all been trained in the United States by the United States Army.

Our riot police, and perhaps you have seen photographs of the riot police in action in Manila where people already lying on the ground are unable to defend themselves are still being truncheoned. Our riot police have been trained – directly or indirectly – by the United States.

The presence of military bases in this country automatically leads to a militarization of society. And the explanation is simple. Regardless of the truth, foreign military bases can be justified only on the basis of mutual protection. Mutual protection means that the government of the country, in this case the Philippines, must have some means of protection which means that it will be given arms, weapons and military training by the United States. In fact, the latest agreement between the Philippines and the United States on military bases gives the Philippine government of Mr. Marcos the sum of U.S. $425 million over the next five years in military assistance: U.S. $125 million in outright grants, and U.S. $300 million in foreign military sales credits but with a ten-year grace period and a twenty-year repayment period. Since the military bases agreement is to expire in 1991, and this military aid will begin in 1984, the grace period alone, not to say the repayment period, goes beyond the term of the bases agreement which can only mean that there is an implied agreement to extend the bases.

---

[7]Symington Sub-Committee Hearings, 1969, Part I, p. 68.

I mentioned earlier that the problem of development is a key to peace and progress in this country. Development, however, means that we must eliminate at least the worst cases of poverty, that we must be able to meet as far as possible our needs with our own resources. But this is not a policy that is favored by the United States and financial institutions connected or controlled or very deeply influenced by the United States, like the World Bank and the International Monetary Fund. The policy is: get involved with international trade, never mind the needs of your people, you can always import them. The trouble is that the time comes when it is almost impossible to import because the entire strategy is one that does not lead to the development of productive capacities that could essentially supply the needs of the nation.

And so today we have approximately 6.4 per cent of our families, that is approximately three million families, living below the poverty line. Our real wages and the real income of our farmers have declined. The value of our currency internally and externally has dropped by several hundred per cent. Internally, the drop from 1965 to today is 682 per cent. Externally it is approximately 300 per cent. Perhaps the cruelest form of this situation of maldevelopment lies in the damage it has done to our children.

In 1965, government figures estimated that 30 per cent of our children were properly nourished – normal. By 1970, that 30 per cent had dropped to 22 per cent. And in 1979, the Philippine Ministry of Social Welfare said that we have one and a half million children of school age who are mentally retarded mostly because of malnutrition. And there is no known medical cure for mental retardation. One and a half million lives blighted. And I think if you stay here long enough you will see this for yourselves.

And that is why we believe that the U.S. bases must go. It is because of the U.S. bases that the United States has made the Philippines a neo-colony. It is because of United States bases that we do not have full control over our lives nor over our destiny. Without that control, we cannot prosper. It is because of United States bases that our society has been militarized and human rights have been totally degraded and violated. And that is why we are fighting against great odds to force these bases out. In doing so, we want to make it very clear that we do not share the sentiments of Mr. Marcos who said that if the United States does not want to comply with the Bases Agreement he will offer the bases to Soviet Russia. The Anti-Bases Coalition is against any foreign base in Asia and in the Pacific. And this is why , while we work to get the bases out of this country, we do not want these bases to go to Guam, Micronesia or any other country in the world. We have suffered enough. We do not want to inflict other nations with the same kind of suffering that we have gone through.

It was a great pleasure to me yesterday to realize that today in this Conference we have people from the two countries that had colonized the Philippines, Spain and the United States. Because, by coming here, by showing their fraternity with us and by associating themselves with our cause, they give us hope that the peoples of the world – all over the world – are one in their demand for peace and for justice. It is my hope that more and more movements, more and more conferences like these will be held in every country of Asia so that in the end, there will no longer be super powers. No longer imperialists. No longer the dominator and the dominated. But that we will all be one people of many races and many creeds and many talents but all working together to make the whole world worthy of humanity.

U.S POLICY AND PRESENCE IN EAST ASIA: AN INSIDER'S VIEW

"It will be extremely difficult to regain our freedom, even more difficult to cut back our ties of dependence with the U.S., and most difficult of all to transform our society." In this address Diokno reiterates the dreary statistics of neo-colonial underdevelopment, dependency and oppression.

Thank you for inviting me to be with you this morning. These are days when the leaders of great powers seem bent, for some perverse motives, to push the world into what may well turn out to be a final immolation. And your presence here, your testimony to a continuing belief in the value of reason, your determination to hold on to sanity in these days, is a bright ray of hope. For doing me honor and for giving me hope, thank you.

Your invitation asked me to describe, and I quote, "the experience of living in East Asia and the impact of U.S. presence and policy on the lives and welfare of those living in the region" which I interpret as simply a polite way of asking me how it is to live under the impact of U.S. imperialism. I hasten to add that I may have misinterpreted your invitation. If so, I hope you will believe that I do not mean to either insult or provoke you by my interpretation. I merely wish to stress a fact. And that is, that U.S. presence and policy in East Asia are nothing more nor less than imperialism. And if our discussions are to be fruitful, I suggest that we must grasp the motives and the nature of that imperialism. For this purpose I hope you will allow me to review, very briefly, its historical roots.

Those roots rest in the urge for westward expansion that William Seward, who was later to become the United States Secretary of State, expressed very clearly in 1853. He said, "You are already the great continental power of America but does that content you? I trust it does not. You want the commerce of the world; that must be looked for in the Pacific." The following year Commodore Perry forced open the doors of Japan to the commerce of the West and this event marked the beginning of U.S. presence in East Asia.

(Keynote address presented at a conference entitled "U.S. Policy in East Asia: Time for a Change," sponsored by the Coalition for a New Foreign and Military Policy, Washington, D.C., May 1, 1980)

When the treaty to formalize this event was signed, Commodore Perry presented the Emperor of Japan with a gift from the President of the United States. To our modern eyes the gift appears quaint but it was also prophetic. It consisted of rifles and pistols, 100 gallons of whiskey, eight baskets of potatoes and one locomotive. And this curious mixture of armaments, farm produce and industrial products symbolizes what was to become and to remain to this day the policy of the United States toward East Asia -- a policy which that great exponent of naval power, Admiral Mahan, expressed in a very brief epigram: "War is not fighting, but business."

Forty-four years later, President McKinley declared war on Spain. One result of that war was the purchase by the United States of my country, the Philippines -- an archipelago of 300,000 square kilometers and, at that time, ten million inhabitants -- for U.S. $20 million, which is either 67 U.S. cents per hectare of Philippine land or U.S. $2.00 per Filipino head. Take your pick. By either computation, the terms of the purchase in today's jargon would probably be described as "on concessionary terms." The purchase also made U.S. presence in East Asia a permanent institution. War had indeed proved to be good business.

Now this event is surrounded by certain myths that must be dispelled if we are to fully grasp the effects of U.S. presence in East Asia. One myth is that the annexation of the Philippines was an unplanned for and unwanted thing. The truth is that plans to invade the Philippines had been made in Washington as early as December 1897. And even before the battleship Maine was sunk at Havana, Dewey had been dispatched with his fleet to Hong Kong, there to await orders to attack Manila, in the event of war with Spain. And four days before the news of Dewey's victory at Manila Bay reached the United States, Senator Albert J. Beveridge told the Middlesex Club of Boston:

American soil is producing more than they can consume. Fate has written our policy for us. The trade of the world must and shall be ours. American law, American order, American civilization and the American flag will plant themselves on shores hitherto bloody and benighted but by agencies of God henceforth to be made beautiful and bright. In the Pacific is the true field of our earliest operations; there Spain has an island empire. Spain's best ships are on the

Atlantic side. In the Pacific, the United States has a powerful squadron. The Philippines is logically our first target.[1]

Later, during the debate over the ratification of the acquisition of the Philippines, the Senator argued that the United States was, and I quote, "the trustee under God of the civilization of the world;" and, in a more worldly vein, that "just beyond the Philippines are China's illimitable markets. We will not retreat from either. The Pacific is the ocean of commerce of the future and most future wars will be conflicts of the commerce."[2] President McKinley himself, despite protestations that his decision to annex the Philippines was entirely due to Christian altruism and humanitarianism, more for the benefit of Filipinos than for that of the United States, did not fail to instruct Dewey to look into and submit a report "on the desirability of the several islands, the character of their population, coal and other mineral deposits, their harbors and commercial advantages." And he made certain that his instructions to the American emissaries to the Paris Peace Conference with Spain included these instructions:

> Incidental to our tenure in the Philippines is the commercial opportunity to which American statesmanship cannot be indifferent. It is just to use every legitimate means for the engagement of American trade.[3]

In the end, of course, the Unite States paid more than U.S. $20 million for the Philippines. To retain the Philippines, to quell what it called the Philippine insurrection, the United States had to deploy 126,000 soldiers in the Philippines, fight 2,800 separate battles and actions, suffer 4,243 American dead and 2,618 wounded, and spend about U.S. $600 million. In the process, the U.S. killed between 16,000 to 20,000 Filipino soldiers and almost a quarter of a million Filipino non-combatants, reconcentrated the people of Batangas, Cavite and Tayabas, leveled Northern Luzon, and turned Samar into a howling wilderness. No doubt these measures were what McKinley had referred to as "every legitimate means" for the enlargement of American trade that he felt just to use.

But despite these costs, the acquisition of the Philippines was for the United States a good investment that continues to pay

---

[1]As quoted by Leon Wolff in *Little Brown Brother*, New York: Doubleday & Co., 1961, p. 63.
[2]Congressional Record, U.S. Senate, January 9, 1900, p. 704.
[3]As quoted by Leon Wolff, op. cit., p. 155.

handsome dividends up to this day. For one thing, the Philippines served as a huge laboratory where the United States tested and perfected the methods that it was later to use in constructing a neo-colonial empire throughout the world. For example, methods of counter-insurgency -- such as the use of the water cure to extort information, reconcentration of villages, civic action groups, and the like. Methods of cultural domination -- such as the use of the system of education, for after all, were not the Thomasites[4] the very first Peace Corps volunteers in American history? Methods of economic domination that led to what the first American Ambassador to the Philippines, Paul V. McNutt, called a dependence of the Philippine economy on that of the United States greater than the dependence of any single state of the Union.

But I think more important than this have been the military and economic benefits that continue to be derived from the Philippine-American relationships. Recent studies in the Philippines show that for every dollar that American investors sent to the Philippines since 1973, they have borrowed U.S. $3.58 for every dollar. Of these profits, U.S. $2.00 have been remitted to the United States and U.S. $1.58 has been left in the Philippines to repeat the cycle of investment, profit, repatriation and reinvestment.

The Philippine government, even the martial law government, despite its subservience to American interest, has attempted to cure this problem. In 1978, President Marcos and his Central Bank issued a decree limiting the debt-equity ratio of foreign companies, but so great is the power of American and transnational capital, that the decree had to have exceptions for "meritorious cases." And the very first exception to the debt-equity ratio was given to General Motors. The second was to the Ford subsidiary in the Philippines. Others who were granted exceptions were Unilever, the Philippines Manufacturing Corporation, International Harvester, and even Colgate Palmolive Company. Name the large transnationals; none of them has been subjected to that limitation on domestic borrowings. Part of the pressure, of course, came from the U.S. Embassy. Ambassador Sullivan on more than one occasion castigated the martial law government for imposing such a debt-equity ratio, arguing that the martial law government was guilty of bad faith in having invited foreign capital to come into the country and then seeking to limit the amount they could borrow locally. In the end, of course, transnationals and the U.S. government won, and transnationals continue to make handsome

---

[4]U.S teachers sent to the Philippines in 1901 aboard the army transport "Thomas."

profits in the Philippines. These same studies show that in the years 1976 and 1977, when the studies were made, transnationals earned an average of 15 per cent profit at a time when the profit rate in the developed world was 7.5 per cent. And in our financial system they earned a whopping 33 1/3 per cent average annual profit over the preceding ten years.

In addition, of course, and equally important, is the presence of the United States Air Force, Navy and Marines in the Philippines. You are all aware that last year President Marcos gave the United States unhampered military control over the military facilities of the United States in Clark, Subic, and who knows where else in the Philippines. Military control that goes to the extent of authorizing American forces outside the base areas for purposes of "the security of the base." And of course, all of you have heard of President Marcos' unconditional and unilateral offer to the United States government on April 21 of this year, that regardless of who is at fault, the Philippines will fight by the side -- I think he meant in front of -- the United States Army. I say in front of because we are the farthermost outpost in the perimeter of American defense.

The consequences of this situation on the people of the Philippines, and in varying degrees, the people of other parts of East Asia, seem to me to be fairly obvious. The first and the most important consequence is that we have no control even over whether we survive as a people or not. And with the governments of certain powers -- let me be very candid -- and with the government of the United States apparently going berserk in its foreign policy, this is a very real danger to us Filipinos. Every day that passes brings closer to home the realization that whether we like it or not – and frankly, we do not like it – we may be dragged into a nuclear war that offers us little chance, if any, to survive as normal human beings. And I think the first question that we must ask ourselves as we review the situation is, how fair is it to deprive the people of any country of any say in whether they survive or not? Forget economic development, forget social change. Let's get down to the nitty gritty of this problem: survival. There can be no right more basic than that. I think once we are all six feet under, we have no human rights.

There is another very important consequence of the presence of American troops in the Philippines. I have mentioned the possibility of war. There is also the possibility of instant incineration by accident, for there is no doubt that nuclear weapons are stored by the United States forces in both Subic and Clark. The Center for Defense Information has made that statement, and we know that that is true for a very simple reason. Nuclear-powered naval vessels call regularly at Subic. Nuclear-bearing naval vessels call even more frequently at Subic. Consequently, there are, in Subic, nuclear warheads.

In addition to being a threat to our survival, the presence of these military facilities diminishes the sovereignty of the Filipino people. No one pointed it out more clearly than Senator Fulbright. Hearing the attitudes and policies of American military leaders during a Senate conference, Senator Fulbright was moved in dismay to explain and let me quote his exact words: "We will always resist any serious change in political and social structure of Philippine government which is very likely to be, in the long run, in your view, a detriment to the people of the Philippines."[5] So we are not only denied the right to survive, we are denied the right to determine what changes in our social and political structure we deem to be better for us. And those changes must be made.

Historically, when the United States came to the Philippines they faced the following basic social problems: first, widespread poverty; second, unequal distribution of wealth; and third, social exploitation as the dominant process that maintained the system. When the Americans left forty-eight years later, they left these same three basic problems behind them and added two more: a totally dependent economy and a military situation so tied to the United States that decisions on war and peace, in fact, rest with the United States and not with the Filipino people. Today, thirty-four years after our flag-independence, we are still faced with the basic social problems. Tremendous poverty, horrendous inequality, social exploitation, economic dependence, military dependence, and two more have been added: widespread corruption in and out of government, and we have lost our freedoms to boot.

Most of you are aware of aspects of these problems, but I think the best way I can give you an idea of the dimensions of the problems is to quote from martial law statistics themselves. In 1979, the martial law government issued a paper which said that, in order to earn a decent living, families outside Manila had to earn ₱43.27 a day for an agricultural family, and ₱45.60 for a non-agricultural family; and within Manila, ₱46.82. Converting this into yearly income in round numbers, the minimum amount that a family would have to earn yearly would be ₱15,000 – that's a little less than U.S. $2,000. Now if you take a look at the productivity of the Philippine economy, this standard does not appear to be impossible to achieve. According to the Philippine Government, in

---

[5]Symington Sub-Committee Hearings, 1969, Part I, p. 68.

1979, the gross national product, after deducting all foreign transactions, taxes, subsidies, and depreciation allowances, amounted to ₱175 billion. And since we have approximately eight million families in the country, if these ₱175 billion had been divided equally among our eight million families, each family would receive about ₱21,000, which is ₱6,000 more than the minimum required for decent existence.

So, the possibility of eliminating poverty is there. And yet, the latest data of the same government shows that 83 per cent of our families earn less than ₱8,000 a year, and another 12 per cent earn less ₱15,000. So that we have 95 per cent of our families earning less than the minimum required to lead a decent life. I submit to you that a society that fosters a situation like this cannot be called a "New Society." It is a decadent society.

But the most disastrous effects have been reserved for our very young people. In 1979 the government reported 45 per cent functional illiteracy for elementary school graduates; malnutrition for one out of every two pre-school children, or worse; mental retardation for 1.5 million young Filipinos by the end of 1979, because of malnutrition. These are the dimensions of the problems we face.

Now, we know what we have to do to solve these problems. We know that ultimately, we must transform our society. We know that to transform society, we have to regain our freedom and we have to regain our sovereignty as a people. We have to regain our freedom because martial law, in destroying our freedom and trampling on our basic rights, has made cowards of us all, has reduced us to being less than human.

Oh, you are going to hear many defenses of martial law. And since the purpose of this seminar goes beyond what I am merely saying, let me try to tell you what they will say. They will tell you that more rice has been produced under martial law; that there are more expressways, bridges, hotels and public buildings; that more of the countryside has been electrified; that several geothermal power plants have been built; and that peace and order have been restored. But they will not tell you that the motivations for these "achievements" were not social and economic development but image building, public relations work to attract transnationals and tourists and to increase the mobility of the military.

And they will not tell you how much they have cost. Heightened inflation, one of the worst in Asia, that by February 1980 pushed our consumer price index to 288 per cent of what it had been in 1972. Heightened dependence: our external debt has increased by 500 per cent since martial law. And the ratio of effective foreign debt to gross domestic product, which was 11 per cent in 1974, jumped to 26 per cent in 1978. So they will not tell you that as a result of all this, despite the greater availability of rice and electric power, more people can buy less goods. Only the rich and high middle income groups can afford to own cars, to travel on the new expressways and bridges, and to take snacks in the new hotels. Military morale is low and criminals are on the rampage again.

Perhaps you may say that this dream of transforming society, of cutting off foreign domination, of regaining freedom, is a dream of the intellectuals, the dream of the rich, the middle class. This is a very common argument. They will tell you the people are happy with the situation in the Philippines. They never had freedom, so this makes no difference. Well, they are lying to you and I can offer no better proof than to cite two people who certainly did not belong to the elite.

One is Salud Algabre, the only woman who was arrested and imprisoned during the Sakdal rebellion in the early 1930's. What was she fighting for, and I quote, "She fought for land, she fought to throw off foreign domination, she fought to rectify an inequitable social system. She fought for all those things but she sought something more. She struggled to create a moral world."[6]

The second quotation illustrates how difficult it is to create that moral world under the impact of U.S. imperialism. It is a quotation from an old general of the Katipunan, General Sandiko, who was called to Malacanang[7] after the rebellion in the early 1930's. By then, Governor Early wanted to know what was happening, why was this so. And this is what General Sandiko told Governor Early: "You Americans have too much respect for property and property rights. Let the United States get out, and the oppressed will soon right things with the bolo."[8]

Now, we know that to accomplish the tasks we must do is not going to be easy. We know it is going to be extremely difficult to regain our freedom, even more difficult to cut back our ties of dependence with the United States, and most difficult of all, to transform our society. We do not know, frankly, whether we will succeed or whether we will fail now. But we take great hope from what Salud Algabre told Professor David Sturtevant when he

---

[6]David R. Sturtevant, *Popular Uprisings in the Philippines 1840-1940*, Ithaca: Cornell University Press, 1976, Appendix D, p. 287.

[7]Presidential palace.

[8]Harvesting tool used as a weapon in Filipino peasant revolts. As quoted by Joseph R. Hayden, *The Philippines: A Study in National Development*, p. 410

interviewed her and he asked her, "Where did you go after the uprising failed?" And Salud said, "No uprising fails. Each one is a step in the right direction."[9]

And so we may fail, but the people like Salud Algabre, the people that has given so much of its blood and its life for freedom, cannot be denied forever. No matter what it takes, how long or at what cost, no matter how repressive our government might be or how oppressive U.S. presence and policy in Asia may be, the Filipino people will prevail. We will regain our freedom. We will restructure our society. We will reorient our relations with the United States.

---

[9]David R. Sturtevant, op. cit., p. 296.

THE MILITARIZATION OF ASIAN POLITICS

". . . by assigning the people the role of uncomplaining acceptance of decisions made by others, all militarized regimes betray a profound contempt for the people's capacity to fashion their own destiny. Such regimes usually enjoy the support of foreign powers." Thus the sovereignty of the Asian peoples governed by militarized regimes has been steadily eroded, and only demilitarization can restore it.

This century has witnessed sixteen major wars, each of which cost between 300,000 and 3,000,000 lives. Ten of these sixteen were colonial or civil wars waged in Asia, wars Asians fought to gain or defend our independence or to overthrow illegitimate regimes supported by foreign powers.[1] Such was the heavy price we paid to end colonialism in our corner of the world.

Unfortunately, we are still paying the price. Phoenix-like, colonialism has been reincarnated as neo-colonialism, less visible but equally oppressive. And our dreams of the freedom and better life that independence should bring have turned into nightmares of dehumanizing poverty, degrading oppression, and apathy born of helplessness and despair.

One sign of our continuing torment is the militarization of our politics: the proliferation of authoritarian, repressive regimes in Asia.

The Meaning of Militarization

Some of these regimes are frankly military. Others are "crisis governments" which called the military out of their barracks to meet an emergency, real or concocted but never ending, and which rule by decree. Still others are civilian in appearance but depend mainly on the military and secret police to stay in power. Harold Crouch of the National University of Malaysia has painted a vivid

(People and Structures of Domination, Christian Conference of Asia-International Affairs Consultation, Kuala Lumpur, Malaysia, February 23-28, 1981)

[1]Stockholm International Peace Research Institute, *Warfare in a Fragile World: Military Impact on the Human Environment*, London: Taylor & Francis, 1980, Appendix 1.1, pp. 30-33.

picture of Southeast Asian politics that, with minor variations, depicts the politics of most developing nations of Asia:

> In each state the governing elite has established a more or less authoritarian political structure making it impossible for opposition groups to capture power by constitutional means. Opposition leaders are arrested or absorbed; newspapers are controlled; and potentially independent mass organizations undermined and supervised, when not banned. Elections, when they are held, always take place in circumstances ensuring victory of the government. The main political battle is thus limited to struggle between factions of the governing elite which, whatever their immediate rivalries, have a common interest in preserving and stabilizing the system.
>
> In the absence of effective constitutional opposition, the most serious resistance comes from insurgents, both communist and regionalist. Insurgencies of one sort or another are in progress in almost all the countries of Southeast Asia but so far they are essentially major irritants rather than immediate threats to the survival of the governments.[2]

The suppression of all effective legal opposition, the use of threats and of violence as the major means to settle political conflicts; and the enormously increased influence of the military in government – these are the hallmarks of militarized politics.

They produce the expected results. Military forces grown in number and armaments, and military budgets soar. Taxes increase; prices rise; and poverty deepens. Military wants take precedence over civilian needs in the use of scarce resources. Military officers assume key civilian government positions. Military behaviour, techniques and values infect the political process. National security becomes the overriding goal. Spying and surveillance replace supervision in and out of government. Command supplants consensus. Discipline banishes debate. Bayonets cast ballots.

Militarization thus perverts both politics and the military itself: politics, because force, not persuasion, becomes its principal process, and coups, not elections, the normal way of changing governments; and the military, because repression, not protection of the people becomes its major mission.

---

[2]Harold Crouch, "Southeast Asia in 1977: "A Political Overview," in Institute of Southeast Asian Studies, *Southeast Asian Affairs, 1978,* edited by Kernial S. Sandhu and others, Singapore: Heinemann, 1978, pp. 10-11.

The Process of Militarization

The process of militarization has not been uniform throughout Asia. Nevertheless, beneath superficial differences, common factors are discernable.

Origins of Militarization

One common factor that contributes to, if it has not caused, the militarization of Asia in this century is the rivalry between the United States and the Soviet Union for control of the world. With missionary zeal, each of these super-powers seeks to make the world over into its image and likeness. At the very least, each seeks to prevent the other from encroaching into its spheres of influence. Whenever the opportunity arises, each is ready to install or maintain a government in any Asian country (and elsewhere in the world), no matter how tyrannical such a government may be, merely to put or keep the country within its camp.

The People's Republic of China has also played a role in the process of militarization. After it had broken with the U.S.S.R., the Chinese Communist Party supported indigenous communist parties in Southeast Asia (Malaysia, Indonesia, Singapore, Philippines); and the growth of these parties served as the rationale for the militarization of the societies of capitalist developing Asia.

It was in this milieu that most Asian countries gained independence. In countries where independence was not accompanied by changes in social structure, the governing elite (including the military in countries like Indonesia, where it became the new elite) opted for the capitalist model of development. They were, however, unable to satisfy the people's demands for land and for a just and humane social order, demands which domestic communist parties capitalized on. So, with the cooperation, if not at the instigation, of the United States, the elite imposed militarization in order to contain their people's demands, and at the same time embarked on a course of forced "development" managed by western-trained technocrats.

In countries where independence was accompanied, or was soon afterwards followed, by radical changes in social structure, leaders had chosen the communist model of development. This required the redistribution of property and a centrally planned economy supervised if not run by technocrats. The West predictably cut off economic and political support. So, apprehensive of a counter-revolution led by the ousted elite of the West, the leaders of these countries, with the cooperation or at the instigation of the Soviet Union, imposed militarization in order to protect the revolution.

Common Factors

In both cases:
>> Militarization was the product of fear; fear of the people in one case, and fear of the ousted elite and colonial power in the other.
>> Militarization required the collaboration of technocrats with the military: without the former's know-how, the latter's coercive power was not enough to govern the country.
>> Militarization would not have succeeded or lasted for as long as it has were it not abetted and aided by the super-powers.

The International Military And Economic Orders

Both the U.S. and U.S.S.R. abet militarization because militarism ties developing nations to them, as ASEAN nations, for example, are tied to the U.S. and Vietnam to the U.S.S.R., and fuel their ambitions to rule the world. Militarism also provides them with testing grounds for new weapons, and areas in which to fight proxy wars, using the armies of their satellites to test each other's strength of will without committing their own armies or their own territories or risking the safety of their own people.

The International Military Order

U.S.-U.S.S.R. rivalry has, in fact, created a new international military order that overlaps the international economic order,[3] and, like the latter, establishes an international division of labor: to the military of Asia and the rest of the Third World has fallen the role of maintaining the status quo nationally; to the military of the super-powers, that of doing so internationally – and of stepping in when national military forces fail to do their job.

---

[3]Jan Oberg, "The New International Economic and Military Orders as Problems to Peace Research," in *Bulletin of Peace Proposals*, Vol. 8, No. 2, 1977, pp. 142 ff: Michael T. Klare, "Militarism: The Issues Today," and Asbjorn Eide and Muzammel Huq, "The Impact of Militarization on Development and Human Rights," both in *Bulletin of Peace Proposals*,Vol. 9, No. 2, 1978, pp. 121-128 and 170-182.

Super-Power Interventions

Of the armed conflicts that have taken place since 1945, 95 per cent have occurred in Third World countries. At the top of the list of states who have intervened in those conflicts are the U.S. and Western European countries, who account for 78 per cent of all interventions. Communist states account for six per cent, and developing nations for the remainder. Recently, the West has been less open in its involvement, and there has been an "increase in hostile communist actions, particularly against other communist regimes, and a rise in hostilities between Third World neighbors."[4] The Vietnamese thrust into Kampuchea and its border incursions into Thailand, and China's "punitive action" against Vietnam, are Asian examples of this trend.

Middle Level Military Functions

In recent years, a trend has also developed towards creating a middle level in the military division of labor: surrogate states who relieve the superpowers of some responsibility for, and assume part of the cost of, the "defense" of particular regions of the world. In Asia, the U.S. is pushing this role on Japan; the U.S.S.R., on Vietnam.

The Role of China

China's preoccupation with the possibility of being invaded by the U.S.S.R., and the consequent need to modernize its armed forces; its rapprochement with the United States; the changes in its foreign policy following the death of Mao Tze Tung and even before that, its policy of supporting only such communist parties in Asia as were self-reliant – these factors have led China to play a secondary role in the international military order, a role limited mostly to moral support of Asian communist movements, with occasional financial help and training of their members. This is not to say, however, that China's role will remain secondary in the future.

Maintaining The Military Order

The processes that maintain the international military order are

---

[4]Ruth Leger Sivard, *World Military and Social Expenditures, 1980*, Leasburg, Va: World Priorities, 1980, pp. 9, 32

well-known, but it does no harm to review them briefly to remind ourselves of the magnitude of the task we Asians face. These processes include:

Transfers of arms. From 1969 to 1978, the total value of arms transfers jumped almost four times, from U.S. $5.86 billion to U.S. $20.6 billion. During the same period, arms imports by developing countries jumped from U.S $3.86 billion to U.S. $16.69 billion, that is, from 65 per cent to 80 per cent of the world's total arms transfers. In 1978, 11 per cent of these imports went to Asia. The largest arms exporters are the United States and the Soviet Union, each supplying about one-third of the world's total, with France, the United Kingdom, West Germany, and Czechoslovakia supplying most of the balance.[5]

Transfer of Police Weapons. Besides arms for the military, weapons for police forces are also exported. Michael T. Klare, of the Institute for Policy Studies, Washington, D.C., who has painstakingly researched the transfer of police weapons and technology by the U.S. to the Third World, reports: "Such weapons include police weapons, prison gear, surveillance systems, torture devices, and other hardware used by the security forces of repressive regimes to suppress resistance," as well as "computers used to identify and to trace victims for torture, assassination or imprisonment." As examples of such sales in Asia, he lists sales of Cadillac Gage V-150 "Commando" armored cars to the Philippines and Malaysia; cannisters of chemical "Mace" and other chemical weapons to Pakistan, Malaysia, Philippines, Thailand, South Korea, and Hongkong; gas generators, grenades and projectiles to Hongkong, Indonesia, Singapore, and Thailand; night vision systems and star-tron viewers to Hongkong, Indonesia, Philippines, Singapore, South Korea and Thailand.[6] Data for

---

[5]U.S. Arms Control and Disarmament Agency, *World Military Expenditures and Arms Transfers, 1969-1978.* Washington D.C.: ACDA, Revised December, 1980; Ruth Leger Sivard, op. cit., note 4; Stockholm International Peace Research Institute, *The Arms Trade With The Third World,* Middlesex: Penguin Books, 1975; Anthony Sampson, *The Arms Bazaar: From Lebanon to Lockhead,* New York: Bantam Books, 1978.

[6]Michael T. Klare, "The International Repression Trade," in *The Bulletin of the Atomic Scientists,*November, 1979; also op. cit., note 3; and with Daniel Volman, *Arms Trade Data: Major Use Arms Transfers to the Third World, 1973-1978; U.S. Arms Sales to Third World Police Forces, 1973-1976,* Washington, D.C.: Institute for Policy Studies, 1979.

similar transfers by the U.S.S.R. are not available; but reports of such transfers have surfaced from time to time in the Western press.

Transfers of arms manufacturing technology. In 1945, India was the only country in Asia capable of producing weapons other than small arms and ammunition. Today, North Korea produces aircraft, warships and small arms, all under license of the U.S.S.R.; South Korea likewise produces aircraft, warships, and small arms, all under license of the U.S.; Pakistan produces aircraft under a 1972 French license and missiles under a cancelled 1964-65 West German license; the Philippines produces aircraft under a 1975 West German and UK license, and small arms under a US license; Singapore produces warships under a 1974 West German license; Taiwan produces missiles under a 1976 US license; and Thailand produces aircraft under a 1973 US license.[7]

Military and Police Training. From 1950 to 1978, the U.S. government's International Military Education and Training Program (IMET) trained 491,721 foreign military personnel, most of them from the Third World.[8] The U.S.S.R. conducts a similar training program; but I have no data about its extent. Police training by the superpowers and their satellites has also been widespread. Apart from normal crime detection and apprehension techniques, police training has included techniques of torture.[9] The similarity in methods used to torture political prisoners throughout the Third World – burning with lighted ends of cigarettes, applying electric shocks to genital organs and other parts of their body, covering their faces with a towel or rag and pouring water or a carbonated soft drink on the towel, stripping them, specially women, before or during questioning and forcing them to stand against an air conditioning or other cooling unit, pushing their faces into toilet bowls filled with feces, inserting sharp needles beneath their finger nails, hanging them by their legs from ceiling beams or head down into wells, isolating them with sensory deprivation –

---

[7]Signe Landgren-Backstrom, "The Transfer of Military Technology to Third World Countries," in *Bulletin of Peace Proposals,* Vol. 8, No. 2, 1977, pp. 110-120.

[8]Michael T. Klare, op. cit., note 6.

[9]A.J. Langguth, *Hidden Terrors,* New York: Pantheon Books, 1978; Michael T. Klare, *Supplying Repression: U.S. Support for Authoritarian Regimes Abroad,* Washington D.C.: Institute for Policy Studies, 1978, and op. cit., note 6; Carol Ackroyd, Karen Margolis, Jonathan Rosenhead and Tim Shallice, *The Technology of Political Control,* Middlesex: Penguin Books, 1977.

this litany of torture, amply documented by country reports released by Amnesty International, attests to the unity of training.

Training of nuclear power transfer. Ruth Leger Sivard, in World Military and Social Expenditures, 1980, reports:

> Over 500 nuclear power reactors are now in operation or under construction in 39 countries. A large but unrecorded number of research and experimental reactors is also at work. The nuclear arms industry operates through hundreds of labs, factories, transit routes, storage sites, many of them secret. Over 50,000 nuclear weapons are deployed in 24 countries and their dependencies.
>
> This is the nuclear world of 1980, but it is in fact more tightly knit than a map or these numbers can suggest. No region is outside of it.
>
> Since 1945 over 1,200 nuclear tests have been conducted throughout the world, in Africa, the South Pacific, Asia, Europe, and North America . . . [10]

Of the thirty-nine countries with nuclear reactors, seven are in Asia: China, India, Japan, Korea, Pakistan, Philippines and Taiwan.

Regional Cooperation. Regional military cooperation has been part of U.S. Policy in Asia since SEATO. SEATO is gone; but efforts are being exerted to make ASEAN its successor. Joint military exercises have become common among ASEAN nations. Recently, Singaporean and Philippine air force pilots were trained by the U.S. Air Force at Clark Air Base in the Philippines. ASEAN countries also cooperate through exchanges of military information and intelligence, officer training exchanges, arms transfers and standardization of logistics and of some arms.[11] Of special significance, given Japan's renunciation of war, was the latest Rimpac exercise, in which not only the U.S., Australia, and New Zealand, but also Japan took part.

---

[10]Ruth Leger Sivard, op. cit., p. 12.
[11]Ho Kwon Ping and Cheah Cheng Hye, "Five Fingers on the Trigger," *Far Eastern Economic Review,* October 24, 1980, p. 34.

Link Between International
Military and Economic Order

The international military order has obvious consequences on the efforts of Asian peoples to determine their own future. It is also part of – and supports – the existing international economic order. Arms transfers, for example, are not one-shot affairs: arms require spare parts, maintenance, and transfers, so arms transfers result in continuing sales. Arms sales, in fact, are often justified by arms exporting countries as decreasing the cost to them of research and development. In recent years, such research has involved one half of the world's engineers and scientists, and has cost more than U.S. $32 billion annually. Between 80 per cent to 95 per cent of this sum is spent by the super-powers.[12]

Militarization Decapitalizes
Asian Developing Nations

In capitalist developing nations, militarization serves another vital economic function: it helps transfer capital, resources and manpower from Asia to the West.

It does this by creating a "favorable climate" for foreign investment and loans, by keeping wages low, suppressing labor's demands for decent and safe working conditions, eliminating political opposition, engaging in huge infrastructure building programs with borrowed funds, streamlining the bureaucracy (the channels for bribery and corruption), and guaranteeing repatriation of profits. These measures reduce operating costs for transnational corporations and increase their profits, which are then repatriated to the West. Asians pay for these measures in low incomes, in higher taxes, and most important of all, in retarded development because the profits repatriated and resources consumed by the West cannot be used for Asia's development.

Some militarized regimes go even further. Their vast power enables them to direct the organization of their national economies and to control what Adam Smith calls "the surplus part of the product," the excess of what is produced over what is consumed. The wise use of this economic surplus is the real key to a family's prosperity.[13] However, militarized regimes do not organize their

---

[12]Ernie Regehr, *Militarism and the World Military Order: A Study Guide for Churches,* Geneva: World Council of Churches, 1980.

[13]Dudley Dillard, "Capitalism," in *The Political Economy of Development and Underdevelopment,* Charles K. Wilber, ed., New

economies to meet their people's needs; nor do they use the economic surplus for autonomous development. On the contrary, because they depend for survival on foreign governments and foreign capital, rather than on the support of their people and their entrepreneurs, these regimes organize their economies to satisfy the wants of transnationals and needs of Western powers; and share with the latter the surplus extracted from their economies. So militarization becomes the passport that guarantees transnationals and the West access not only to Asian natural resources, labor forces and markets, but also to Asian savings and financial resources. The result is that capital-poor Asia capitalizes capital-rich West.

Philippines An Object Lesson

The Philippines provides an object lesson for the rest of Asia. From 1950 to 1975, for every U.S. $1.00 that U.S. transnationals invested in my country, they borrowed the equivalent of U.S. $8.33 from Philippine banks and financial institutions.[14] During that period, for every U.S. $1.00 they invested, they made a profit of U.S. $3.58, U.S. $2.00 of which were repatriated and U.S. $1.58 re-invested to repeat the cycle of investment-local loan-repatriation-reinvestment.[15] Is it any wonder that, despite the wealth of its resources and the talent of its people, the Philippines remains underdeveloped?

The Trend Towards A Democratic Facade

The situation has not been changed by the recent tendency of military rulers to doff their uniforms and don mufti, as in South Korea, and of militarized regimes to abandon forms of blatant repression and adopt a facade of democracy, as in my country. These moves have little more than deodorant effect for two reasons:

---

[14]Edberto M. Villegas, *Foreign Investments and the Multinational Corporations in the Philippines,* Philippines in the Third World Papers Series, No. 11, Diliman, Quezon City, Philippines: University of the Philippines, August, 1978, p. 3.

[15]Mamoru Tsuda, Rigoberto D. Tiglao and Edith Sangalang Atienza, *The Impact of TNC's in the Philippines: A Summary Report,* Quezon City, Philippines: U.P. Law Center, June, 1978, p. 4.

Reactions Not Actions

First, the moves are not actions but reactions. They are not spontaneous and are not motivated by an authentic desire to restore power to the people. They are calculated responses, more or less forced upon the regimes, to overcome world-wide condemnation of their gross violations of human rights, a condemnation which reduces their prestige in international politics and makes it increasingly difficult for them to get, and for their patron states to give, the aid and loans without which most such regimes would soon collapse. By these moves, the regimes also accommodate themselves to U.S. foreign policy, which the secret Supplement B to U.S. Army Field Manual 30-31 bluntly describes as follows:

> U.S. concern for world opinion is better satisfied if regimes enjoying U.S. support observe democratic processes, or at least maintain a democratic facade. Therefore, a democratic structure is to be welcomed always subject to the essential test that it satisfies the requirements of an anti-Communist posture.[16]

And, the supplement adds, subject to the requirement also that it does not "drift into extreme nationalistic attitudes which are incompatible with or hostile to U.S. interests."[17]

Since the moves towards "democracy" are designed merely to change the appearance of militarization, they cannot be expected to, and in fact do not, change its substance.

Consolidation Of Power
Precedes "Democratization"

Second, force is the only language the military know, and they will not deny themselves its use as long as they feel that their survival is threatened. Militarization rams this reliance on force into politics. Consequently, in spite of world condemnation, militarized regimes use force to seize power; and it is only after they have consolidated their hold over power:

>> Over political power, by pulverizing the traditional

---

[16]W.S., "The Mysterious Supplement B; Sticking it to the Host Country," in *Covert Action*, No. 3 (January 1979), p. 14.

[17]Ibid, p. 14. See also note 5.

opposition, destroying people's organizations, rigging elections, and creating a rubber stamp parliament;

\>> Over legal power, by emasculating the courts, creating military tribunals, and, worse, by enacting laws or amending constitutions to legalize and make ordinary such extraordinary powers as preventive detentions, travel bans, prohibitions on strikes and the like;

\>> Over psychological power, by controlling media and the educational system;

\>> Over physical power, by confiscating arms held by the people; expanding the armed forces; integrating the police into the military; and arming previously brain-washed para-military forces; and

\>> Over economic power, by entering into joint ventures with transnationals to establish key industries; by creating, through decrees, new investment opportunities for themselves, their cohorts, and foreign investors; and by controlling, through state corporations or agencies usually run by loyal retainers or relatives, the country's principal agricultural exports and the basic grains, food processing and marketing industries, and the financial infrastructure of the country-side;

only after all these forms of power have been effectively monopolized – and the war, so to speak, has been won – do militarized regimes sheathe their bayonets. Even then, the regimes do not order the military back to barracks. On the contrary, they keep the military on the alert, ready to fix bayonets again should the people dare question the new face of the old order. Mr. Marcos' recent "termination" of martial law in my country is a classic example of this type of "democratization."

The Consequences of Militarization

To our sorrow, most of us Asians have experienced the militarization of our societies and we know we cannot live with it. But some men of good will, not having experienced militarization, look upon it as a necessary evil if our societies are to develop. So let me spell out the major reasons that impel us Asians to end militarization.

Militarization's Heavy Burden

Militarization puts a back-breaking burden on our poorer societies, among which it is most prevalent. Data for 1977, the most recent available, show the appalling weight of this burden. In that year, twenty developing nations of Asia, communist and non-communist excluding the People's Republic of China, maintained standing armies of 4.85 million men and women. By comparison, the armies of the fifteen NATO nations had a strength of only 4.8 million, and the armies of the seven Warsaw Pact nations, only 4.75 million – and the Asian total does not include the armed forces of Kampuchea for which data are not available.

To maintain these armies, Asian nations spent U.S. $13 billion, 4.4 per cent of their combined gross national product (GNP). This is the same percentage that NATO spent but less than the Warsaw Pact's 8.1 per cent. And Asian states spent less on education, U.S. $8 billion, 2.7 per cent of GNP, and on health, U.S. $2.6 billion, 0.9 per cent of GNP, which are relatively less than NATO's six per cent for education and 4.3 per cent for health, and the Warsaw Pact's 4.6 per cent for education and 2.3 per cent for health.

The military burden was heavier in Asian communist states than in non-communist states: 6.1 per cent to four per cent of combined GNP. On the other hand, communist states spent more on education and health than did non-communist Asian states: 3.9 per cent to 2.7 per cent for education; and 1.4 per cent to 0.9 per cent for health.

Opportunity Costs Of Militarization

What is really important, however, is not that money is spent on the military. Given the present state of the world, some military spending may be, if not necessary, at least arguably prudent. What is important is that every penny spent on the military cannot be spent on anything else. So in nations where the majority of the people are as desperately poor as we are in most of Asia, simple justice and common sense would seem to demand that military spending be pared to the bone, and every available penny used to eradicate poverty.

Take the Philippines again as an example. Some 15,000 people died violently in my country in 1974, perhaps half of them because of clashes between the military and rebel or dissident forces.[18] But in that same year, some 46,000 people died of pneumonia; 31,000 of tuberculosis; 15,000 of avitaminosis and other forms of nutritional deficiency; and 12,500 of malignant neoplasms, all

[18]David K. Whynes, *The Economics of Third World Military Expenditures,* London: MacMillan, 1980, p. 151.

76,500 of causes that could have been prevented or cured.[19] Yet that year, the Philippine government spent only U.S. $3 per capita for health, compared to U.S. $8 per capita for the military.[20] As David K. Whyness says: "The moral is clear: guns kill in more ways than one."[21]

Increasing Burden of Militarization

What is alarming is that, as Whynes shows, in eleven of fifteen Asian countries for which he has compiled data, military expenditures grew from 1971 to 1977 at higher annual rates per capita income. And in seven, military manpower increased annually at higher rates than their population.

The increase in both military spending and military manpower has been specially marked in the five ASEAN nations. In 1975, total Asean military spending was U.S. $2.85 billion. In 1980, it was U.S. $5.47 billion, an increase of 92 per cent. In 1975, ASEAN's regular forces totalled 628,100. In 1980, they had increase 11 per cent to 693,400. An even greater increase in manpower took place in Vietnam, whose regular forces jumped from 700,000 in 1975 to 1,029,000 in 1980, an increase of 47 per cent.[22]

Whether the increase in ASEAN's military forces and expenditures was a response to a similar increase by Vietnam or vice versa is not too important. What is important is that an armaments race is in progress, and no one knows when or how it will end. And while it goes on, the peoples of ASEAN suffer heavier taxes, heightened tension, retarded development and lost chances for a better life.

Violations of Human Rights

These are reasons enough to put an end to militarization, but there are more.

Militarization carries within it a deadly virus that kills human rights. If democracy rests on the premise that it is better to count heads than to break them, militarization proceeds from the premise that it is easier to break heads than to change minds. The very logic

---

[19]NEDA, *1977 Philippine Statistical Yearbook,* Manila: no publisher, 1977, p. 94.
[20]Ruth Leger Sivard, op. cit., note 4, Table III, p. 26.
[21]David K. Whynes, op. cit., note 18, p. 152.
[22]Ho Kwon Ping and Cheah Cheng Hye, op. cit. note 11, p. 34.

of militarization requires prolonged detention without trial (often without charges) of those who dare oppose the regime, torture, unexplained disappearances, murder committed unofficially but officially secretly approved, control of all media of communication, suppression of mass organizations and trade unions, denial of the right of peaceful assembly for redress of grievances, destruction of judicial independence, legislation by decree, and emasculation of popular representation. These violations of human rights are sadly prevalent throughout Asia.

Contempt For The People

Militarization also introduces the hierarchical and paternalistic features of the military structure into politics. That structure assigns the soldier the role of almost automatic obedience, reserving the discussion of strategy and tactics to the officers' corps. So militarization assigns the people the role of silent acquiescence, reserving debate over policy and programs to the governing elite or the ruling party. And just as the military establishment, in exchange for the soldier's unquestioning loyalty, feeds, clothes, and cares for him, so too militarized regimes, in exchange for the people's passivity, promise to feed, clothe, and shelter them.

The promise is often broken, but that is beside the point. The point is that all militarized regimes proclaim themselves defenders of the people against any number of evils: against exploitation by the strong and the rich, incompetence and corruption of traditional politicians, or against the deceptive blandishments of an evil ideology. Yet by assigning the people the role of uncomplaining acceptance of decisions made by others, all militarized regimes betray a profound contempt for the people's capacity to fashion their own destiny.

Militarization Brings Increased Dependence

There are still more reasons for putting an end to militarization, but I shall limit myself to just one more: militarization deepens Asia's dependency. Because it is the military or depends on the military, every militarized regime requires more and newer weapons for its armed forces, even though these weapons may never be used. And because it rules over a developing country, the regime cannot develop or produce the weapons the armed forces want. So it becomes more and more dependent on external supply.

In 1979, for example, in exchange for U.S. $500 million in military aid, the militarized regime of my country assured the U.S. government of "unhampered military operations involving its forces within the Philippines;" worse, it granted the American military the right to "participate in security activities" and "contribute security forces" outside the base areas.[23] These concessions give the United States blanket authority both to involve people in nuclear war and to intervene in our internal affairs. Today we Filipinos live with a loaded gun pointed at our temple – and the finger on the trigger is not a Filipino finger.

One Argument For Militarization

I have heard only one argument that defends the militarization of Asian politics and even that argument is advanced apologetically. Briefly, it is this: that there are so many divisions and centres of power in developing countries that their governments become "soft," and when confronted by the conflicts of interest that economic development produces, become paralyzed. Only the military or militarized regimes, it is argued, possess the discipline and the power to weld the nation together, settle conflicts, enforce decisions, and push the people firmly along the road to development. Nations most often cited as examples to support this argument are Singapore, South Korea and Taiwan, and more recently Indonesia and the Philippines, the last two because of recent high economic growth rates.

Despite its apparent logic, this argument does not hold water.

Economic Growth
Not Economic Development

For 'one thing, it confuses economic growth with economic development. It concentrates on how much is produced and disregards what is produced and who consumes it. More is not always better; and the people cannot eat guns or bullets.

---

[23]*Exchange of Notes Between the Government of the Philippines and the Government of the United States,* January 7, 1979, par. 3; Annex III, par. 6.

Militarized Development
Highly Inequitable

Another flaw is its premise, unspoken but transparent from the examples usually cited, that development comes through locking Asian economies into the existing international economic order. This was, in fact, the explicit proposal of the study that Hla Mynt of London University's School of Economics made for the Asian Development Bank in 1970, a study which has since become dogma for militarized regimes.[24]

Locking domestic economies into the international economic system, however, subjects domestic economies not only to the ups but also to the downs of developed economies. Last year, for example, the Philippine economy grew by only 4.7 per cent, according to official estimates (more realistic estimates put growth at only 3.8 per cent), a rate which the regime, with refreshing candor, admits is "lowest experienced in the 1970's"[25] And South Korea experienced negative growth.[26]

Moreover, the effort required to lock the national economy into the international economic order deflects attention from the important task of seeking solutions to the fundamental problems that afflict most developing nations. So, in most militarized regimes, poverty has worsened, inequality has been aggravated, and discontent increased.

A Case In Point

The Philippine is a case in point. Before our politics became openly militarized by the imposition of martial law, the Philippine situation could be summarized in four cruel paradoxes: a country that was a state but not a nation, formally independent but not sovereign, with a democratic constitution that proclaimed equal freedoms for all but which only a few actually enjoyed, a rich land filled with poor people. Much the same, I believe, could be said of other developing nations of Asia.

After eight years of militarization dedicated to locking the domestic economy into the international economic order, these

---

[24]Hla Mynt, *Southeast Asia's Economy in the 1970's,* Manila: Asian Development Bank, 1970, pp. 24-25, 63-64 and others.

[25]Philippine National Economic Development Authority (NEDA), "The National Income Accounts CY 1978-1980, Advance Estimates as of December, 1980."

[26]Bulletin Today, February 3, 1981, p. 10.

paradoxes have become even sharper.

To lock a national economy into the international economic order requires at least three things: pushing exports, attracting transnational investment, and getting the World Bank-IMF seal of approval for foreign loans. To push exports and attract transnationals, labor must be cheap, docile and easily trained; but since laborers must eat lest their productivity decline, basic staples must also be cheap. So in eight years of militarization, real wages dropped 40 per cent[27] and rice farmers' real incomes, 53.4 per cent.[28] The economy, of course, has grown; but the poor are not only poorer, they are also more numerous. So much for economic progress under militarization.

Much the same could be said of sovereignty. To get the World Bank-IMF seal of approval and borrow money from them and from private foreign banks, the conditions they impose must be accepted. This requires that the economy be kept open not only to foreign investments but also to foreign goods. So tariffs must be reduced, import and exchange restrictions eliminated, and currency devalued. In eight years of militarization, the exchange rate of the Philippine peso has dropped from P6.75 to P7.68 to the U.S. dollar[29] which contributed to raising the consumer price index to its present level of 319 per cent of what it was in 1972;[30] luxuries and non-essential commodities are imported,[31] though the lack of

---

[27]The Central Bank Report for 1980 disclosed that real wages for skilled workers were 63.7 per cent and for unskilled workers 53.4 per cent of what whey had been in 1972.

[28]Bureau of Agricultural Economies Study, 1980, cited in Joel Rocamora, *U.S. Imperialism and the Economic Crisis of the Marcos Dictatorship,* p. 4, paper submitted to the Permanent People's Tribunal, Antwerp, Belgium;

[29]Central Bank Annual Report, 1973, p. 49; *Business Day,* February 20, 1981. As a condition for the IMF standby loan and the IBRD structural adjustment loan, Finance Minister Cesar Virata, in a letter dated August 12, 1980 to the World Bank pledged the Marcos regime to allow the Philippine peso to float freely which means in effect, to devalue the peso.

[30]Extrapolated from the September, 1980 consumer price index of 304.5 reported in NEDA, *Philippine Economic Indicators,* Vol. III, No. II, November 1980, p. 24.

[31]The requirement that the Philippine government remove restrictions on imports is a condition of the structural adjustment loan granted it by the World Bank in August, 1980. See the Report of then World Bank President McNamara, to the World Bank's Board of Governors, dated August 21, 1980, Appendix IV, p. 66.

foreign exchange has increased our external debt 600 per cent;[32] Filipino industries have had to shut down or sell out to transnationals as a result of competing imports, and plans for establishing basic industries have remained pious intentions because tariffs have been reduced. So much for enhanced sovereignty under militarization.

Militarization has not even solved the problems of law and order that were the given reasons for its being. In fact, it cannot do so. Because militarization is inherently repressive, it breeds dissent and resistance. And because it brings impoverishment in its wake, it encourages crime, violence and disorder. Militarization is a self-fulfilling prophecy: it creates the very conditions which "justify" it..

Continuing with the Philippine example: by the regime's own admission, crimes in 1980 were 41 per cent more than in 1971; the crime rate, the number of crimes per person, was 8.5 per cent higher.[33]   And despite claims that it had "neutralized" 3,261 dissidents between 1979 and 1980, the regime admits that the New People's Army – whose armed strength had been estimated at 900 regulars in 1976[34] – had a strength of 2,800 regulars in 1980.[35] Perhaps even more significant, the regime admits that new groups, unknown before martial law, and distinct from the New People's Army and Moslem rebels, have since organized in violent opposition to it.[36]

Ending Militarization

Militarization, then, is a monstrously heavy burden that has worsened the poverty of the peoples of Asia, an unforgivable affront to their dignity – and a failure to boot. It must be ended.

But how?

Let me venture some suggestions which, because of my limited experience, are addressed primarily to capitalist developing countries like my own.

---

[32]Central Bank Report for 1980.

[33]Maj. Gen. Fidel Ramos, "A New Approach to Crime Suppression" in Fookien Times, *Philippines Yearbook 1980*, pp. 84, 86.

[34]Television statement of Pres. Ferdinand E. Marcos, 1976.

[35]Defense Minister Juan Ponce Enrile, "The National Security Situation," in Fookien Times, *Philippines Yearbook 1980*, p. 80.

[36]Ibid., pp. 80, 92.

Need for New Defense Strategy
And New Development Strategy

I know only two ways by which government policies may be changed: the people must change the mind of the government, or change the government.

However, if either step is to prove fruitful, the people should have an alternative policy to adopt. This is particularly true of militarization because, in the present state of the world, defense against external attack seems necessary. To end militarization then, we should evolve an alternative strategy of defense that will not abet militarization.

But militarization is not an isolated phenomenon. It is part of the larger problem of domination, of internal colonialism and imperialism. It is linked to the national and international structures and processes of politics, economics and culture that other papers delivered at this seminar deal with. So, to end militarization, an alternative defense strategy is not enough. We should also evolve a strategy of economic, cultural and political development that complements the alternative defense strategy.

Defense Based On Self-Reliance

What principles should inform such a strategy? The most important, I suggest, is the principle of self-reliance: the alternative defense strategy should be based on the application of native resourcefulness to native resources. A dependent defense system is a contradiction in terms. Dependence implies vulnerability, at least to the foreign power depended upon; and to be vulnerable is to be defenseless. In concrete terms:

(a) Dependence implies importing armaments and the technology of using imported armaments. But, as Mary H. Kaldor points out, technology is a social system; importing the organizational structure, the ways of behavior, and the values of the society that produced the armaments.[37] Dependence thus impairs our national identity, the preservation of which is one of the major functions of defense.

(b) Dependence also requires that our officers be trained by a foreign power. Such training always involves ideological indoctrination, open or subtle; and so creates added vulnerability.

---

[37]Mary H. Kaldor, "The Significance of Military Technology" in *Bulletin of Peace Proposals*, Vol. 8, No. 2, 1977, p. 121.

On this point, the following passage of the Supplement to the U.S. Army Field Manual from which I quoted before is instructive:

> Standing directives to U.S. training establishments require the study of (foreign) officers ... from the point of view of political loyalty; immunity from Communist ideology and their devotion to the democratic ideals of the United States. The Secret Annex to the final training report on each ... (foreign) ... officer passing through a U.S. training programme contains an assessment of his prospects and possibilities as a long-term agent of U.S. Army intelligence.[38]

(c) Dependence reinforces, if it does not cause, militarization. Every militarized regime justifies its seizure of power by some domestic situation or event, but behind all such excuses, as I said above, is the U.S.-U.S.S.R. rivalry for control of the world. El Salvador, for the United States, and Afghanistan, for the U.S.S.R., are current vivid examples of this. I have no doubt that the militarization of Asia received much impetus from the declaration by the United States in the 1950's of eleven "forward defense areas," eight of which are in Asia: Pakistan, India, Thailand, Laos, South Vietnam, South Korea, Taiwan and the Philippines.[39] Nor have I any doubt that militarized regimes in Asia would have crumbled long ago were it not for their links with the international military and economic orders. Parenthetically, that the United States has lost two of its forward defense areas in Asia and one outside Asia (Iran), as the U.S.S.R. has lost its influence over Ethiopia, Somalia and Egypt, shows how inherently bankrupt is the policy of viewing other nations simply as outposts for one's own defense, without regard to the wishes and the welfare of the people of those nations.

If we Asians are to put an end permanently to the militarization of our societies, the new defense strategy we devise must be self-reliant. Otherwise, like colonialism, militarization will rise again.

**Self-Reliant Economic
Development Possible**

A self-reliant defense strategy, however, implies a self-reliant economic development strategy. Can Asia develop its economy

---

[38]W.S., op. cit., note 16, p. 17.
[39]Gavin Kennedy, *The Military in the Third World*, New York: Scribner's, 1974, p. 160, footnote 6.

without relying on either the First World or the Second World? I have no doubt that we can. Twelve years ago, the eminent development economist Sir W. Arthur Lewis categorically said there is no reason why the countries of Asia, Africa, and Latin America should not continue to develop "even if all the rest of the world were to sink under the sea." What we have to do, Sir Arthur pointed out, is gear our industrialization to generating employment, and concentrate our efforts, not on light manufacture, which requires that we import needed machinery, but on establishing our own metal-fabricating industries "which is where employment is really to be found."[40] These propositions were recently echoed by Wassily Leontief in the United Nations study "The Future of the World Economy."[41]

Elements Of New Defense Strategy

Since self-reliant economic development is possible, so, too, is a self-reliant defense strategy. What should such a defense strategy comprise? Johan Galtung, the noted peace researcher, has elaborated twelve strategies he calls NMD, non-military defense, and which can be organized into three groups of four basic strategies each. This is his outline:

    I.   Antagonist oriented defense strategies.

          A.   "Attack should not pay."
              1.   Self-inflicted sabotage.
              2.   Non-cooperation and civil disobedience.
          B.   "Incapacitation of the antagonist."
              3.   Creating empathy.
                  (a) positive interaction before attack;
                  (b) cooperation with the person;
                     non-cooperation with the status.
              4.   Creating sympathy through suffering.

    II. Defense strategies aimed at protecting oneself.

---

[40]W. Arthur Lewis, "Some Aspects of Economic Development," quoted in Geoffrey Barrachlough, "The Haves and the Haves Nots," in the *New York Times Review of Books,* May 13, 1976, p. 8.

[41]Wassily Leonfief, Anne P. Carter and Peter A. Petis, *The Future of The World Economy,* New York: Oxford University Press, 1977, pp. 10-11.

5. Efficient communication inside one's own group
6. Effectively hiding selected people and objects.
7. Decreased vulnerability of the population.
8. Communication and enaction of one's own values.

III.   Defense strategies aimed at deterring the antagonist.

9. Organization of NMD prepared in peacetime.
10. Communication of preparedness through maneuvers.
11. Communication of commitment to NMD.
12. High levels of satisfaction in one's own group.

Galtung stresses that "these strategies must be combined" and "the primary idea is to deter the antagonist so that he does not attack at all; if that fails, the idea is to see to it that his 'attack does not pay' and to 'incapacitate him.'"[42]

Guerrilla Defense Also Needed

Galtung's strategies are sound, but they may not prove sufficient. Unlike Galtung, I am not constitutionally opposed to violence: I believe that violence is justified in self-defense. For this reason, I suggest that one other strategy be added to Galtung's list of defenses against external attack: the use of guerrilla warfare. The Vietnam War has proved, as has the current Afghanistan conflict, first, that against a determined people, superiority in numbers and armaments does not ensure victory; and second, that guerrilla war can make invasion so costly that the game is not worth the candle. The Vietnam War has also proved that guerrilla war buys time to win the sympathy of the invader's own people and paralyze their government's will to continue to fight. True, a similar result had earlier been obtained by Ghandi's *satyagraha*, which did not involve guerrilla warfare, but world conditions are different now. A strategy based on Galtung's non-military defense plus guerrilla warfare would be, I believe, economically less expensive and militarily more effective for developing nations than mantaining a

---

[42]Johan Galtung, *The True Worlds: A Transnational Perspective.* New York: The Free Press, McMillan, 1980, p. 208.

large standing army.

A standing army would still be required, of course, but it need not be large. Only a small contingent of professional soldiers would be needed to train the people in guerrilla tactics and to help maintain their weapons. Its small size would deter it from usurping political power. To minimize that risk, the standing army should be trained to respect not only individual human rights but also the collective rights of the people. Professional soldiers must learn that the government is not the people, and that their loyalty to the government must be subordinated to their loyalty to the people. In any case, a small standing army, faced with a citizenry trained in guerrilla war, would be foolhardy to try to take over the government.

No Need For
Internal Defense

Such a strategy would obviate the need for any strategy of internal security. If militarization were ended, power restored to the people, and a new economic development strategy implemented that provides for people's basic needs, there would be no reason to fear the people and, therefore, no need for internal defense. "Subversion" would find no support from the people, since they hold power and the government is their government. Besides, a people trained in non-military defense and guerilla war against external enemies would be more than capable of dealing with whatever internal security problems agitators may try to stir up.

Controlling
"Intelligence"

Still a word about secret police or intelligence forces would not be superfluous. The ideal would be a world where such organizations are unnecessary; but that seems far away, if not unattainable. As Sun Tzu said, "There is no place where espionage is not used;" and the distinction between external and internal security in intelligence work is blurred and indistinct. There is need then to control such activities, and perhaps the most practical way of doing so would be to place all such organizations under the control of civilian authorities, including representatives of the legal opposition, who will be required to scrutinize their use of funds, place clearly defined limits on what they may do, hold every member strictly accountable for keeping within the limits, and approve all non-routine operations before they are carried out.

People's Organizations Are
The Answer To Militarization

The question remains: how can militarized regimes be demilitarized, so that the alternative defense strategy can be implemented?

Militarized regimes are perched on a three-legged stool: the passivity of the people, the obedience of the armed forces and technocrats, and the support of a foreign power. To end militarization we must cut off at least two of these legs. And if we are not to substitute one tyranny for another, the one leg we must cut off is the passivity of the people, a passivity born of their sense of powerlessness, of the feeling that it is futile to act since a new government may turn out to be as bad or worse than the existing regime.

The answer to militarization, then, is people's organizations. To end militarization, we must, at all risk to ourselves, arouse the people's consciousness not only of the causes of their plight but, equally important, of their power to achieve their goals if they act together; help them organize themselves; and encourage them to invent and to use meta-legal tactics[43] to exert pressure on the regime to demilitarize itself. If that fails, there is always the last resort: revolution.

While helping the people to get organized, we must also seek to cut off foreign support for the regime. Here the tactics Sandinistas used to cut off U.S. and Latin American support for Somoza deserve careful study, although I warn against tie-ups with foreign governments or foreign government-supported organizations, lest we merely substitute dependence on one state for that on another. Here also, links with international non-governmental organizations and like-minded national organizations in other countries are extremely valuable. For creating such links and learning from each other's successes and failures, conferences like this offer rich possibilities.

---

[43]I use *meta-legal* in its two senses: as something beyond the law and as that which underlies the law, not as something against the law. Meta-legal tactics then would be tactics that go beyond normal legal or judicial procedures yet remain faithful to the basis of those procedures in that they unequivocally express the will of the people. Such tactics would include strikes, boycotts, ostracism, confrontation, etc.

Appeal To Military
And Technocrats

Nor should we neglect the military-technocrat partnership.

The military are not just the generals, the colonels and the commanding officers, but also and more importantly the soldiers they command. These soldiers are our countrymen; they are sons and daughters of the people – the poor, the dispossessed and the oppressed – and share the people's hopes and fears, pains and joys; when they are abusive, it is often because they are themselves abused.

Technocrats, as a class, are highly educated and intelligent, and many resent the subordinate positions they occupy vis-a-vis foreigners. Their nationalism can be appealed to and they can be shown that their talents would be better used in the service of the people.

So, if we do our job well, if we can raise our people's consciousness of their power and help them act together in organized, purposeful mass actions, we will create so much doubt in the minds of our soldiers and our technocrats about the legality and morality of what the regime is and of what it is doing, so much sympathy for the people's cause, that they may well refuse to continue to support the regime and the people may never need to resort to the ultimate recourse. The recent example of Iran and the 1973 example of Thailand give substance to this belief.

The Road Is Long
But Must Be Travelled

By the strategy outlined, militarization can be ended. But the road to demilitarization is long and full of pitfalls. And we here present may not reach its end. Yet we must travel this road, whether we like it or not. We must brave its dangers, whether we finish the journey or not. We are not Asians if we believe that what counts is to succeed, and not to acquit ourselves as human beings.

POLITICAL LIFE: ITS PLACE IN FULL HUMAN DEVELOPMENT

A government in which people do not participate is useless; it denies them the right to grow in self-governance and sovereignty.

It is the fashion these days for statesmen of all stripes to insist that political life is essential to full human development, and then to so constrict the scope of political life that it becomes meaningless.

In our country, for example, Marcos argues that:

A philosopher once said that complete humanitas implies civitas, that the fully developed man is necessarily a citizen. The end of human development is citizenship, while the end of all his actions is the political good. And so, to participate in the political process is an inherent responsibility of every citizen--this every Filipino must not only internalize; this he must also exercise. For is it not often said that a people gets a government that it deserves?

Whatever our individual persuasions might be, all of us share a responsibility to get involved in and to utilize the political process to reflect our collective political thinking. We should exercise our right of suffrage in a civic and patriotic spirit without regard to personal selfish ambition. We should recognize that the right of suffrage is no less a fundamental obligation we owe to the nation as it is articulation of the political faith we live by.[1]

Yet in 1978 his government blatantly subverted the right of suffrage of the people of Metro Manila; and for the last seven years, we Filipinos have had no real political life, no meaningful share in determining what the powers of government are, who

---

(Delivered in the Seminar, "A New World Order Among Nations: An Exchange of Views on the Implications of the Mutual Interdependence of Nations in Full Human Development," Cagayan de Oro City, May 23-26, 1979)

[1]Ferdinand E. Marcos. *Five Years of the New Society,* no publisher or place, 1978, p. 186.

should exercise them, and when, for what purposes and for whose benefit they should be exercised.

The situation is the same throughout Southeast Asia and in many parts of the world. The Institute of Southeast Asian Studies of Singapore describes the political situation in Southeast Asia in these depressing words:

> Few major changes took place in the domestic politics of the countries of Southeast Asia. In each state the governing elite has established a more or less authoritarian political structure making it impossible for opposition groups to capture power by constitutional means. Opposition leaders are arrested or absorbed; newspapers are controlled; and potentially independent mass organizations undermined and supervised, when not banned. Elections, when they are held, always take place in circumstances ensuring victory for the government. The main political battle is thus limited to struggle between factions of the governing elite which, whatever their immediate rivalries, have a common interest in preserving and stabilizing the system. In the absence of effective constitutional opposition, the most serious resistance comes from insurgents, both communist and regionalist. Insurgencies of one sort or another are in progress in almost all the countries of Southeast Asia but so far they are essentially major irritants rather than immediate threats to the survival of governments.[2]

It is appropriate therefore that we go back to the basics, that we ask ourselves:

>> Why is political life essential to full human development, and what must political life include in order to be meaningful?

>> What reasons have been given to constrict political life and how valid are these reasons?

>> How do international relations affect political life?

If full human development is -- as I think most will agree -- the optimal development of all that is human in all humans, the bringing to full flower of the native genius of each and of all, then

---

[2]Harold Crouch, "Southeast Asia in 1977: A Political Overview" in *Southeast Asian Affairs 1978*, edited by Kernial S. Sandhu and others, Singapore: Heinemann Educational Books (Asia) Ltd., 1978, pp. 10-11.

there are at least two reasons why political life is essential to full human development.

The first is that, as Aristotle puts it, we are, by nature, political animals. To deny us political life, then, is to deny us the full development of our nature. Why are we political animals? Because we are social animals with a difference. We are social animals because we cannot be born alone and cannot become fully human unless we relate to and communicate with other humans. But our social nature is different from that of ants or bees: we are not, by nature, compelled to relate to each other in set, immutable ways. On the contrary, because we have a sense of what is right and wrong, just and unjust, expedient and inexpedient, and the faculty of speech to communicate our thoughts, our feelings and our will, we have the capacity to determine how our social relations are to be carried out, how, that is, our society is to be governed. It is this capacity that makes us political animals. And it is this capacity that is stultified when we are denied political life.[3]

The second reason is that, whether we are by nature social or political and whether we like it or not, we do live in society and under government. The quality of our life and the extent of our development as human beings depend in large part on the state of the economy of our society; and, as we know by sad experience, economic issues are often resolved politically: for economic life is not merely a network of exchange; it is a network of power;[4] and political power exercised through government is often the strongest of all powers, power that can be and has been used in ways that can threaten human existence itself. A recent example is the decision both to establish a nuclear plant in Bataan and to award the contract for the reactor to Westinghouse. And who can overlook the glaring presence in our society of political entrepreneurs whose only capital is their political power or their proximity to those who wield political power? In a very real sense, politics is "concentrated economics;"[5] so that to deny people's participation in political life is to deny them participation in determining at least the type and direction of their economic life, and so to deny them the opportunity to attain full human development.

---

[3] Aristotle, *Politics*, 1253 a.

[4] F. Perrous, "The Domination Effect and Modern Economic Theory" in *Power in Economics*, edited by K.W. Rothchild, Middlesex: Penguin books, 1971, p. 56.

[5] Attributed to Lenin by Regis Debray, *A Critique of Arms*, Middlesex: Penguin Books, 1977, Vol. 1, p. 185.

In insisting upon political life as essential to full human development, I am not to be understood as insisting that political life is all there is to human development. I insist only that it is essential; I do not say it is enough. There is much more to life than politics; there is faith and love, work and play and leisure, wife and children and home and earning a living; yet, in today's societies, even these are affected by political life. "Everything," Gustavo Gutierrez says, "has a political color. It is always in the political fabric -- and never outside of it -- that a person emerges as a free and responsible being, as a person in relationship with other people, as someone who takes on a historical task."[6]

To those who may believe that preoccupation with political life is of purely western origin, let me cite two examples out of the many available. The first is a lesson from Confucius of particular relevance to our age:

> Tuan-mu Tzu inquired about the essentials of good government.
> "They are these: sufficient food, sufficient armament, and the confidence of the people."
> "Suppose a necessity arose and despite oneself, it was impossible to have all three. Which should be dispensed with first?"
> "Armament."
> "And if one of the remaining two had to be dispensed with?"
> "Food. Everyone has always been subject to death, but without the confidence of the people there would be no government."[7]

The second is from our own Mabini's True Decalogue:[8]

> QUINTO. Procura la felicidad de tu Patria antes que la tuya propia, haciendo de ella el reinado de la razon, de la justicia y

---

[6]Gustavo Gutierrez, *A Theology of Liberation: History, Politics and Salvation*, edited by Sister Caridad Inda and John Eagleson, Maryknoll: Orbis Books, 1973, p. 47.

[7]James R. Ware, tr., *The Sayings of Confucius*, New York: Mentor Books, 1955, pp. 77-78.

[8]Apolinario Mabini, *La Revolucion Filipina*, Manila: Bureau of Printing, 1931, Vol. I, pp. 106-107.

del trabajo; pues si ella es feliz, felices tambien habeis de ser
tu y tu familia.[9]

SEXTO. Procura la Independencia de tu Patria porque tu solo
puedes tener verdadero interes por su engrandecimiento y
dignificacion, como que su Independencia constituye tu propia
libertad, su engrandecimiento tu perfeccion, y su dignificacion
tu propia gloria immortalidad.[10]

SEPTIMO. No reconozcas en tu Patria la autoridad de
ninguna persona que no haya sido eligida por ti y por tus
compatriotas, porque toda autoridad emana de Dios, y como
Dios habia en la conciencia de cada individuo, la persona que
designen y proclamen las consciencias individuales de todo un
pueblo es la unica que puede ostentar la verdadera autoridad.[11]

OCTAVO. Procura para tu pueblo la Republica y jamas la
Monarquia: esta ennoblece a una o varias familias y funda una
dinastia; aquella constituye un pueblo noble y digno por la
razon, grande por la libertad y prospero y brillante por el
trabajo.[12]

What must political life include to become meaningful, to lead
to full, human development? That is a fit subject for a book; but in
outline, most would agree that, if all are to have the opportunity
and the means to fully develop their inborn talents, physical and
spiritual, political life must include at least:

---

[9]Fifth. Thou shalt strive for the happiness of thy country before
thy own, making of her the kingdom of reason, of justice and of
labor for if she be happy, then, together with thy family, thou shall
likewise be happy.

[10]Sixth. Thou shalt strive for the independence of thy country, for
only thou canst have any real interest in her advancement and
exaltation, because her·independence constitutes thy own liberty; her
advancements, thy perfection; and her exaltation, thy own glory and
immortality.

[11]Seventh. Thou shalt not recognize in thy country the authority
of any person who has not been elected by thee and by thy
countrymen: for authority emanates from God, and as God speaks in
the conscience of every man, the person designated and proclaimed
by the conscience of a whole people is the only one who can use
true authority.

[12]Eight. Thou shalt strive for a Republic and never for a monarchy
in thy country, for the latter exalts one or several families and
founds a dynasty; the former makes a people noble and worthy
through reason, great through liberty, and prosperous and brilliant
through labor.

>> The right of every adult citizen not only to express views on the power and policies of government, but to do so in circumstances where one may be listened to by his fellows and those who do exercise those powers;

>> The right to learn the truth about public affairs, which includes the right to listen to the views of those other than in government about those affairs;

>> The right to contain public officials within the limits of their powers;

>> The right to change those who exercise governmental powers;

>> And the right to exercise all these rights peacefully, without risk to one's person, and free from that repressive tolerance that allows dissent only when it is ineffective.

Political life includes much more than these, but if any of these elements is missing, political life is ineffective and meaningless.

Why is it that these rights are so widely denied in practice, both in our country and in other parts of the globe, despite the avowal of all governments that they act for or in the best interests of the people?

The justifications -- or rationalizations, if you will -- are differently worded, but they all sound the same.

For example, Mao Tze Tung insists on the need for "the people's democratic dictatorship" to "consolidate national defense and protect the people's interests . . . [and] . . . to advance towards a socialist and communist society."[13] Marcos insists on the need for "constitutional authoritarianism" for "the institutionalization of the democratic revolution . . . [and] . . . the laying of the legal foundations of the New Society."[14]

The Singaporean elite argues the need for "a three way trade-off between economic growth, individual liberty and nation-building . . to find a right mix of these desirable objectives, often sacrificing a measure of one to get more of another."[15] David Rockefeller's Trilateral Commission warns against "an excess of democracy" because "in many situations, the claims of expertise, seniority, experience and special talents may override the claims of democracy

---

[13]Mao Tze Tung, "On the People's Democratic Dictatorship," in *Selected Works of Mao Tze Tung,* Peking: People's Publishing House, Vol. IV, pp. 417-418.

[14]Ferdinand E. Marcos, *Notes on the New Society of the Philippines,* no publisher or place, 1973, pp. 170-172.

[15]Goh Keng Swee, "A Question of Choice," in *Insight,* May, 1973, p. 35.

as a way of constituting authority;" "the effective operation of a democratic system usually requires some measure of apathy and non-involvement on the part of some individuals and groups;" and "a value that is normally good in itself is not necessarily optimized when it is maximized . . . there are potentially desirable limits to economic growth. There are also potentially desirable limits to the indefinite extension of political democracy."[16]

All these justifications suffer from the same fallacy: paternalism. Whether the argument be that, in this technological age, the problems are so complex that only experts may solve them -- the classic argument for government by technocrats, in itself a derivation from Plato's idol, the philosopher-king -- or that, unless political life is denied temporarily to the "enemies of the people," the people may be deceived, their will, which the State claims to embody, subverted, and their aspirations frustrated -- a variation of the Lockean justification for colonialism from which the justification for "crisis government" is derived -- whatever form the argument may take, I repeat, it rests on the same premise that the people are not capable of exercising the prudence and judgment needed to protect themselves from deception because they are, as a Filipino political scientist says, "by and large, political innocents;" in short, that although adults, the people are still politically children who need a strong, wise, prudent father, whose thoughts must guide their lives.

There are at least two things wrong with this argument. First, it is unjust, under any circumstance, to treat adults as though they were children; and to do so stunts their development. Second, neither government by technocrats nor crisis government works, as our continuing experience with martial law has amply proved.

Let me add a few words on government by technocrats. No one has castigated technocrats more severely than L. Costa Pinto, the Brazilian sociologist. Out of the anguish of his experience with the Brazilian model -- the same model that, with some overtones from the Chinese model, Marcos is foisting on our people -- L. Costa Pinto wrote:

---

[16]*The Crisis of Democracy,* as quoted by Craig S. Karpel, "Who Runs Jimmy Carter?," *Oui,* September, 1977, p. 127.

The technocrat is a specialist in the manipulation of means, who was born to be commanded and dies desiring to be the "eminence gris" of those who command. He serves anyone and solves any problem as long as he is given the key to the solution. He is more arrogant and sophisticated than the old type bureaucrat, but cultivates the same vocation of being a human tool. Not even if they had invented them for the role of sargeants without uniform could the military have found a mental and social type more adequate for that role than the civilian technocrat.

In fact, there is much in common between the technocrat and the new type military. Both are products of the first stages of our development; both are interested in changing the stereotyped image of the social types that historically preceded them: the civilian technocrat is the most unregenerate critic of the liberalistic "thinker" and rhetorician of the past, and the military technocrat of the "pajama general," whom folklore ironically describes as the man who wakes up early every day to do nothing. Both, convinced of that collection of logical half-truths that impedes seeing the whole truth, display the inhuman and mechanistic angles of efficiency, of organization, and of discipline; and have as implicit models the totalitarian centralization of the garrison State of which Harold Lasswell spoke, in which, at the end, what decides is the computer and what imposes order is institutionalized violence that dispenses with debate and cannot be questioned because it is revealed and imposed from the mountain to the plain.[17]

Costa Pinto is not the first to denounce government by technocrats. Three hundred years before Christ, the mythical Chinese sage Lao Tzu said:

> Get rid of the wise men!
> Put out the professors!
> Then people will profit
> A hundredfold over.[18]

---

[17]L.A. Costa Pinto, *Nacionalismo y Militarismo,* Mexico: Siglo xxi Editores, Sa., 1972, pp. 77-79.

[18]Lao Tzu, *The Way of Life,* translated by R.B. Blakney, New York: Mentor, 1955, p. 71.

One need not go so far as either Costa Pinto or Lao Tzu. It is enough to point out that technocrats may be experts in means, in know-how: they are not necessarily experts in ends, in know-what. In deciding what are the proper ends of government and what is best for himself and his fellowmen, every man not mentally retarded or deranged is as expert as the most expert of technocrats. In fact, though he may know less about things, he probably knows more things: for the more expert the technocrat, the more specialized he becomes, the more he learns about less. And, frankly, as one who has suffered the consequences of the expertise of our technocrats for almost seven years, I have little reason to trust their prudence, much as I may admire their technique: for I find myself, as do the vast majority of our people, worse off today than seven years ago.

Let me turn now to the theory of "crisis government." Here I would like to stress that "crisis government" is the first cousin of the "white man's burden;" and just as the "white man's burden" was used to justify external colonialism, so "crisis government" is being used to justify internal colonialism.

Consider McKinley's famous rationalization of his decision to colonize our country:

> . . . that we could not leave them to themselves -- they were unfit for self-government -- and they would soon have anarchy and misrule over there worse than Spain's was; and that there was nothing left for us to do but to take them all, and to educate the Filipinos, and uplift and civilize and Christianize them, and by God's grace do the very best we could by them, as our fellowmen for whom Christ also died . . . [19]

Isn't this hauntingly similar to Marcos' rationalization of "crisis government" as necessary not only to save our society, but to reform it; and once reforms are institutionalized, there will be "not only . . . political normalization but also . . . restoration of political power to its rightful owners, the people?"[20]

---

[19]Garel A. Grunder and William E. Livezey, *The Philippines and the United States,* Norman: University of Oklahoma Press, 1951, p. 37; and Thomas R. McHale, "The Development of American Policy Toward the Philippines," *Philippine Studies,* Vol. 9, No. 1 (January 1961), p. 49.

[20]Ferdinand E. Marcos, *Five Years of the New Society,* op. cit., p. 170.

Yet after forty-eight years of American colonialism, when independence finally came in 1946, were we any better prepared to govern ourselves than our forefathers had been in 1898? If we were, was it because of American tutelage or in spite of it? If we grant that Marcos declared martial law in good faith and without thought of personal advantage -- which is granting a lot more than seems reasonable -- we can come to only one conclusion about our capacity for self-government: that we did not acquire it under American tutelage; if we had, there would have been no reason for declaring martial law. Yet if we did not learn enough in the forty-eight years that we were an American colony to become fit to govern ourselves, is it reasonable to expect us to learn to reform ourselves no matter how long we remain a Marcos colony? The basis of crisis government is martial law: and martial law, Marcos has said, connotes command and coercion.[21] Can people be coerced into reforming themselves? Seven years of coercion and command have gone by, and corruption in government, which martial law pledged to stamp out, has become worse.[22]

In this roundabout way, I hope I have made two points clear:

One, neither government by technocrats nor crisis government leads to full human development because, like the external colonialism they internalize, neither allows men to govern themselves; and men cannot learn to govern themselves except by governing themselves. One can learn to swim only by going into water.

Two, crisis government, with its connotations of coercion and command, cannot reform society. Reform implies conversion; but men cannot be converted by force or command. If men could be reformed by these means, then prisons would be ideal reformatories -- and we know they are not. And what is society under crisis government but a prison without walls?

This brings me to the last question that the subject of our seminar evokes: how would the "mutual interdependence of nations" affect political life? I say would because the "mutual interdependence of nations" -- the global society of nations all equal in rights, where none tries to control another, and all exchanges of goods and values are equal and just -- is still a hope in search of fulfillment, a dream aspiring to become reality.

---

[21] Ferdinand E. Marcos, *Notes on the New Society in the Philippines,* op. cit., p. vii; *Five Years of the New Society,* op. cit., p. 169.
[22] Ferdinand E. Marcos, *Five Years of the New Society.* p. 187.

What does exist is a world divided into two 'blocs': the capitalist bloc headed by the United States and the Socialist bloc headed by Russia, with China linked to but not in the capitalist bloc; each bloc seeking to expand or at least prevent the other from expanding; and both keeping a precarious peace mainly because each knows the other can obliterate it.

Each bloc holds itself together by a system of differing degrees of domination and dependence. Sometimes domination takes blatant forms: show of force, open intervention, invasion, occupation. Normally, however, domination is exercised more subtly, yet nonetheless effectively, by the process known popularly as neo-colonialism, the key to which is the congruence of interests between the ruling elite of the dominant power and the ruling elite of the dominated nation, at the expense of the people of both nations, but more so of the people of the dominated nation.

On the political life of the latter, such domination produces disastrous effects. First, it deprives them of the power to make ultimate decisions on the kind of government, economy and society they believe is best for them: nothing that would impair the interests of the dominant power is allowed. Second, it perpetuates inequality in wealth, prestige and power: for without such inequality an elite could not exist in the dominated nation, and without an elite, there would be no neo-colonialism. Third, it produces a sense of inferiority, a feeling of impotence that converts the people of the dominated nation into a supplicant people who not only bend their knees but their minds, and whose politics are the politics of patronage and bribery. Fourth, it alienates them from their own culture, even to the point where, as in the Philippines, we do not communicate with one another in our own language, and celebrate our defeats, rather than our victories. Fifth, it makes it more difficult for the people of the dominated nation to liberate themselves: for they must struggle not only against internal but also against external forces of domination.

The Philippines provides an almost perfect example of the effects of the five types of neo-colonialism: political, military, economic, cultural, and communications; but there is neither time nor space to explore that subject here.

Here I can point out only if a new world order of equal interdependence among nations were ever achieved and if domination by one nation over another abolished, full human development would still require the people of the once dominated nations to free themselves from their internal structures of domination to enjoy a truly meaningful life in all its aspects: political, cultural and economic. Indeed, unless they do so before or simultaneously with the birth of the new world order, the latter would be stillborn.

One last word.

Because of the academic setting of your seminar, I have tried -- though not always successfully -- to keep the discussion of political life on an essentially abstract, theoretical level.

But politics is concrete and eminently practical.

Above all, political life is action -- people's action.

FOREIGN POLICY AND PHILIPPINE-AMERICAN RELATIONS: PAST AND PRESENT

An absorbing account of Philippine Foreign Policy from the 50's through the 60's to the 70's, its major feature being the mendicancy and subservience of our foreign policy process to the U.S. Even our posturings against imperialism, while pleading to Third World associates to act with reason and moderation, help the U.S. maintain its hegemony in the Asian region. Nowhere is the subservience more manifest than in the continued presence of the U.S. military bases in our territory.

"In the context of realities, the real issue posed by these bases is whether they are to remain or not."

The United States and Third World Diplomacy

Foreign policy is a powerful tool in the hands of a government determined to enhance the nation's progress and security. England is the outstanding example of an island nation whose once commanding position in the world was due in large part to the adroitness of her foreign policy and the skillful diplomacy of her government.

For our purposes, however, the United States offers the more relevant example. Once herself a developing nation like the Third World countries of today, "an agrarian republic in a revolutionary age," carved out of a continent where the super-powers of her time, France, England and Spain, extended their struggle for world supremacy, the United States adopted, from the beginning, a foreign policy of independence, neutrality and non-alignment. Through this policy, she was able to steer clear and remain aloof from international power politics and to concentrate on nation building during her formative and critical years. In 1805, she carried out one of the most dramatic coups in diplomatic history: the Louisiana Purchase which, in one stroke, doubled her territory and laid the basis for her phenomenal rise as a continental power. In explaining how President Jefferson succeeded in acquiring the

(Paper written for the Civil Liberties Union of the Philippines, February 8, 1977.)

Louisiana territory, which embraced the land mass comprising the Missouri and Mississippi Valleys, Walter Lippmann recalls:

> The famous words are "peace, commerce and honest friend-ship with all nations, entangling alliances with none." Shortly after this disavowal of entangling alliances, Jefferson performed the diplomatic feat of buying the Louisiana territory from Napoleon Bonaparte. He seized a golden opportunity which was presented to him because France and Great Britain were at war. Jefferson, having no entangling alliance, did in fact negotiate with both powers, and he used his neutral position to make a bargain which brought into the union the Mississippi and Missouri Valleys.[1]

In pursuing a non-aligned course, Jefferson simply followed the foreign policy established by his predecessor, America's first president. George Washington had proclaimed America's neutrality in 1793, and, in his Farewell Address, explained the rationale for a neutral, non-aligned policy. Written in 1796, almost two hundred years ago, that document remains a classic formulation of the case for non-alignment and neutrality in the foreign policy of developing nations, and the relevant portions are well worth quoting for their applicability to Philippine conditions which special relations with America have brought about.

So, likewise, a passionate attachment of one nation for another produces a variety of evils. Sympathy for the favorite nation, facilitating the illusion of an imaginary common interest in cases where no real common interest exists, and infusing into one the enmities of the other, betrays the former into a participation in the quarrels and wars of the latter without adequate inducement or jus-tification. It leads also to concessions to the favorite nation of privileges denied to others, which is apt doubly to injure the nation making the concessions by unnecessarily parting with what ought to have been retained, and by exciting jealousy, ill-will and a dis-position to retaliate in the parties from whom equal privileges are withheld; and it gives to ambitious, corrupted, or deluded citizens (who devote themselves to the favorite nation) facility to betray or sacrifice the interests of their own country without odium, some-times even with popularity, gilding with the appearances of a virtuous sense of obligation, a commendable deference for public

---

[1] Walter Lippmann, *Public Opinion and Foreign Policy in the United States,* p. 18.

opinion, or a laudable zeal for public good the base or foolish compliances of ambition, corruption, or infatuation.

As avenues to foreign influence in innumerable ways, such attachments are particularly alarming to the truly enlightened and independent patriot. How many opportunities do they afford to tamper with domestic factions, to practice the arts of seduction, to mislead public opinion, to influence or awe the public councils! Such an attachment of a small or weak nation toward a great and powerful nation dooms the former to be the satellite of the latter ... Real patriots who may resist the intrigues of the favorite are liable to become suspected and odious, while its tools and dupes usurp the applause and confidence of the people to surrender their interest.[2]

It is fitting to recall the beginnings and original nature of American foreign policy in order to better and more fully appreciate that independence, neutrality and non-alignment, which the United States has consistently opposed in contemporary developing countries since the last world war, are in fact the only logical and rational option for young and comparatively weak nations faced with the problem of survival in an age of big power rivalry. If the United States found it imperative for her survival to be non-aligned and neutral in the European power struggles of the 18th century, what more for developing countries today caught in the crossfire of nuclear adversaries? This is the option understandably adopted by most of today's developing states, led by India, Yugoslavia, Algeria and Sri Lanka, who comprise more than half the world's population.

Twentieth century neutralists, preeminent of whom are Nasser, Nehru, Tito and Gandhi are now legends and by-words for the astute, non-aligned diplomacy they have conducted on behalf of their respective nations and peoples. They have demonstrated that economically underdeveloped nations can be strong through the unyielding independence of their international position; that a non-aligned nationalistic foreign policy when honestly pursued by leaders of incorruptible integrity, can tap the wellspring of deep and fervent popular support, and thereby galvanize a people into dynamic self-reliance and national unity, the indispensable requisites for political stability and economic development.

---

[2]George Washington, "Farewell Address," in Richard B. Morris, *Great Presidential Decisions,* Philadelphia: J.B. Lippincott Co., 1965, pp. 43-44.

Non-aligned countries have been the recipients of sizable economic favors and assistance from contending parties in the ideological war, without relinquishing their national identity and sovereignty.

Philippine Foreign Policy:
Alignment, Dependence and Subservience

In contrast with Third World diplomacy, however, Philippine foreign policy, from the beginning, has been one of alignment, dependence and subservience. From our inception as a republic, we not only aligned with, but tied ourselves to, the United States economically and militarily, and did so under conditions which made a sham of our sovereignty. To be sure, we were coerced into this by the United States, who exploited the ravaged condition of our post-war economy: but too many among our political and economic leadership yielded to that coercion only too easily and willingly, accepting it as necessary -- and even desirable.

The Formative Years: 1946-1949

In the formative years following our independence, we entered into a package of agreements that made our foreign policy simply an extension of United States foreign policy in the Pacific: The Bell Trade Act extended the system of free trade, which had molded our economic relations with the United States into one of exploitative dependence and prevented us from industrializing. Worse, it gave American nationals and American goods a preferred status in our economic system and international commerce. The Military Bases and related agreements, on the other hand, drew the Philippines within America's defense perimeter, a magnet designed to attract the nuclear fire of America's adversaries away from her mainland shore, as the late Claro M. Recto repeatedly pointed out during his lifetime. In addition, the agreements made us totally dependent on the United States as our sole external source of arms, equipments and military "advisers," and relinquished the nation's sovereignty over the sizable areas covered by the bases.

These agreements not only aligned us economically and militarily with a super-power, but insured that our relations with it would be relative of total subservience and dependence. They were to determine the nature and goals of our foreign policy as a supposedly sovereign nation; bring us to the brink of nuclear war; isolate and alienate us from the Third World community, particularly our Asian neighbors; create a deep and traumatic division in our national life; and involve us in the criminal adventure of America in Vietnam, an act documented as one of the most barbaric and savage ever inflicted by a nation against an entire people.

Philippine Foreign Policy in the 1950s: Recto's Role

Having established the basis for its alignment and subservience during the critical years 1946-1949, the Philippine government entered the decade of the fifties with a foreign policy described so aptly by Claro M. Recto as "mendicant." The voting record of the Philippine delegation to the United Nations was predictably "American," unquestioningly trailing the position of the U.S. government on virtually every issue of significance. As Recto charged:

> Our foreign policy was conducted from the very beginning, and is being pursued, on the erroneous assumption of an identity of American and Filipino interests, or more correctly, of the desirability, and even the necessity of subordinating our interests to those of America.[3]

"Thus," he continued --

> On the fourth of July, 1946, it was announced that our foreign policy would be to follow in the wake of America. We have, indeed, followed. We followed America out of Spain and back again: we followed America in her aimless pilgrimage in the Holy Land, from Jew to Arab and Arab to Jew, as the American need for Arab oil and the American administration's desire for Jewish votes dictated: we recognized the independence of Indonesia when America did, and not one moment before. In the world parliament of the United Nations, it is no more difficult to predict that the Philippines will vote with the American Union than that the Ukraine will vote with the Soviet Union. American policy has found no more eloquent spokesman and zealous advocate, and Russian policy no louder critic and more resourceful opponent, than the Philippines. Americans may disagree violently with their

---

[3]Claro M. Recto, *Our Mendicant Foreign Policy*, April 17, 1951.

own foreign policy, but it has no better supporters than the Philippines.[4]

The Formosa Resolution

That mendicancy was vividly demonstrated when, in 1955, the Magsaysay administration, backed by our Senate, gave its blind support to the Formosa Resolution of the American Senate. Under that resolution, the United States government, at the plea of Chiang Kai-Shek, pledged that it would defend the offshore islands of Quemoy and Matsu against any claim or assertion of sovereignty by mainland China. The U.S. government prevailed upon the Magsaysay administration to endorse and support the Formosa Resolution. These islands were generally regarded, by the Western and Asian allies of the United States, as properly belonging to mainland China. They were certainly not a part of Philippine territory, nor of any relevance to our national security. The U.S. pledge to defend Quemoy and Matsu was deemed necessary by the American State Department only for the purpose of sustaining the morale of Chiang Kai-Shek, who saw in those islands a necessary stepping stone to his imaginary invasion of the Chinese mainland.

Recto immediately saw the military implications to the Philippines of its support of the Formosa Resolution. Should the U.S. government engage the People's Republic of China in a nuclear war over the defense of Quemoy and Matsu, Philippine support of that Resolution could automatically drag Filipinos into a nuclear war over foreign territory which, although important to the mental condition and emotional stability of Chiang, had no relevance whatsoever to Philippine security, much less any connection with Philippine territory.

That the State Department actually contemplated the use of nuclear weapons against mainland China had the latter asserted its claim over the offshore lands, has been confirmed in a recent biography of John Foster Dulles, then America's Secretary of State. In what is considered a classic biography of Dulles, the following narration appears:

> But Dulles was not too engaged as political advocate and tactician to see the matter with detachment. He accepted Taipei's argument of linkage. Therefore, as he saw it, the only

---

[4]Ibid.

way out of the deepening dilemma was to apply more pressure -- to force the Chinese Communists to back down by threatening the use of nuclear weapons. "If we defend Quemoy and Matsu," he further told Eisenhower, "we'll have to use atomic weapons."[5]

Philippine support of the Resolution was a crystal clear illustration of the suicidal blindness with which our foreign policy followed in "the wake of America."

Recto waged a massive and scholarly assault in the Senate against the Resolution. Although the Magsaysay administration eventually had its way, Recto's espousal served as an invaluable contribution to the development of public awareness that something was fundamentally wrong in the way the nation's foreign policy was being conducted. In the course of his opposition to Philippine support of the Formosa Resolution, Recto gave Filipinos our first major concrete insight into the nuclear implications of the Philippine-American alliance.

The Premature Recognition of the Diem Government

But it was over the issue of the premature recognition of the Diem government that Recto's prophetic insight into Asian affairs demonstrated itself with a timeless quality. In 1955, he took to the floor of the Senate to assail an announcement of the Magsaysay administration concerning its plan to recognize the Diem government of South Vietnam. It was a move obviously directed and inspired by the State Department in an effort to secure international support for one of her Southeast Asian puppets, in whose assassination the CIA would later be involved when Diem outlived his usefulness, and to seal South Vietnam's violation of the Geneva Agreement.

Recto took the floor to show that any move to recognize Diem's regime at that time was premature and could embroil the Philippines in Vietnam's internal affairs. Among his arguments were that Diem did not command the support of the South Vietnamese, that his regime was illegitimate and "founded on usurped authority." The details of Recto's arguments need not concern us here, but what is noteworthy is the fact that the apprehensions he expressed in 1955 were materially fulfilled and vindicated by later events.

---

[5]Hoopes, *The Devil and John Foster Dulles*, p. 277.

The two closing paragraphs of his Senate speech on the issue more than speak for themselves. As early as that time, in 1955, he already anticipated the debacle of Diem and the eventual involvement of the Philippines in an Asian war, provoked by "power politics and international intrigue." He warned then:

Asians as Sacrificial Victims

I find also good reasons to believe that we were pressed into recognizing Diem's government in order to legalize and continue the training of Vietnamese military officers by our army which has been secretly going on at Camp Murphy, and to justify Diem's request for sanctuary for his exiled government should his government fall or South Vietnam be invaded by Ho Chi Minh's army. Diem's American-backed regime is facing a three-cornered threat: from the Vietminhs, from the belligerent "sects," and from the same powerful clique, the Revolutionary Junta, that helped him into power but which now may drive him out because of his refusal to reform his government according to the demands of the Junta. Indeed, as I see it, our government is again courting unnecessary trouble by interfering in the civil war of a neighboring country, thru military aid given in the form of training of South Vietnamese army officers, and by encouraging Diem in his stand of frustrating the plebiscite under the Geneva Agreement.

Time and again, I have consistently opposed dangerous and provocative entanglements, such as these, because they distract our attention from our own local problems, which are of the gravest and most urgent, because they dissipate our already limited strength and energy which we need so much to establish our political, social and economic security, and because we expose thereby our people to the fearful consequences of another war, a war which will be fought on Asian soil with only expendable and bewildered Asians for sacrificial victims on the altar of power politics and international intrigue.[6]

---

[6]Claro M. Recto, *My Crusade,* Manila: Pio C. Calica & Nicanor Carag, Publishers, 1955, p. 122.

Recto on Other Issues
of Foreign Policy

Recto did not confine his policy pronouncements to occasions when he took a dissenting position on particular issues provoked by specific acts of the government. For a full decade he converted his life into a full time crusade against the colonial structure of Philippine-American relations, insisting that it be replaced with one reflective of the people's interests, concern for their security, solidarity with Asian countries and respect for the nation's sovereignty. He was a strong and early advocate of trade and diplomatic relations with the socialist countries. More than anyone, he exposed the anti-developmental nature of our foreign economic policy as expressed in our acceptance of the Bell Trade Act and the Laurel-Langley Agreement. He spoke repeatedly on the question of military bases, pointing out the mortal danger that they posed to our national security, and persistently demanding that our government assert its sovereignty over them.

Although the decade of the fifties witnessed the manifestation of the nation's alignment and subservience in such humiliating specifics as the Formosa Resolution, our accession to SEATO, the premature recognition of Diem's regime and the ratification of the Laurel-Langley Agreement, that decade also witnessed the steady and unrelenting development of anti-imperialist thought which flowed out of Recto's Philippines. The dialectics of Philippine-American relations in fact worked itself in the process of Recto's herculean struggle against the orthodoxy of his time, in his scholarly expose of the unreal premises and treasonous workings of special relations, in his defiance of Presidents, in his debates with the small, opportunistic and vicious brown Americans whom the U.S. Embassy pitted and unleashed against him, and who populated Congress and the Department of Foreign Affairs.

For his patriotic struggle against American imperialism in the fifties, Recto was ousted by the Magsaysay administration from the Nacionalista Party. The move was palpably CIA-inspired, designed to kill Recto's political carrer and the nationalist awakening he embodied.

The purpose of recalling Recto's role in the fifties is to remind ourselves that the seeds of what today has been self-servingly described as an "innovative" and "independent" foreign policy, were planted by the man whom the political gods of his time sought to destroy. The rhetoric of today's "independent" foreign policy is a virtual plagiarism lifted from Recto's foreign policy pronouncements by the very people who attacked him and the very ideas he espoused, or who maintained a callous silence in the midst of Recto's struggles. One only has to recall the bitter exchanges between Recto and Romulo, whom Recto considered the principal instrument of the Americans, in the course of their foreign policy debates to realize the ironic twist of today's events.

As then Secretary of Foreign Affairs, Romulo would rhetorically ask in the course of his attack on Recto:

> Is it desirable that a small nation like the Philippines should cling to the shadowy kind of independence at the risk of losing the only strong friend and ally we have in the world?[7]

The entire premise of Philippine foreign policy may be found in the assumptions implicit in Romulo's question, and the way he obviously intended that question to be answered.

To Romulo, America was a real friend and ally, and any attempt at independence on the part of the Philippines could at most be "shadowy."

Any foreign policy structured on such a premise could not be anything but mendicant.

As Constantino would narrate, "observing the fawning attitude of Romulo towards Americans, Recto marveled at the man's temerity in presenting himself as an independent-minded, patriotic Filipino. Recto in attacking Quirino had flushed out the one individual he had all along suspected of being a principal instrument of the Americans, and with great pleasure cut him down to size and exposed him for history."[8]

The "independent" stand which the Department of Foreign Affairs has assumed today is certainly a far cry from its traditional posture, particularly that of the Foreign Affairs Secretary who, during his debates with Recto, saw nothing wrong that the United States can do, nothing good that can come out of dealing with the socialist community, and nothing much that can result from closer ties with the Third World. Secretary Dulles, who condemned as immoral the doctrine of non-alignment and neutrality postulated by Nehru of India, could not have found a more zealous supporter than our Foreign Affairs Secretary during those cold war years.

---

[7] For an extensive narration of the Recto-Romulo debates, see Renato Constantino, *The Making of a Filipino*, Quezon City: Malaya Books Inc., 1969.

[8] Ibid., pp. 161-162.

In the last part of this paper, we shall examine the current "independence" and "nationalism" of our nation's foreign policy, but before we do so, let us review how our foreign policy fared during the decade of the sixties.

Philippine Foreign Policy in the 1960s

Foreign policy in this decade was dominated by one traumatic issue. That was Vietnam, and our involvement in that tragedy through Philcag. Much was made at that time of the claim that Philcag was a non-combat contribution of the Philippines to America's war in Vietnam, but, whether non-combat or not, the fact is that, through Philcag, we became a direct and active accomplice in America's aggression against fellow-Asians, an act which U.S. Secretary of State Cyrus Vance now admits was a "mistake" and which world opinion had long ago condemned as criminal. It fulfilled the stark apprehensions of Recto when he counselled against the premature recognition of Diem's regime.

Initiated by the Macapagal administration, Philcag provoked a bitter national debate and major demonstrations against the United States Embassy and President Johnson. President Marcos, in his campaign for the presidency in 1965, pledged to withdraw Philippine involvement in Vietnam, but within 24 hours of his election, he reversed his pledge and proceeded to expand Philippine participation, with American money.

The Philcag issue demonstrated the lowest depth of puppetry to which our foreign policy can descend and earned us nothing but the contempt of the non-aligned Third World with which we now seek frantically to identify ourselves. By refusing to take an independent stand on Vietnam during those years, Philippine foreign policy forfeited a brilliant opportunity to demonstrate at least its potential and capacity for independence. It involved us in America's savage aggression against an Asian people whose only crime was to insist on the integrity of their independence against American imperialism.

With the foregoing historical background of Philippine foreign policy in mind, we now turn to an evaluation of the nation's foreign policy in the decade of the 1970's.

Contemporary Foreign Policy
in Action -- Its "Innovativeness"
and "Independence"

Beginning with 1970, particularly with the advent of martial law, the myth has been assiduously cultivated that Philippine foreign policy has, finally, shed off its longstanding subservience to the United States and taken on a Rectonian direction.

The martial law government's claim to "innovativeness" and "independence" is anchored on three developments. These are (1) the establishment of trade and diplomatic relations with the socialist countries; (2) official identification with the aspirations of the Third World, particularly the demand for a new international economic order; and (3) the government's assertion of Philippine sovereignty over the U.S. bases.

This is a claim, however, that completely collapses when examined in the light of the nation's domestic policy and changed international realities. For the truth is, and this is the central thesis of this paper, that the "bold" and "innovative" moves taken by the Department of Foreign Affairs, which it passes off for "independence" are in fact the latest variation of its traditional subservience to America's global interests.

The character of a nation's foreign policy starts with its domestic policy. As Recto reminded us, a nation's foreign policy is only an extension of its domestic policy.

Export-orientation and Diplomatic
Relations with Socialist
and Third World Countries

The decision to establish trade and diplomatic relations with the socialist countries did not stem from any qualitative change in the government's view of how foreign policy should be conducted. Relations with the socialist world, particularly China, were dictated by the logic of the nation's colonial export-oriented development program and the requirements of the multinational companies who see in the Philippines an ideal "export platform" for their operations in Asia. There simply would have been no point in an export-oriented development policy if the country's foreign policy continued to prohibit trade with socialist economies.

Philippine decision to adopt an export-oriented development program in turn was evidently dictated by a shift in the strategic thinking of the Nixon administration. In the late sixties, multinational corporations began to perceive the futility of the

Vietnam war and the need to resume normal relations with China. This was dramatized by Nixon's trip to China in 1971. The American decision to normalize relations with China in turn was dictated by the requirements of America's multinational companies, and the American economy itself which was then facing a deepening recession. In fact, the devaluation of the dollar at about that time signaled a decline in the American economy and the need to expand American exports at all costs. In this drive, the Philippines, as an export base, would play a critical role. As early as 1971, this had already been perceived by political economists of the nationalist school, and the following analysis, made at that time, is relevant:

. . . the recent decision of the U.S. government to capture the China market means that America will have to intensify its hold and control over Philippine policies in order that these policies may serve the imperatives and requirements of America commercial interests. These are interests fighting desperately for survival and who see in the vast China market one possible source of escape from the profound dilemma that confronts the American economy today. The American economy has been in a deep recession these last several years, and this threatens to evolve into another Great Depression. Ironically, the U.S. government is now forced to look to Communist China as a factor that might possibly save the American economy from a tragic collapse.

Our government which has demonstrated unprecedented servility to American demands, even if these demands are directed against the very interest of our people, may now be expected to intensify further its so-called export-oriented approach to economic development, open the country to multinational companies which would exploit cheap Filipino labor and resources in order to produce goods for export, and pursue policies, such as tight credit, which incapacitate Filipino entrepreneurs from making use of domestic labor and resources to produce goods for the consumption of our own people.

This is the new colonialism, as dictated by the contemporary requirements of the American economy, and as reflected in the dramatic turn of American policy in Asia.

We are witnessing today, in a magnified scale, the reproduction of the very considerations that resulted in our colonization at the turn of the past century.

American imperialism in the Philippines has entered a new stage.[9]

This is not to argue against diplomatic relations with the socialist world, but what this paper points out is that the decision to establish such relations certainly did not stem from any heroic aspiration to independence on the part of the Martial Law government. On the contrary, such a seemingly "bold" and "innovative" act, when viewed in the context of the nation's colonial domestic policy and changed international realities, is easily seen as the latest variation of our government's traditional subservience to the pragmatic changes in American global objectives.

As was wryly observed in a book, published in 1974, dealing with global corporations and the economic motivation underlying the shift in U.S. policy towards socialist countries:

> Even before President Nixon had arrived in Peking, soft drink manufacturers were speculating in print what it would mean to sell China's 800 million just one Coke a week.[10]

As that well-documented book points out, explaining the shift in U.S. policy towards the socialist countries:

> In the 1960's, the ground rules of the revolution changed radically. The United States, it turned out, lacked the power to eliminate socialist enclaves within the global market, even in such a weak and obscure place as South Vietnam, and the 20-year attempt to do so had disastrous consequences for the American economy. At the same time, all hopes were abandoned of overturning the socialist revolutions in Russia and China through military pressure. These shattered hopes were replaced by new hopes of integrating the workers and peasants of Russia and China into the new global economy.[11]

The Philippines, a rich source of cheap labor and raw materials, with its export-oriented development program and an investment

---

[9]Alejandro Lichauco, "Dollar Devaluation: New Design on the Philippines," published in *Graphic*, Vol. XXXVIII, No. 14, September 8, 1971, p. 8.

[10]Richard J. Barnet and Ronald E. Muller, *Global Reach*, New York: Simon & Schuster, 1974, p. 61.

[11]Ibid., p. 68.

policy lavishly generous towards multinational companies, having full relations with China and the socialist world, would evidently play an important role in the furtherance of the economic objectives of the U.S. and its multinational companies to penetrate the economy of China.

Our Third World Identification

The decision to trade with the socialist world and establish diplomatic relations with her made it imperative that we should go through the motions of identifying ourselves with the Third World, particularly with its declared aspiration for a new international economic order. Noise had to be made in this connection, and much noise was certainly made. We hosted the ministerial meeting of the Group of "77" and President Marcos was given the honor of submitting the Manila Declaration in Nairobi.

But what, actually, was the Philippine intellectual and ideological contribution to the Third World Movement which, until last year, we had virtually ignored? Who, in the hierarchy and firmament of Philippine officialdom, may be said to be a credible spokesman for Third World aspirations?

On the other hand, there is respectable basis for the suspicion that Philippine participation in the Third World movement is in the nature of a Trojan role, with the Philippines evidently functioning to moderate the growing radicalization of the movement. This was made very evident in the position taken by the Martial Law government on the question of debt moratorium at the last IMF-World Bank meeting. The demand by Third World countries for relief on their excessively accumulating debt burden through a moratorium on debt repayments was opposed by the Martial Law government, consistent with and supportive of the position taken by the industrial and creditor countries.[12]

But a more basic factor makes our Third World involvement highly suspect, and that is our position on foreign investments and the give-away policy that we have adopted toward multinationals. Ours is a development philosophy which is in direct variance with the spirit that pervades Third World attitude toward these global corporations and of its conscious attempt to regulate and limit their activities radically.

It is obvious that our assumed role in the Third World is to inject a tone of sweet reasonableness and to serve, by that, as a

---

[12]*Sunday Express,* October 5, 1976.

moderating vehicle through which the industrial countries may pacify the demands of radical Third World leaders like Gandhi, Tito and Khadaffi.

We could not assume this Trojan role for America if we persisted in our traditional policy of open alignment with her, of having nothing to do with socialist nations, of viewing neutrality as immoral, and isolating ourselves from the Third World and socialist camps, as we had done for nearly a quarter of a century.

Changed international realities, not the least of which is America's decision to come to terms, finally, with growing socialist and Third World power, and the desire to assume a more sophisticated and effective role as America's chattel, and stalking horse, rather than a genuine resolve to assert and pursue our national independence, explain the "innovativeness" and "dynamic flexibility" of our new foreign policy.

This interpretation is in fact sustained and confirmed by the position the government has taken on the question of the military bases.

On the U.S. Military Bases

The assertive posture taken by the martial law government on the question of the bases ha ot concealed the fact that, basically and in the ultimate analysis, have assumed the role of assisting the United States maintain a military and naval presence in the Pacific. President Marcos himself has made this commitment. As he announced in a policy speech before a conference of bankers and economists organized by the Financial Times of London:

> We want to assume control of all these bases and put them into productive and economic, as well as military use.
>
> At the same time, we are willing to enter into new arrangements that would help the United States maintain an effective presence over the air and sea-lanes of the Pacific.[13]

How else can the Philippines "help the United States maintain an effective presence over the air and sea-lanes of the Pacific," other than by allowing these bases to remain on Philippine soil.

In the context of realities, the real issue posed by these bases is whether they are to remain or not. Questions of jurisdiction,

---

[13]*The Times Journal,* December 29, 1976, p. 10.

although paramount in Recto's time, are no longer as important, considering the intensification of the nuclear race. The danger of a nuclear war today is infinitely more than it was in Recto's time. What has now become the paramount issue is nothing less than our people's survival. Whether or not the Phillippines acquires jurisdiction over these bases, in the event of a nuclear war these bases will not be spared. Surely, we cannot expect America's nuclear adversaries to spare these bases simply because they shall have acquired a Filipino commander. Survival being the paramount issue, the question of jurisdiction becomes almost peripheral. Either these bases stay or they are dismantled. The realities and the risks present no other alternative. In fact, they dictate only one option, and that is dismantlement.

The fact that we continue to negotiate means that the President has indeed decided to allow these bases to remain, if the United States should so persist.

It is true that in a speech before the UP Law Alumni homecoming, President Marcos announced that he is now considering the option of dismantling and denouncing these bases -- should a study committee he had created so recommend. The fact that he made that announcement in evident response and angry reaction to a "leak" made by the State Department of the supposed terms and conditions agreed upon for the rent of the bases, considerably casts doubt on the seriousness and integrity of his latest posture. By this time, he should know, and he should have made up his mind, whether or not these bases do constitute a threat to the survival of a people he has elected to lead unilaterally and alone. The fact that he continues to await and hope for a favored smile from the Carter administration indicates that dismantlement is not anywhere at all in his mind, and that he has mentioned it only out of pique, and in a transparent attempt to add to his leverage. Our government continues to angle and maneuver to retain its position as America's "right hand man" in Asia.

Why should it be our business, as a people, to "help the United States maintain an effective presence over the air and sea-lanes of the Pacific?" To commit ourselves to this role automatically aligns us with a nuclear superpower engaged in a lethal adversary relation with another, or a combination of others. It is a role which automatically precludes neutrality, and independence.

The conclusion is difficult to resist that all these aggressive, and even belligerent, posturings against the United States are nothing more than a grand moro-moro designed to give our continuing subservience a new look, conceal it underneath the rhetoric of militant nationalism, and thereby give subservience respectability.

This, indeed, is the new thrust of Philippine foreign policy in the ongoing decade of the 1970's. If, during the decades of the fifties and sixties our foreign policy was unashamedly subservient and openly mendicant, in this decade it has assumed an activist Trojan role. It now glosses and conceals its historic and traditional nature with a deceptive nationalism made possible by changed international conditions. To persist in open subservience, as our foreign policy did during the previous decades, would be self-defeating. It would be self-defeating for the United States in whose service our foreign policy has always been, and remains, enlisted. America, in the post-Vietnam period, in a period of Socialist and Third World power, cannot afford to have an arm in Asia openly aligned with her. If that arm is to continue being useful to her, it must be one that must speak in the rhetoric of national liberation, defiant even in posture. But not too defiant. Defiant enough to be able to capture the leadership of the Third World, or at least, of ASEAN which is now evolving into another SEATO; defiant enough, that is, to be able to make a respectable bid for that leadership, but not too defiant to be able to make a deal with the United States and Japan -- the former concerning its military presence in ASEAN's, and the latter concerning its need for continuing access to ASEAN's raw materials. It is an arm whose usefulness to the United States and Japan derives from its capacity to posture belligerently against imperialism while pleading to its Third World Associates to act "with reason and moderation" in defending themselves against it.

On the Intervention of
Libya in Mindanao

With mendicancy and subservience so deeply ingrained in the psychology and structure of our foreign policy process, it is not surprising that the government should have taken the step of soliciting the intervention of the Libyan government for the resolution of the secession problem in Mindanao. A government in whom mendicancy and subservience are ingrained, inevitably looks to the foreign management of its internal crisis. In fact, whether in crisis or not, the fundamental elements of our internal affairs have always been under foreign management. Before martial law, the U.S. government, through the CIA, openly intervened in our presidential election. This was one of the open secrets of our political life. Martial law was a joint venture between the administration and the United States government, seeking relief from a resurgent nationalism sweeping the nation then. Some factions of the political opposition to martial law in turn brazenly seek endorsement of the U.S. government. Why not Libyan intervention in Mindanao?

Concluding Remarks

The birth anniversary of the late Claro M. Recto, an illustrious member of the Civil Liberties Union, is always an occasion for our people to re-examine the fundamental premises of our national existence, to ask where our nation goes, and where the incumbent leadership is taking them. For Recto symbolized and embodied not only an intellectual and moral integrity of the highest order, qualities which our people have always sought in those who would lead them, but a ferocious concern for the independence of our nation. He had always believed that a cause of the nation's socio-economic problems lies in the colonial mentality of the nation's leaders who have allowed a foreign power to make a mockery of our sovereignty. This, to him, was the ultimate corruption that made the mismanagement of our national affairs inevitable. The mismanagement of our foreign policy all these years in fact is the distilled expression of the truth to which Recto alluded.

Recto spoke not only for himself. His real significance was that he echoed the thoughts, and feelings and longings of a movement whose revolutionary nationalism was the one pervasive force that forged these disparate islands into a nation, and which alone can save it from the perceptible process of national disintegration unleashed by martial law.